Polity, Practice,

and the

Mission of

THE UNITED METHODIST CHURCH

Updated Edition

Thomas Edward Frank

ABINGDON PRESS / Nashville

POLITY, PRACTICE, AND THE MISSION OF
THE UNITED METHODIST CHURCH

Copyright © 2002 by Abingdon Press

This book is printed on recycled, acid-free, elemental-chlorine–free paper.

Library of Congress Cataloging-in-Publication Data

Frank, Thomas Edward.
  Polity, practice, and the mission of the United Methodist Church / Thomas
Edward Frank.—Updated ed.
    p.   cm.
Includes bibliographical references and index.
  ISBN 0-687-02356-4 (alk. paper)
  1. United Methodist Church (U.S.)—Government. I. Title.

BX8388 .F73   2002
262' .076—dc21

2002041513

Unless otherwise noted, all Scripture quotations are from the New Revised Standard
Version Bible, copyright © 1989 by the Division of Christian Education of the National
Council of the Churches of Christ in the USA. Used by permission.

Unless otherwise noted, all paragraph and page references in the text are to *The Book of
Discipline of The United Methodist Church 2000* (Nashville: The United Methodist
Publishing House, 2000).

Unless otherwise noted, all references to Wesley's *Works* are to *The Works of John Wesley,*
ed. Thomas Jackson, 14 vols. (London: Methodist Conference Office, 1872; reprinted
Grand Rapids: Zondervan Publishing House, n.d.).

03 04 05 06 07 08 09 10 11—10 9 8 7 6 5 4 3 2

MANUFACTURED IN THE UNITED STATES OF AMERICA

Polity, Practice, *and the* Mission of The United Methodist Church

To

Mom and Dad

Contents

Acknowledgments

This book, like so many labors to which I commit myself, turns out in the end to be a gift. I offer it to the laity, clergy, and scholars of the church, in the knowledge that whatever I have to say that is worthwhile has already been a gift to me.

I have been gifted first with the challenge of writing a critical study of United Methodist polity. This came at the initiative of the United Methodist Studies Advisory Committee of the General Board of Higher Education and Ministry, which in cooperation with Abingdon Press is offering a new series of books in doctrine, history, and polity. I am grateful to the committee for its faith that an ambitious outline would become a book, and for a grant from the board to support a year's sabbatical in which to complete the work.

I was gifted second with stimulating and supportive places in which to do my research and writing. The sabbatical began with a semester of study in the library of the United Methodist Archives and History Center at Drew University. I am grateful to Kenneth Rowe and the library staff for their hospitality and many acts of kindness. Ken Rowe has been a most helpful conversation partner in the preparation of this book. I am also thankful for a few months' absorbing the energy of New York City, living in Mr. Alex McFarlane's art studio, from which sunsets over the Hudson were a continual inspiration.

For a semester devoted to writing I am grateful for a place that has nurtured many theological works from idea to word, the Institute for Ecumenical and Cultural Research at St. John's University in Minnesota. I express my thanks especially to Patrick Henry, executive director, for many provocative questions and comments as well as encouragement of my approach. Much of the introduction and chapter 2 were published at his behest in the

Occasional Papers of the Institute. My thanks also to Sister Dolores Schuh and Father Wilfred Theisen for making my stay so pleasant. The staff of the Alcuin Library was unfailingly helpful, and the monastic community welcomed me and other guests to the steadying rhythms of daily prayer in community. The other Research Fellows who shared the semester at the Institute with me, particularly Richard and Barbara Bell of the College of Wooster, became friends and intellectual companions in this work, and I appreciate their many gifts as well.

Third, I was gifted with a brief stay at Garrett-Evangelical Theological Seminary in Evanston. I am thankful for the support of President Neal Fisher and the seminary staff for offering me use of the library to substantially complete the book.

Other work in which I have been involved during the last few years has been a great stimulus to my thinking. I have benefited from the opportunity to work with David Lundquist and Harold Wright on a challenging research project on connectional issues for the General Council on Ministries. Some of the results of that study appear here. I have found numerous conversation partners in the Lilly Endowment/Duke Divinity School research program on "United Methodism and American Culture." I express my appreciation particularly to Dennis Campbell and Russell Richey. Collaboration with William J. Everett on constitutional order has been especially helpful to me, and I am thankful to Randy Maddox not only for discussing ideas with me but for reading a draft of this book. My continuing participation in a research group of the General Board of Discipleship convened by Ezra Earl Jones and Alan K. Waltz has given me useful occasions for exploring polity issues.

I have been gifted as well with marvelous colleagues of the Candler School of Theology. I am thankful particularly to Dean Kevin LaGree and Dean of the Faculty and Academic Affairs Rebecca Chopp for their interest and support for my sabbatical. John and Adrienne Carr, John Freeman, Susan Henry-Crowe, and Theodore Runyon have helped me think through this project at various points. I am thankful to Janet Gary for her diligent work in preparing the manuscript.

Above all, I have been gifted with a connection of United Methodist people whose lives have taught me and whose faith has shaped me. Some were early mentors, among them Dana Dawson, Ferdinand Sigg, and Wesley Hager. Others have supported me through the years, particularly my parents, Eugene and Wilma Frank. My pastoral mentor, Clarence J. Forsberg, taught me much about how to find grace and freedom in United Methodist ministry. Roy C. Clark, Judith Craig, William B. Grove, W. T. Handy, Jr., Nolan B. Harmon, Robert W. Huston, James T. Laney, Jeanne Audrey Powers, Margaret and J. W. Sonnenday, and James L. Waits are among those who encouraged me to use my gifts for the general church. I have found deep support for my faith and work in St. Paul United Methodist Church of Atlanta and in friends around the connection, among whom I thank especially Stephanie Anna Hixon and Craig R. Hoskins for reading the manuscript.

For all those who have gifted me with encouragement, support, and faith, I am thankful. Now it is my joy to offer back what I have received.

Thomas Edward Frank
Candler School of Theology
Emory University

On Learning the Connection

Whene I was growing up, my sister Susan and I often spent our weekends riding with our parents on Dad's episcopal rounds through the state of Missouri. Bishop Frank took his circuit seriously, putting over 35,000 miles on his car each year. He seemed to know every road in the area and drove them all with a confidence undiluted by rain, snow, ice, or darkness.

When he began his itineracy as bishop in 1956, interstate highways were just beginning to be designed. We traveled most frequently on the old federal routes, and before long I could call the roll of every town along the way. From St. Louis west on Highway 40 we would pass by Wentzville, Wright City, Warrenton, Montgomery City, Fulton, Columbia. From there north Highway 63 took us past Sturgeon, Moberly, and Macon. A turn to the west on Highway 36 led to Marceline, Brookfield, Chillicothe, and Cameron.

I was learning, of course, not the town names alone, but a fundamental feature of the American landscape. In virtually every settlement, town, or city in Missouri there was a Methodist, Evangelical United Brethren, or later United Methodist church. And Dad could drive to each one of them and call the pastor and usually several laypeople by name. Any time we came to a town new to Dad, we had to drive around until we found the United Methodist church. It wouldn't do—even on family vacations—to pass through a place without spotting the edifice and reading aloud the name of the pastor posted on the church sign.

This would lead to my parents' favorite pastime for whiling away the miles. "Why, their sign says John Smith, now he used to be in Higginsville, and he's married to the daughter of Weldon Jones, who was pastor in Warsaw before he retired. They have a son who's just started at Central Methodist College. That makes me think, who is at Warsaw now? Oh, of course, Wiley Williams moved there from Joplin. Well, who followed Wiley? That's where Paul Sapp is now, but he's been ill, you know."

Today we would call this "networking." Certainly it was gossip of the richest, most complex sort. But I think a better name would be "making the connection." Their lore, their living memories, their repetition of names and places and relations, was a vital embodiment of the United Methodist connection in Missouri and many other places for the sixteen years Dad served there.

At last we would arrive at a church. Whether we pulled into the parking lot for the early service on Sunday or raced in a few minutes late for Dad's fifth engagement of the day, we were always greeted with great fanfare. Dad set the tone for all of us with a wide smile, firm handshake, and startling capacity for calling people by their first name. Typically we would be ushered to seats of honor near the front of the congregation (I never understood why the seat of honor wouldn't be where the members actually liked to sit), asked to stand and be recognized during the service, and taken out at the last hymn to assume our places in a receiving line in Fellowship Hall.

As a nine-year-old I found such lines intensely boring and a terrible invasion of my privacy. I didn't know their significance then. On the long drive home, yawning and stretching in the backseat, I would try to make sense of the trip, reviewing and revisiting towns, sanctuaries, people, and words. Even today I can feel the hands and see the faces of people who—I know now—were experiencing a larger fellowship through our presence.

Having caught this geographic virus and built up untold amounts of my own connective tissue, I cannot drive through any town today without slowing by the churches to see their affiliation and pausing at the United Methodist church to see who the pastor is. Even wheeling along the interstate I conduct a mental roll call of the churches in each town and who serves them now.

Just west of Columbia, old Highway 40 forks off to the right with signs pointing to Fayette, Missouri. Another right on state road 240 takes me around sharp bends, up and down some steep grades, and across the rises of fields and pastures. Soon I can make out the rooflines of a cluster of buildings, and after driving across a wide stretch of bottomland I come up into the town.

During my youth and young adulthood, every annual conference, pastors' school, youth convocation, or other major United Methodist event was held here at Central Methodist College. The slope of the hilltop site, the vistas from Brannock Hall to the old science building, and particularly the grand gothic sanctuary of the college church, are permanent features of my landscape of memory.

I cannot go into Linn Memorial Church without thinking of the conference sessions there, the air-conditioning beating against the tide of June's heat and humidity, the pews crowded with pastors and laity sitting shoulder to shoulder, balancing piles of papers and reports on their laps. I hear the organ belting out a Bach prelude and the congregation rising to sing "And Are We Yet Alive." I can still see Wesley Hager, in the 1960s one of the conference's most senior and respected clergy, planting his feet in the aisle to denounce a resolution about China that was little more than anti-Communist propaganda—this only a few years before President Nixon's eventful trip. The arches echo in my memory with the reading of every pastor's name and the church he (or, then only rarely, she) would serve. And I can still feel myself kneeling up by the altar, my hands on a book and many hands resting weightily on my head, and hearing the awesome words, "Take thou authority. . . . "

Even the college steps down into the town square carry me back to a kind of march from years ago. Several of us from the statewide youth convocation, led by our counselors, were walking down to see the mayor. We had discovered that our group of a hundred or more youth was welcome to use the municipal swimming pool, as long as we had white skin. We decided to speak with the mayor of Fayette about this.

Our little delegation was guided by Mary Longstreth, a white lay speaker who was a living repository of the lore of Methodist missions, and by the Reverend H. M. White, erect, dignified, soft-spoken, one of the first black pastors I ever knew as a friend. We met the mayor, introducing ourselves. "So White is black," he said with a big chuckle to Reverend H. M. None of us was amused. We told him our concern; we reminded him of the civil rights laws Congress was about to pass. He was impervious to our words. Blacks could use the swimming hole down at the creek just like he had when he was a boy, he declared. The federal government would

17

never tell Fayette what to do. Sure enough, when we came back to the college the next summer, the municipal pool was closed.

This was my most memorable encounter as a young man with the intractability of prejudice and the crying need for reconciliation between peoples. And it came about through the church. I would never have known this determined woman named Mary Longstreth or this persevering man named H. M. White had we not been brought together by a denomination that gathers people of many backgrounds, connecting them and giving them a sense of mutual care and responsibility.

I remember these stories not out of nostalgia, for I have utterly no desire to go back—or see the church go back—to those days. I remember them because they are woven into the fabric of my being. I remember them because they are shared by others with whom I am joined in a community of witness.

Our practices of remembering and connecting, of gathering and gossiping, of singing and preaching and praying, are what constitute us as a church. No book or written text of any kind can capture what it means to be part of such a community of memory and hope. Least of all, one might think, could the *Book of Discipline* be anything but the hardest soil from which to grow an understanding of church.

But I would not be writing this book had I not come to see the *Discipline* more fully in the context of this storied and vital community. True, it is the legislative record of United Methodist polity and as such must provide the backbone of this work and any other understanding of the subject. But the *Discipline* is also one major form of the church's story, told in sometimes cumbersome ways, but recorded and even advocated there nonetheless.

To study United Methodist polity and the *Discipline* is to come in on a conversation that began long before I knew of it and will continue long after I am gone.[1] Its dialogue is in varied tongues, sometimes opaque, often tangled. It can be difficult to find one's way into the jargon. But it is astonishing how many very different people have made their voice heard here.

The *Discipline* represents a living stream of personalities and relationships, crises and changes, ways of working and avenues for organizing, prejudices, assumptions, values, and beliefs—a stream that cannot be confined to the banks of numbered paragraphs.

Through it flow currents of words, ideas, assertions, claims, and mandates that have originated at various periods of the church's life, some to sweep into major significance, others remaining as forgotten rivulets.

Side by side in one paragraph one can read the passions, the deepest concerns, and the fondest hopes of people of widely variant views. In many cases they do not really fit together, or are made to fit only with a heavy gloss. But such is the outcome of work together in a diverse communion.

I have heard people argue vehemently that the *Discipline* is only a tool of the powerful, that its words are written by an elite who want power over the church's resources. I have heard it said that most laity and many pastors could care less what the *Discipline* says and see no connection between their congregation and a book coming down from on high. At one level the anger and alienation of such claims could be a measure of the populism that regularly brings any American organization down to size. Such feelings may also have roots in the hurts and disappointments people have suffered in the church.

But it is also true that the church is scrutinizing its polity today as sharply as at any of the most critical times in its history. Just as American business and the whole independent sector is vibrating with calls for a "new paradigm" of organization, so many United Methodist people are questioning the givens of the system—clergy appointments, financial apportionments, established agencies for mission, and most generally the connectional structure of parallel units for program and administration in all congregations, conferences, and boards. Some pastors speak of their unwillingness to teach new members about a system they view as irrelevant. Some lay leaders complain of resources being drawn away from their congregations by the costly bureaucracy of denominational agencies.

On the other hand, many other United Methodists hold tenaciously to structures they consider to be the foundation of the church's effectiveness in mission. They argue that the United Methodist connection has provided channels for congregations to be vitally involved in local and global mission through decades of drastic social change. The connection offers a system of clergy placement that avoids costly and time-consuming pastoral searches.

It fosters a network of friendship and collegiality that spans generations. Many United Methodists do not want to put these values at risk.

These are times, then, for a searching assessment of what we most value in our tradition, what patterns of authority and decision making will hold us in good stead for the future, and what can be changed or let go. In the forefront of our thinking about the church are foundational questions: What is our polity really for? What is a denomination, and what are the strengths and weaknesses of this form of organization? What are the distinctive forms of United Methodist polity that would strengthen the church that is emerging today?

I write this book in love and appreciation for a connection of churches and people that has deeply shaped my life. With all the startling social changes that have swept the world since those drives down Missouri highways, I am amazed at how connected United Methodist people still are through webs of friendship, collegiality, vocation, and prayer.

I write also in the spirit of pursuing the fundamental questions and issues that face us as a church today. The connection is being reborn in ways that no one is prescient enough to name. The new forms that endure will be created through a shared process of discernment and consensus including many diverse voices. Mine is only a small part of the conversation—and sometimes uproar—that is continuing these days. I invite you to hear my voice in these pages, and—because we are a connection of common witness—I look forward to hearing yours.

The Rhetoric of Crisis and United Methodist Polity

Mainstream Protestantism is in crisis. If you did not already think so, surely you would after reading books not only about The United Methodist Church but also about other denominations—such as the Christian Church (Disciples of Christ), Episcopal Church, United Church of Christ, or Presbyterian Church (USA)[1]—or listening to speeches at church conferences, or perusing articles in newsletters and periodicals.

- The church is in disastrous decline, commentators agree. If present trends continue there will be no denomination in the next century.

- Clergy are demoralized. Laity are disillusioned. Our leaders are afraid to lead. Our people do not know our basic church teachings.

- It's time for "new paradigms" of organization. The days of bloated bureaucracy and top-down programming are over. This is the era of local initiative and control.

- The church is at the crossroads, a critical turning point, a time of decision. It's now or never, change or die.

The church is immersed, in short, in a rhetoric of crisis. So pervasive is this manner of speech that no speaker at a pastors' school or conference would dare omit a litany of ills or fail to promise a coming revolution.[2] The recitation of alarming statistics and their reduction to tabloid headlines seems to get everyone's attention. A speaker who can persuade a church audience of their impending doom will be talked about for years, and maybe even touted for the episcopacy.

I have chosen this time in history to write a book on United Methodist polity. My colleagues and friends think I'm crazy to take on such a topic. Even I have joined in the sarcasm about the project, telling friends that I'm writing a book about how the church works—it's going to be a novel.

Indeed I must begin by making clear that I recognize that the polity I describe and interpret here will continue to be modified while the book is in circulation. Yet I hope that the perspective from which I write will be of some enduring value. In particular, I conceive of my task in what I consider an entirely different frame of reference from many commentators on American mainstream Protestantism in general, and United Methodism in particular.

A Rhetoric of Power

I first began to speak and write about United Methodism less than ten years ago, when a shift from nine years of pastoring to full-time teaching gave me more time to focus my thoughts. At first I joined fully in the rhetoric of crisis. I found that it gave me entree to audiences; listeners would become very intent as I described the denomination's problems. If I could put the right statistics together, I would have them gasping in horror. I could then dazzle them with metaphors for how the church ought to look in the future.

I began to get uneasy about my zealous viewpoint for three reasons. For one thing I found myself part of a cadre of interpreters who were touring the denomination saying things that seemed to procure more and more invitations to say more and more potent and decisive things. I began to realize that the rhetoric of crisis is a rhetoric of power. It gives power to the speaker who can manipulate the data; it ascribes power to distant experts who have organizational and religious knowledge that the laity lack; it conveys power to groups who have a plan or program for (what they call) change.

Conversely, the rhetoric of crisis takes power away from laity and pastors by diminishing the significance of their work—they who meet week after week in sanctuaries all across the landscape to worship God, pray for guidance, and struggle to raise the money and rally the volunteers to carry out their ministries. The rhetoric of crisis makes judicatory officers, conference lay leaders, and others who are charged with connectional work look lazy and uninformed or worse, pathetic.

Second, I began to understand how the rhetoric of crisis profoundly serves American culture's idol of success. An obsession with declining numbers and loss of influence is the mirror image of a compulsion for growing numbers and increasing influence and notoriety. In America bigger is better or more attention-grabbing no matter what the product or effect of the bigness. The public thrills to stories of hamburger empires without asking questions about where the beef is raised. People are glued to their televisions to see who won the biggest state lottery pot in history, but few seem to wonder who is buying all the tickets and at what price to their families.

By this way of thinking in the church, only a congregation with thousands of members, crowded with upwardly mobile (subtext: white or at the very least, professional black) people, is considered a success worth talking about. No one goes to a small church to study methods of attracting new members or getting people involved. A church flourishing in a poor neighborhood, or a growing church that conducts services in a language other than English, or a congregation of a hundred members that works tirelessly to respond to needs in its community, cannot "count" as a sign of vitality in the denomination.

The choice of numerical decline and institutional crisis as the central issue for discussion is itself an exercise of power. It draws attention and energy away from the pressing concerns of the communities in which congregations minister. It preoccupies conferences and conversations with talk of success or failure instead of such persistent issues as gender, racial, or economic justice, which must be resolved in the church if we expect them to be resolved anywhere in the human community.

Worse, the rhetoric of crisis distracts the church from the gospel it has been entrusted with proclaiming. It focuses on the institution instead of the message the institution represents to the world. A church that talks constantly about its loss of members, tells nostalgic stories about how wonderful everything used to be, continually scolds its pastors and laity for not being more productive, and harangues people about finding a vision for the future is focusing

focus on the gospel

on itself and its own compulsive needs. A church that announces the good news of Jesus Christ, identifies with the poor, cares for the brokenhearted, welcomes the stranger, pours money and volunteers into places of crisis, acts for justice, and pleads for the beauty and integrity of God's good creation is being true to itself. And it is God who gives the increase when the church is thus faithful.

hmm... I don't know if I agree

Change as Loss

My discomfort with the power of words to disrupt, to hurt, or subtly to rearrange and appeal to organizational power and social status was accompanied by a third realization. The rhetoric of crisis was blinding me and other commentators to a realistic assessment of denominational trends and the emerging outlines and possibilities of a church of the future.

For the past thirty years many mainstream Protestant scholars and leaders have been preoccupied with decline. Having begun their professional work in the denominations in the 1950s and 1960s, they tended to view this period as an era of failure, fragmentation, and loss. Many of the flagship churches of their youth had a remnant of their previous membership. Nationally known figures in preaching and scholarship retired or died and were not replaced by equally well-known leaders. Denominational units for mission, education, or other connectional causes were under severe financial duress. Many church-related institutions approved new charters diminishing or deleting their church affiliation and continuing with self-perpetuating boards of trustees.

A brief review of membership data also seemed to confirm a paradigm of loss, though how precisely to account for the trends has been hotly disputed. The five largest denominations generally considered the core group of mainstream Protestantism (listed above) all reported their highest membership totals around 1965. From then until the end of the 1980s, the Presbyterians reported losses of a third of their membership, the Episcopalians almost 30 percent, and the Disciples astonishingly close to half.

United Methodism in the U.S. peaked at over eleven million members, and in 1999 reported about 8.3 million, a drop of about 2.7 million or almost 25 percent. Worship attendance, at one time

24

over 4.3 million on an average Sunday, stood at about 3.5 million. Church school attendance fell from well over 3 million on an average Sunday to about 1.6 million.[3]

The problem was what to make of these statistics. For interpreters viewing the data through a framework of loss and decline, the figures were nothing short of disastrous. At the very least they indicated a diminished significance for mainstream Protestantism and perhaps even the demise of denominations as Americans have known them.

One prominent explanatory metaphor for the denominational trend was sickness and the need to return to health. American Presbyterianism was thoroughly studied through a series of seven volumes of essays called *The Presbyterian Presence*. One of these volumes was even titled *The Mainstream Protestant Decline*. The summary volume, *The Re-forming Tradition*, made clear the assumptions of the primary editors and authors. "We approached our subject as a study in pathology," they wrote, beginning with questions such as, "What is going wrong?" They went on to discuss their subject around metaphors of health and sickness, like analysts circling the body detailing the signs of aging and disease. Everything in recent Presbyterian history was framed by the perspective of decline.[4]

"Statistics such as these are indicative of an illness," claimed the authors of a major United Methodist study.[5] Another widely read book about the United Methodist need for church growth referred to the numbers as a "hemorrhage" in a chapter titled "sick unto death."[6]

Such metaphors function primarily as rhetorical devices, of course; they indicate no actual analytic categories. The rhetoric of malaise can stir feelings of remorse and guilt; evidently it is intended to spur self-examination and new resolve to seek the right medicines and outlooks that will lead to recovery. Whether trying first to make people feel bad by getting them to acknowledge that their organization is sick will lead them to desire healthy change is, of course, questionable. It has long since been rejected as a therapeutic approach. But some interpreters apparently think it will work.

This is only one of many strategies for interpreting the data and stirring people to action. Among the others:

Loss of influence. United Methodist affiliation has been declining as a percentage of the U.S. population in recent years. As late as

1950 The Methodist Church (MC) and Evangelical United Brethren Church (EUBC) together comprised 6.4 percent of the American populace. Lately the United Methodist (1968 union of MC and EUBC) portion has fallen closer to 3.6 percent. Membership has not only failed to grow with the U.S. population, it also has experienced actual decline even in high-growth areas such as California or the east coast megalopolis from Boston to Washington.[7]

Therefore—this argument goes—United Methodism and other mainstream denominations are threatened with loss of influence in shaping their communities. Fewer business and civic leaders attend their churches. The cultural hegemony once enjoyed and exercised by mainstream Protestant churches, embodied in such practices as Sunday closing laws, the printing of a sermon or inspirational column by a prominent pastor in each Saturday's newspaper, or free access to radio and television time, has dissipated. If the denominations want to regain their footing, they must exert their views more forcefully from the pulpits of growing local churches with access to public media. But that will require a more uniform definition and declaration of their doctrine and moral teaching.

Failure to be strict in discipline and evangelical in message. Ever since Dean Kelley's argument in 1972 that so-called conservative churches were growing because of their strictness in doctrine and discipline, some United Methodists have interpreted the data of decline as evidence that United Methodists in general are indifferent about their beliefs, or do not really believe anything specific enough to attract and hold new members. For many advocates of this view, more evangelical preaching, clearer confessional statements of belief, and more expectations of membership—particularly a verbal commitment to Jesus Christ—would turn the denomination around.[8]

Assimilation into the culture. A related framework for understanding decline has been to argue that United Methodists have been too much assimilated into the wider American culture. Accepting the basic values of human rights movements, the "free exercise of religion" of the First Amendment, and faith in education, science, and technology, mainstream Protestants have lost their voice for speaking out against moral wrong. One prominent

26

we don't have that ar much

book argued that "the church is a colony, an island of one culture in the middle of another." Christians must live like "resident aliens" in their "outpost," teaching their "distinctive language and life-style" to the next generation and being faithful to the truth and way of Jesus. The book was subtitled "a provocative Christian assessment of culture and ministry for people who know that something is wrong."[9]

A Broader View of Denominational Change

All of these interpretations first assume decline, not only in numbers of denominational members, but also in the vitality of the church and the place of the church in the culture. Each of them offers a rhetorical strategy for recovering from what appears (to them) to be a fatal course. They all belong to an interpretive framework of failure and loss—a rhetoric that "something is wrong."

This framework obviously has limited what these observers were able to see in the data. There are a number of demographic and sociological factors that more clearly account for the numbers, help to reinterpret the past, and point toward the contours of an emerging church.

Population shifts and mobility. Methodism was wildly successful in nineteenth-century America, following European settlers to the farthest reaches of new towns and crossroads, organizing congregations among Africans—slave or free—Native Americans, Hispanic and Asian people, and moving with the urban, mainly white middle class through its successive waves out from the city centers. At the end of the twentieth century the church still enjoys the legacy of that enormous accomplishment. Over 35,600 United Methodist local churches serve the American populace. Only 140 out of 3,105 counties in the U.S. lack a United Methodist church, a statistic matched only by Roman Catholicism.[10]

Yet many of these churches are located in areas of severe population loss or shift. Some rural counties have lost three-fourths of their population in fifteen years. The megachurches of the 1920s, built on prime sites along trolley lines in city neighborhoods and accommodating huge auditoriums, gymnasiums, and even bowling alleys, have seen their members migrate to the suburbs. American cities have burgeoned, spreading across the land, following the patterns of expressways that make towns sixty miles from a city center effectively part of the metropolis. Only in the last few years have United Methodists begun to organize new congregations at a pace that is responsive to this metropolitan growth.

On a national scale, the old Methodist Episcopal (MEC) and EUB heartland stretching from Maryland and Pennsylvania across Ohio and into Iowa has found itself labeled the "rustbelt." While both the states and the annual conferences in those states continue to drop slowly but steadily in numbers, the Sunbelt has witnessed stunning growth in metropolitan areas such as Atlanta and Houston as well as in entire states such as Florida. In 1993 ninety-one of the one hundred largest United Methodist churches in the U.S. were located in the band of states from Virginia to Florida and across to Texas.[11]

These shifts, combined with the startling estimate that over one-fourth of the American population changes residence in any given year, mark a severely dislocated society. Many residents of any metropolitan area are not natives and view themselves as transient. Long-term, committed church membership has traditionally been more typical of community natives or permanent residents. Church affiliation has become notoriously difficult even to count, much less to count on, as congregations plan their programs.

Generational change. The generation of Americans born in the fifteen years after World War II experienced some of the sharpest changes in the history of American culture. While all the so-called revolutions in civil rights, sexuality, gender relations, social mores, and artistic expression has roots deep in previous generations, the baby boomers came of age just as those changes began to flourish. New cultural attitudes, combined with sharp divisions over America's war in Vietnam, helped to foster a deep suspicion of institutions and associations earlier generations had taken for granted. Thus not only the established churches, but also fraternal organizations, civic clubs, and many other voluntary associations found themselves facing a generation with the least inclination to join of any in memory.[12]

As the boomers were heading into their thirties—the decade in which young adults have traditionally found their way back into churches—books, workshops, and videos on how to reach this institutionally less committed generation were springing up like weeds. But no sooner were they in print than another generation with still different social experiences and outlooks came to adulthood. Clearly the challenge for mainstream denominations was not simply to adapt to one generation, but to read the signs of the times and discern ways to enable diverse people of all ages to experience the riches of tradition that were these denominations' greatest gifts.[13]

Education and birth rate. United Methodists of the nineteenth century were prolific college builders. They believed that educated Christians could be more effective leaders of a Christian civilization. What they did not seem so aware of was that the more higher education people pursue, the fewer children they tend to have. According to one of the most thorough and reliable studies of mainstream religious groups, the low birth rate accompanying higher levels of education is itself enough of a demographic factor to account for most contemporary membership decline. The boomers postponed children and have had smaller families. As the post-boom children of the 1960s—fewer in number already—have relatively few children themselves, the demographic pool from which mainstream Protestant churches have usually drawn their membership gets even smaller. The significant effect of birth rate in membership trends is confirmed by the recent slowing of the statistical decline, reflecting the time lag from the initial diminished birth rates in the early 1960s. Many UM annual conferences show stable or growing numbers, and the Episcopal Church is beginning to report modest growth.[14]

All of these factors are helpful in broadening the picture of mainstream membership and reducing the rhetorical temperature. As sociologist of religion Robert Wuthnow argued,

the present woes of the liberal mainstream denominations are more a matter of demographics (low birth rates), geographic mobility (especially among the young), and sunk costs (often in declining neighborhoods) than it is [*sic*] of anything basically wrong with their teachings. . . . The liberal churches should not abandon their views and become more like evangelicals . . . they should in fact provide an alternative to fundamentalism.[15]

Similarly, evangelical denominations should continue to offer an alternative to liberalism. No one should think that overheated rhetoric and polarization will do any more than induce a declining quality of discourse and discussion. The characteristic emphases of each way of thinking are essential to the balance and well-being of the church, especially in a denomination like United Methodism that encompasses many varieties of people and viewpoints.

In the same vein, David Roozen and Carl Dudley responded to a *Newsweek* article hinting that mainstream Protestantism was headed for a "dead end." Roozen and Dudley pointed out that mainstream Protestant membership is still large, that a high percentage of members show long-term commitment, that at least two-thirds of their congregations are stable or growing, and that these churches collectively raise billions of dollars a year in charitable giving. The United Methodist share alone is over 4.5 billion dollars annually.[16]

The authors went on to criticize commentators for not distinguishing between denominational reform and congregational vitality. The older denominations have an enormous overhead to carry from their previous institutional successes. That this has become a burden to be reorganized or reshaped in some way should not distract attention from the vitality of ministry and mission in local church congregations. Nor should struggles over denominational structure be interpreted to mean that congregations no longer want or need their connection through denominations.

As for the fear that mainstream Protestantism has lost its influence in society, James D. Davidson's recent research on religious affiliations of persons listed in *Who's Who* showed that mainstream Protestants continue to hold prominent leadership roles in all American institutions, far out of proportion to their numbers in the population. The question then would be what kind of witness the churches hope their laity will make in such positions of influence.[17]

Here the prevalent theology of diversity and inclusiveness practiced by mainstream denominations comes into play. A plurality of ethnicity, social status, political views, and theological stances can be, in Roozen and Dudley's words, "organizationally unsettling."

All national—much less international—organizations that hope to encompass a diversity of peoples face this enormous challenge of maintaining a coherent structure and program.

The white leaders of denominations—people of predominantly northern European background—have too often confused their sense of normativity and self-assurance with what they think of as the identity or center of the church. As the participation of Christians of many cultures increases, denominational identity does indeed become more diffuse. But is this to be viewed as a loss, or as a gain that vastly enriches the church's witness? Do current developments represent a decline from an imagined past in which the world was simpler, or are they not the fruit of the effectiveness of evangelism and mission over the last two centuries?

Outlines of a New Church

There is a startling difference between viewing recent church history through a paradigm of illness, decline, and fragmentation, and seeing it as a story of an emerging church encompassing many cultural ways and becoming a global communion. The lines of development that have brought mainstream Protestantism to this point run deeply through its history.

Wesleyan Methodism has always been by nature a movement bursting with activism and energy for mission. It has touched people of many cultures, many economic and social locations. A paradigm of flourishing new forms of church is far more suited to understanding the emerging contours of a United Methodist Church (UMC) of the future, contours that a paradigm of loss filters out as insignificant.

An international church. Nineteenth-century Methodist, Evangelical, and United Brethren bodies were missionary in character. They viewed themselves as part of a sweeping movement that would bring Christianity to all Americans and ultimately to the whole world through "the evangelization of the world in this generation" (circa 1900, that is). They planted churches in many countries, built hospitals, and supported schools in which were educated many of the new leaders of modernizing societies.

These newly trained leaders eventually argued for national independence from colonialism and for self-determination as churches. Some of these churches have become autonomous from United Methodism; some have maintained their denominational affiliation. Many have flourished under indigenous leadership, enjoying remarkable growth in recent years.

Even without the numbers for autonomous Methodist churches, United Methodist membership in Central Conferences (non-U.S. regional conferences) alone now comes to over 1.3 million, a nearly threefold gain in the past decade. This figure represents over 13 percent of the denominational total of 9.7 million. Why this is not the whole picture regularly reported and discussed in denominational bodies, instead of the U.S. figures alone, indicates the endurance of the loss paradigm and its American preoccupations.

A multiethnic church. Not only from an international perspective, but also within the U.S., United Methodism continues to encompass many distinct ethnic and cultural groups. As the U.S. continues to add significantly more Hispanic, Asian, and other people to its predominant population of European and African heritage, the churches will be challenged to respond by founding even more diverse congregations and raising up leaders from within various ethnic groups.

Current data do not show much membership growth among nonwhite ethnic groups in United Methodism. However, data on ethnicity has only recently been collected and so far is not very reliable.[18] In any case, many annual conferences recognize a significant need for expansion of their work among new immigrant groups. Denominational programs such as an emphasis on the Ethnic Minority Local Church or Hispanic or Native American initiatives have made a start on ministries that will come to fruition only over a sustained period of support and action. Meanwhile, many church facilities are hosting congregations of first and second generation immigrants from regions such as Korea, the Pacific Islands, Central America, the Philippines, the Caribbean, and sub-Saharan Africa.

A church in ministry with the poor. Wesleyan Methodism has a long history of passionate concern for the poor. One of John Wesley's definitions of "doing good" in the General Rules was a

32

paraphrase of Matthew 25: "giving food to the hungry . . . clothing the naked . . . visiting or helping them that are sick or in prison." The Methodist, Evangelical, and United Brethren churches carried out this mandate in ministries that gradually became institutionalized in schools, hospitals, and many other services.

Today the challenge of the church's witness with the poor is even more pressing. Few United Methodist congregations include poor persons within their membership. Yet with much of the world's population going hungry each day, and with persistent and growing poverty and unemployment in Western societies, churches have responded with new efforts in feeding the homeless, building affordable houses, and sending mission teams of skilled laity into crisis areas. Moreover, many annual conferences are seeking to identify leaders from within poor communities to organize congregations that can be catalysts for health and stability.

A church of historic resilience. Given the astounding social changes of the fifty years since World War II, the endurance of mainstream traditions is nothing short of amazing. Hundreds of mainstream congregations are still going strong after 150 or more years of ministry in their place. Older city churches continue to find new forms of ministry even as the landscape of urban life around them has been drastically altered. Many small town congregations have come through the enormous economic transitions of their communities with steady membership and expanded mission. While the total numbers of members in the U.S. have continued to go down, less than a thousand American United Methodist churches—mainly in rural areas—have been closed in the last decade.

Unquestionably congregations face difficulties. They gather in all the distractedness and confusion of American culture, contend with social prejudices, compete with television and computer games for people's attention and passions, and suffer with their communities from bouts of economic recession. But they endure, and not just on their own, but as bodies within historic denominations that at the very least provide them their pastors, many of their mission opportunities, and much fellowship in the work.

A distinctive ecclesiology. As later chapters will make clear, United Methodism has a form of organization that distinguishes it from any other church as well as from other kinds of associations such as civic government or business corporations. Among many notable features, the UMC is structured first and foremost for mission. By tradition and polity it is set up to invite people to Christian faith and life, to provide them the disciplines of Christian discipleship, and to send them into their communities as catalysts of a loving and just society. United Methodist clergy itinerate as missionaries in local places, and local churches are organized as mission outposts.

United Methodists make decisions in conference. The church has no single presiding bishop, no chief executive officer, and no executive committee. United Methodist bishops have great influence and hold the power to appoint clergy, but they are not elected by annual conferences. They are responsible not just for the annual conference(s) in which they preside, but for the whole church.

In all these ways United Methodist connectionalism is distinctive. It is the denomination's unique contribution to the church catholic. In its Constitution and its practices, United Methodism expresses itself as a movement within the ecumenical church *ad interim* on the way to helping form a new church that is truly catholic, truly evangelical, truly reformed.

A Connection of Vital Congregations

Many denominational programs and campaigns in recent years have called for "re-vitalization" of churches. The last congregation of which I was pastor, located in an older, racially balanced, in-town suburb of St. Louis, was considered ripe for "re-vitalization," and I used the term quite a bit myself.

I used it, that is, until the day I decided to clean out the cabinets in the pastor's study and found the box of old photos. There was a picture of Bob Baker with the Men's Bible Class of the 1950s, the wooden chairs all in rows, the podium on a little platform in front, Bob in his bow tie and suit. Here was the Youth Choir, over sixty strong, freshly scrubbed kids, the girls with collar length page-boys, the guys with buzz cuts—not a hair over the ear. And here was a clipping from the society page of the *St. Louis Post-Dispatch* detailing a 1950s Christmas Tea of the Women's Society of

Christian Service, complete with silver tea sets, china cups, linen cloths, and corsages for the servers. And everyone in every picture was white.

The prefix *re* means "again" or "back," suggesting a re-turn, going back to something, getting things back the way they were, having life (vitality) again—presupposing that there once was indeed life. But I could not imagine my church ever re-capturing the kind of vitality found in the photo box. The community was multiracial now; few women had time or inclination to pour tea. The vitality reflected there may have been right for its time, but it would never be adequate for these times.

Nor could I imagine United Methodism as a whole ever going back to the forms of vitality of times past. Among other things, the older vitality included all-male clergy and lay leadership; it was marked by segregation of black and white churches, and an endemic paternalism of Western Christians toward the rest of the world. Surely this is not a vitality which the UMC must "re-vive."

Instead anyone who wishes to get a glimpse of United Methodism tomorrow must look for the signs of life springing up in local churches and activities around the globe. Contrary to the rhetoric of crisis, the emerging vitality of the church today has been developing for a long time. The flourishing of a more hands-on ministry style in congregations is the outgrowth of decades of teaching about the ministry of the laity in each place. The phenomenal spread of Bible studies is the vine that has been nurtured by generations of scholars, pastors, and laity working for a more conscious place for scripture in liturgy, preaching, and church ministries.

In 1990 the United Methodist bishops issued a foundation document on *Vital Congregations—Faithful Disciples*. I was privileged— and deeply challenged—to have the responsibility of drafting this book. It began with a statement that sounds in retrospect like it belongs to the crisis mentality.

> We, the people of God called United Methodist, have come to a critical turning point in our history. The world in which our heritage of faith seemed secure is passing away. We must choose now to follow the call of Jesus Christ into a new era. . . . The obvious decline in membership of many of our congregations troubles us. We feel burdened by the increasing financial load our congregations are carrying.

The point of this initial recitation, however, was to invite United Methodist congregations to consider the signs of vitality in their own life and mission.

> The realization is dawning among us that we must be more intentional about being the church God calls us to be. . . . A deep spiritual hunger is awakening our congregations. . . . The Spirit is calling us, in all our congregations, to a time of discernment.[19]

The book went on to invite congregations to tell their stories, to share their experiences of their life of worship and service together, and to consider how their stories expressed the greater story of God's mission in the world. Many of these stories were actually printed in the book as a kind of commentary on the ecclesiological text.[20]

The whole document was arranged in a pattern of worship, partly because praise of God is the central act of the church, and partly because worship is the form through which Christians seek to discern God's leading. Thus after the movements from gathering to praise to confession to pardon to hearing the word, congregations were invited as an offering of response to discern the signs of life in Christ in their own work. This was no mere group exercise, but deeply significant, for "a new imagination for tomorrow's church will arise by God's grace from the creativity and vitality of congregations who find their life in Christ."[21]

The method of this book was itself an ecclesiological statement of critical importance to how United Methodists should understand their polity. Rather than issuing a document as the chief executives of the denomination telling local churches what vitality is and mandating ten steps that every congregation must take—with accompanying reports to the district office—the bishops invited United Methodists to join them in a disciplined journey of discovery. Rather than talking *about* congregations, the episcopal leaders of the church asked them to contribute what they knew and experienced in each place of ministry.

Many local churches did not seem to know how to handle such a process. They did not believe their story was really of profound interest to anyone else. Others reacted with surprise and excitement. As one response put it, "Thank you for including the laypeople, for turning the process the other way around."[22] Many people simply stated that this was the first time anyone representing the denomination had asked them to tell their story.

United Methodists are inveterate keepers of statistics. From the beginning of Methodism as a society in England, John Wesley continually remarked on numbers of hearers and members in all his meetings. Questions about "What numbers are in Society?" have always been significant to Methodist conferences as they weighed the effectiveness of their work.[23]

But statistics can also become demonic institutionally when they are the sole means for local churches to communicate their ministry and mission. The yearly meeting of United Methodist "charges" presided over by the district superintendent, called the charge conference, requires reports that are compiled into a journal for the whole annual conference. As a result United Methodism has a remarkable historical record of membership and money for every local church and for districts, conferences, jurisdictions, and the church as a whole. In the computer age this data is a dream, making for no end of charts, graphs, and spreadsheets.

These reports provide no means, however, for congregations to tell anything about the life experience of which numbers are only the merest—and least adequate—expression. Most people would fill in their personal demographic data on a survey with some reluctance, and resent being packaged and labeled in numerical categories. But in its recent crisis and survival mentality the UMC has increasingly grabbed hold of statistical abstraction to categorize what is happening in local churches.

This, too, is very much an issue of power since numbers can be manipulated for many institutional and rhetorical purposes. Denying people the opportunity to tell their story is disempowering and immobilizing. Numbers without the narratives of the real people so inadequately represented in them are "a noisy gong or a clanging cymbal" (or clanging symbol, as I hear Paul's words).[24] They cannot communicate the love and compassion, the conflict and struggle, the fears and hopes of trying to be a Christian community in today's world.

A deep restlessness about these institutional patterns is sweeping through the church today. The 1994 report of the General Council on Ministries summarizing views of annual conference leaders put forward as its first conclusion:

The local church congregation is the primary base for ministry and mission and the foundation of everything that happens in the church.[25]

The primary question that follows from this claim is how the connection can empower local churches for ministry. District superintendents are trying varied ways of hearing congregational stories. They and the pastors of their districts are experimenting with forms of worship as a means for celebrating, evaluating, and planning ministries in what used to be church "business meetings." Leaders are trying ways to incorporate prayer and Bible study into decision making, rather than relying solely on agendas governed by Roberts' Rules of Order, formal motions, and votes.[26]

Out of this ferment will come new perspectives on the vitality of the United Methodist connection. As the bishops stated it,

> Through our mutual support as congregations in covenant, we share resources and hold one another up in the joys and sorrows of ministry. Together we undergird the whole outreach of the church. . . . *But the connection is only as vital as the congregations that comprise it.*[27]

Like breathing in and breathing out, the local churches of United Methodism and the connection through which they are linked together are both vital expressions of the church. Each local church is gifted in its own way for worship, fellowship, education, and care—breathing in deeply the life of Christian community. Each is drawn into mission in company with churches of a broader connection, breathing out the witness and service of the church in the world.

Conclusion

I have undertaken to write this book because I believe that United Methodism needs a fresh understanding of what its polity is for and what its organizational arrangements can make possible in the church's continuing witness to the Reign of God. Writing is itself a space of discernment. I am trying to see for myself how the unique gifts and strengths of the United Methodist way of being church can be a foundation that will support the church that is emerging today. I invite my readers to join in this reflection.

I believe that in order to grasp a fresh perspective we will have to keep before us the actual daily life and action of particular Christian congregations and other forms of Christian community. United Methodist polity makes no sense and has no enduring significance except as a means by which the denomination nurtures and supports the vitality of the gathered people of God in ministry. Polity always has an end in view, namely, the community of wholeness, justice, and hope that God has revealed in Jesus Christ. That end cannot be separated from the actual communities of faith that in myriad ways embody and fail to embody God's vision for the world. Staying close to the ground of a lived faith will save this book—and United Methodist polity—from abstraction, and bring the church closer to the community of witness of which polity is an expression.

Nurturing a connection of varied congregations and cultures is no easy task. The coherence of this undertaking must form gradually from the conferences of many voices who participate in creating the church for the future. Yet United Methodism is gifted with some particular strengths in its ways of being church on which it can continue to draw. The purpose of this book is to identify those strengths and ways in which they could be even more clearly articulated for the church that is to be.

The first two chapters that follow establish a historical and cultural context for understanding United Methodist polity. Chapter 1 addresses the question of what polity is and how United Methodist polity has emerged from its distinctively Wesleyan heritage. Chapter 2 examines how denominations have developed in America, with United Methodism serving to illustrate those developments. The book goes on to follow the outline of the *Book of Discipline.* My critical analysis of polity begins in chapter 3 with the foundational elements in the church's Constitution. In chapter 4 I examine the relationship of theology, authority, and polity in the church. Thereafter I proceed to forms of ministry, superintendency, conference, and administration. I conclude with brief comments on issues that call for attention, most apparent among them the need for critical reflection on the long-neglected subject of ecclesial polity.

CHAPTER 1

Polity as Ecclesial Practice and Practical Discipline

olity is not a commonly used word in American English. Few people know immediately what the term means, though it is widely applicable to any form of governance, secular or religious. To the extent people think about it at all, they often misunderstand polity in two basic ways.

First, the word *polity* itself sounds to many ears like a mispronunciation, as though the speaker surely meant to say "politics" or "political." Among church folk this may quickly lead to the old bromide that "politics has no place in the church." By this people may be thinking more in a pejorative sense of politics as "smoke-filled rooms," the down-and-dirty brawl of greed and competing interests. But politics in the sense of polity—means of governance, patterns of order, authority, participation, and decision making— #1 not only has a place in the church; polity is essential to its life if it is to function effectively as a community of faith.

A second misconception is that polity is simply a euphemism for #2 the established rules, regulations, offices, and authorities devised by past generations. These now comprise an iron cage that today's participants must subvert or ignore. Certainly for those who have been excluded in the past or otherwise treated unjustly, the church's system has seemed incorrigible.

At the same time, though, the basic character of polity as a political practice means that people who want change are always free to organize, advocate, and write legislation or resolutions for reform. It may take generations, but the collective mind and will of the church does change. Nineteenth-century Methodist bodies finally gathered themselves to oppose slavery. Twentieth-century Methodism eventually reached consensus for ordaining women as clergy.

Moreover, whatever may be written in books of church law, the people of the church are the ones who must live out the polity and in living it must continually adapt it to new situations and contexts. Those who practice polity have a wellspring of past wisdom on which to draw—some of which is written down, some borne by oral tradition—as well as their own creativity in responding to new challenges.

Most important, a healthy polity serves not the institution itself, but the institution's mission. In ecclesiological terms, ecclesial polity is the practice of creating, ordering, re-forming, and sustaining the church's witness and service of the Reign of God. As John Wesley put it most forcefully in 1746,

> What is the end of all *ecclesiastical order*? Is it not to bring souls from the power of Satan to God, and to build them up in his fear and love? *Order*, then, is so far valuable as it answers these ends; and if it answers them not, it is nothing worth.[1]

Wesley was not claiming here that "anything goes" in church order. On the contrary, his words were a manifesto for preaching to people who were outside the *established* order. This preaching would demand its own discipline in the service of proclaiming the gospel.

Polity and politics are rooted in the same Greek word *politeia*—the government, constitution, and practices of citizenship in the *polis*, the city or state. Aristotle argued that *politeia* is fundamental to human life. "Man is by nature a political animal," he asserted, for no one can live—or live completely—outside human community. Therefore the central *praxis* of human life is politics. Only through politics and the polity that results can human beings reach "the greatest of goods," that is, the common good of the whole city, which is the *telos* or end of politics.

At the heart of political responsibility Aristotle placed participation in the *ekklesia*—literally a calling out (from *kaleo*) or calling together in assembly. In the Greece of his day the free, male, and property-owning citizens *(polites)* of the city would gather to consider issues affecting the whole community. In assembly they would work out the common good.[2]

As the early Christians began to gather for worship and fellowship, they assumed the term *ekklesia* for their own meetings. Apparently they were drawing on its reference to a public assem-

Ecclesia - the gathered together.

bly of people called together for a purpose. Now, though, the *ekklesia* was open to all—women as well as men, slave as well as free—and strove for an even broader ideal of common good, a community of shared life anticipating the Reign of God.[3] The term itself later came over into Latin *(ecclesiasticum)*, Spanish *(iglesia)*, French *(église)*, and English. But since the English "ecclesiastical" has developed such a connotation of institutionalism and hidebound tradition, many contemporary Christians have adopted the neologism "ecclesia" or "ecclesial" in an effort to capture the original dynamism of Christian community in formation.

Discourse about ecclesia, "ecclesiology," has always had a central place in Christian theology. Beginning with descriptions of life in Christian community in the New Testament, classical ecclesiology typically described a vision of the church perfected with all the saints under the headship of Christ. Ancient creeds named distinguishing marks of the true church: unity, holiness, catholicity (universality), and apostolicity. Sixteenth-century reformers defined the church as a congregation (which they took to be a literal translation of *ekklesia*) gathered for Word and sacrament. In all these distinct emphases, ecclesiology generally has specified a continuous ordered ministry through which Word and sacrament could be rightly preached and administered, and a ministry of oversight through which the whole *laos,* the people of God, could be inspired and held accountable to their calling.[4]

In this century ecclesiology has been transformed by the dynamic sense of Christian ecclesial communities assembling for practices of worship, hospitality, education, and service. Leonardo Boff's term "ecclesiogenesis" captured this "church-in-the-making" power of basic Christian communities in Latin America.[5] Many contemporary theologians view ecclesiology as a *praxis*, a continuous practice of action, reflection, and new action seeking faithful witness and service of God's Reign. They conceive of ecclesiology as a form of practical theology, which may be defined as critical and transformative reflection on the practices of Christian ecclesia.[6] In this way ecclesiology is a task not only for scholars, church councils, or denominational governing bodies, but also centrally a practice of particular local church congregations as they organize their ministries, choose their leaders, and carry out their mission.

43

Ecclesiology in both traditional and contemporary forms by definition incorporates the practice of politics. Like any human community, the congregations, councils, and connectional bodies of the church have had to work out a polity—arrangements of authority and power that made ordered practices possible.

Most basically, ecclesial polity has to do with the organization and maintenance of an ordered ministry and with the disciplines of Christian discipleship both communal and individual. Polity provides the church with a way to test and confirm the calling of its leaders. It specifies the ordination and orders by which the church names and blesses those who preside over its ministries. It sets standards and responsibilities for participation in the church's life of worship, sacrament, study, prayer, fellowship, care, and service.

Polity is a living process because the church is a living, continuous, yet ever-changing community. One generation's verities are the next generation's straitjacket. In each era the church has to work out the political arrangements that will structure the people of God for effective witness to the gospel. Likewise the context within which polity is practiced is continually changing. Some elements of order may stay the same for generations because the church believes they are central to its continuity. Other elements may change often to enable the church to adapt its witness and ministry to a society in flux.

Through ordination the church sets apart persons in whom it discerns gifts of leadership. To them the church entrusts a particular concern for polity. In the case of United Methodism, elders are ordained to "Service, Word, Sacrament, and Order" (¶137). Much ink has been spilled about the first three terms, relatively little about the last.

Through ordination to "Order" the church sets apart certain persons to take special responsibility for the polity of the community of faith. A ministry of Order is grounded in the Word, to be sure, as congregations and other bodies seek to bear witness to the Reign of God of which scripture testifies. A ministry of Order is vitally linked with the sacramental life of the church as well, for the work of preparing and administering baptism and Holy Communion is designated to the ordained for the sake of the good order of the community. These are critical tasks, for through the sacraments

God calls, reconciles, and nourishes a people for God's work of healing and justice.

But the practice of "Order" also goes beyond Word and Sacrament. The church sets apart persons to represent the community of faith in its definite political responsibilities. They are in biblical terms stewards (*oikonomoi*) of the household (*oikos*) of faith, entrusted with making sure that every member of the house is able to serve (or minister, *diakonia*) in the most effective way possible.[7]

Leaders ordained to Order care for the common good of the whole body. They bring to focus the concern of the whole community of faith to organize for ministry in a way that will best enable it to witness to the Reign of God. These leaders hold the people to "the one hope of [their] calling," in the words of Ephesians. They help the people of God discern their vocation and use their gifts to fulfill their particular ministries. Through their own gifts of leadership, they "equip [the Greek *katartismon* is 'fit together' the gifts of] the saints for the work of ministry" in order to promote "the body's growth in building itself up (*oikodome*) in love."[8] They "order the life of the Church for mission and ministry" in a way that holds people accountable, keeps them in community, and empowers them to do ministry (¶323).

Order is a practice that can only be learned in a continuous shared process of action, reflection, and new action. Like any essentially political practice, Order is refined in the crucible of joys, celebrations, conflicts, wounds, loyalties, and disaffections that comprise life together in a human community.

Yet at the same time the ministry of Order is grounded in the church's collective experience, much of which is contained in a book of canon law, order, or discipline. A book of order lays out a pattern for organization that bears the authority of broad consensus and shared wisdom. Those set apart as stewards of the body cannot lead without being immersed in the continuing conversation that is distilled in the book.

No book, of course, can explain to anyone ordained to "Order" how to apply its measures in every situation. For example, a book of order contains mechanisms for resolving conflict mainly in the most dire circumstances. It describes "limit situations" of how to start or how to close a congregation. But it does not detail the dailiness of Order in a living community of people with their own stories, ideas, commitments, and interests. It does not provide a method for building consensus or for persuading people that their gifts match a job that needs doing. In that sense, a book of order must be used in the context of the whole scope of pastoral care and administration. Order is inseparable from a vital and disciplined life of prayer and Christian experience.

Polity as Discipline

United Methodists have called their book of polity a "discipline" from the time predecessor bodies organized in the late eighteenth and early nineteenth centuries. The term had roots well back in Christian traditions, particularly in Puritanism and Presbyterianism as evidenced by the Books of Discipline of the Reformed Church of Scotland in 1561 and 1581.[9] But in the United Methodist heritage "discipline" was peculiarly related to the "methods" of Methodism—disciplines of growth in the Christian life and practices of love in Christian community.

John Wesley did not devise a distinct book of canon law for the Methodists, since to his death he clung to the illusion that he had not created a polity separate from the Church of England. Yet through the Methodist conferences he convened, Wesley built up a body of material entitled the "Large Minutes," which contained the order governing Methodist societies. Conference proceedings were an exercise in practical theology—critical examination and reflection on the practices of Methodist societies—encompassing both doctrine and the ways in which doctrine was being lived out in holiness of life.

The practice of critical self-examination was evident from the Minutes of the first conference of preachers that Wesley formally convened in 1744.

> The design of our meeting was proposed; namely, to consider, 1. What to teach; 2. How to teach; and, 3. What to do; that is, how to regulate our doctrine, discipline, and practice.[10]

The minutes were organized around a question and answer format much like a catechism[11]—to select a few:

What was the rise of Methodism, so called?
What is faith?
What is it to be sanctified?
What is the office of a Helper?
What is the business of an Assistant?
How many circuits are there now?
How may we raise a general fund for carrying on the whole work
of God?

Each sequentially numbered Question was followed by paragraphs of Answers.

For the Methodists, doctrine and discipline were inseparably bound up with each other in the practices of holiness. Doctrine without discipline degenerated into antinomianism, which Wesley decried as "liberty from obeying the commandments of God . . . or to do good works."[12] Wesley equally feared discipline without vital doctrine.

> I am not afraid that the people called Methodists should ever cease to exist either in Europe or America. But I am afraid, lest they should only exist as a dead sect, having the form of religion without the power. And this undoubtedly will be the case, unless they hold fast both the doctrine, spirit, and discipline with which they first set out.[13]

Thus in effect Wesley encouraged and taught Methodist people to be practical theologians. When the American Methodists organized their work as an independent church in 1784, they took over and revised the "Large Minutes." The title page of the first book of order in America (first published in 1785) read:

> Minutes of several conversations between Coke, Asbury and others composing a form of Discipline for the ministers, preachers and other members of the Methodist Episcopal Church in America.

Beginning with the 1792 edition of the book the title became more formally "The Doctrines and Discipline of the Methodist Episcopal Church in America." Subsequent editions of the Methodist Episcopal (ME), African Methodist Episcopal (AME), African Methodist Episcopal Zion (AMEZ), Evangelical, and

United Brethren books of order originating in the period from 1784 to 1820 were also titled "doctrines and discipline." At the same time, the early American Methodists moved many longer doctrinal tracts considered essential to Methodist teaching into a separate volume published in various editions throughout the nineteenth century, entitled *A Collection of Interesting Tracts*. This was issued at the request and under the guidance of the General Conference.[14]

The combined "doctrine and discipline" name continued into the mid-twentieth century, disappearing at various times among the Methodist and EUB churches in favor of the simpler title "The Book of Discipline." The UMC adopted *The Book of Discipline* when the new denomination was formed in 1968. The books still contained basic doctrinal statements, to be sure, such as the EUB Confession of Faith or the Articles of Religion. But one could legitimately ask whether the change of title did not also indicate a weakened sense of the interdependence and inseparability of what the church teaches and what the church practices.

In the broadest sense, of course, in its ecclesiastical use the term "discipline" means

The system or method by which order is maintained in a church, and control exercised over the conduct of its members; the procedure by which this is carried out; the exercise of the power of censure, admonition, excommunication, or other penal measures, by a Christian church.[15]

(margin handwritten note: THE DISCIPLINE)

But for the early Methodists the word was peculiarly appropriate. It expressed the inherent quality of their common life, namely, their sense of mutual accountability.

Discipline was practiced first and foremost in the societies of Methodists through their structure of class meetings and bands. Anyone of any denomination or religious persuasion was welcome in a Methodist society as long as they desired salvation—"to flee from the wrath to come, to be saved from their sins"—and agreed to the rules or disciplines of holiness. These latter Wesley summarized as early as 1743 in the General Rules.[16] In this original sense the "Nature, Design, and General Rules of the United Societies" belong in their primary place in today's *Discipline* (pp. 71-74), for from them—and the practices of accountability that surrounded them—flows the character of Methodist discipline and polity.

48

The Rules embodied and expressed the Methodist conviction—in Henry Knight's words—of "the Christian life as involving change over time within an ongoing relationship with God, or as a continual growth in love." They described a life that was both a response to God's grace and a means of enjoying God's continuing presence. They specified ways in which Methodist people could refrain from doing harm, do good, and attend upon "the ordinances of God."

> It was Wesley's insight that, to faith, God is immediately present in the means of grace. To the person of faith, prayer becomes a conversation, scripture becomes the voice of God, and the Lord's Supper a meal with the risen Christ. Such faith must be nurtured in small communities in which each person is accountable to a common discipline.

Class meetings were created not so much to monitor adherence to rules, then, as to nurture a deeper love of God which members would manifest in "the practice of Christian love in the world."[17]

At the same time, the rules made clear, as David Watson stated it, that "acceptance of God's grace . . . brings immediate obligations." Critics of Methodism regularly confused this stance with works righteousness, when the Rules were intended to be a framework of scriptural *oikodome* (building up) in a life of faith.[18] In fact,

> the genius of Wesley's organization of the Methodist societies lay in his recognition that Christian discipleship was first and foremost a response to God's grace, and not a striving for virtue, nor yet an expectation of instant salvation.[19]

In Wesley's view the believer was co-operant or responsible in receiving God's grace. As Randy Maddox summarized Wesley's chief theological concern,

> without God's grace we *cannot* be saved; while without our (grace-empowered, but uncoerced) participation, God's grace *will not* save.[20]

The point was subtle but critical: participants in Methodist societies were not trying to earn points with God, but to enter more fully into a life of love—love of God and neighbor—because "God has first loved us."[21] This could not be achieved alone (though personal prayer, study, and action were essential) but only in a community of mutual support and accountability.

In the class meeting the Leader was to

> carefully inquire how every soul in his class prospers; not only how each person observes the outward Rules, but how he grows in the knowledge and love of God.[22]

The practices of prayer, "searching the Scriptures," fasting, and "Christian conversation," together with the sacrament of the Lord's Supper available in the parish churches, were means of grace by which class members and leaders were drawn closer to God in love.[23] Particularly in the questions and answers of Christian conversation they submitted themselves to these disciplines and examination of their consequent spiritual growth—or lack thereof.

Wesley knew by experience that discipline could only be sustained with constant attention. He directed preachers to "go into every house in course, and teach every one therein, young and old, if they belong to us, to be Christians inwardly and outwardly." Not only adults, but "the rising generation" were included as well. Preachers were to meet with a society's children "at least an hour every week" and to "diligently instruct and vehemently exhort all parents at their own houses."[24]

In the meetings of the bands, comprised of persons already well along the path of holy living, the questions and discipline were even more intense.

1. What known sins have you committed since our last meeting?
2. What temptations have you met with?
3. How were you delivered?
4. What have you thought, said, or done, of which you doubt whether it be sin or not?[25]

The point of such questioning was not to drive people out but to draw them to "walk closely with God."[26] Of course, Wesley regularly purged the rolls of Methodist societies, but mainly for indolence or lack of participation, and less commonly for blatant violations of the rules. Many who came hoping for conversion were put off by the rigorous accountability of the disciplined life. Wesley "preferred a smaller group of the committed to a large group of the lukewarm" anyway, and so held steadfastly to the rules through controversy and tension with those who saw other ways to holiness.[27]

Polity as "Connexion"

Discipline belonged foundationally to the societies and their class meetings and bands, then, but more fully to the whole "connexion" that related to John Wesley. The term "connexion" had no more an exclusively ecclesiastical sense than the word "polity." "A trademan's clientele, and even more . . . a politician's personal following" was then called a "connexion," what some today might call a network. Since Wesley kept personal control of the Methodist movement through most of his life (except the Americans after 1784), the term could easily fit the Methodists as Wesley's "personal, religious following."[28]

But there was always more to the connexion than that. Wesley did not make himself into a cult figure idolized by indiscriminate and unthinking groupies. He was a spiritual guide for many people, but a rigorous and sometimes cantankerous one for sure.[29] In fact, he argued endlessly with many of his "followers," peppering them with letters, tracts, and sermons intended to turn their hearts, cajoling those who resisted his rules, and parting company with those whose doctrines and discipline he found wanting.

The connexion was discipline writ large, to which Wesley himself was also subject—and judging from his own self-critical observations, at times among the least malleable followers of this way. Discipline was the defining practice not only of class meetings, but of the whole structure of leaders, helpers, assistants, and preachers which Wesley over time devised. Everyone was under the same accountability for their time, their faithfulness to scripture, prayer, and fasting, and their doing of good works. The conference of preachers was no less searching than the Christian conversations with seekers in every cottage where Methodists met.

Much has been made of the word "Methodist," which as a term of derision from Wesley's student days at Oxford and elsewhere nevertheless captured something true enough that Wesley accepted the name. He did use methods of spiritual discipline in his own life and in the societies he organized.[30] But this is sometimes viewed in retrospect as though he first developed a system of methods adding up to a comprehensive discipline which he then installed as a pattern of his growing movement. Nothing could be farther from the truth. As Henry Rack stated it,

> "Mr. Wesley's Connexion" had emerged as a result of a complex process of revival and controversy. Wesley had been insensibly led into defining his position and drawing societies under his sole control by doctrinal disputes sharpened by rivalries for leadership. . . . This led him to define his doctrines but also his disciplines more clearly—hence the preoccupations of the first few Conferences.

Far from being planned from the start, Wesley's connexion

> emerged through a series of accidents and improvisations. . . . The various institutions were developed by a process of trial and error, borrowing and adaptation, occasionally outright invention.[31]

Rack's is a somewhat iconoclastic way of describing the practical theological method that was endemic to Methodist ways. Wesley was eclectic in his reading, broad in his interests, and malleable in many of his opinions. In Richard Heitzenrater's assessment, Wesley attempted "over a long lifetime, to deal with organizational and missional questions from a theological perspective, which itself was open to development and change."[32]

Wesley was determined to construct a "middle way" between various parties of antinomianism, enthusiasm, formalism, and quietism.[33] Certainly he was pragmatic in his artfulness of securing a place for Methodism in a society with an established and culturally entrenched church. Necessarily, then, disciplinary practice grew with the Methodist movement, its emerging leadership and situations of ministry. The Minutes captured a dynamic process, not a static structure.

Wesley met annually with his preachers "in connexion," who with him evolved over the years a pattern of piercing questions of accountability.

> Why is it that the people under our care are no better?
> But why are we not more knowing?
> Why are we not more holy?
> What is the best general method of preaching?[34]

Gathered in conference, they faced up to their own work in company with a leader as self-searching as they were. Gradually they brought to conference more and more concerns about the managing of an increasingly complex movement. These, too, were worked out in Christian conversation. Then, based on his judgment of their gifts and the available places of work, Wesley would assign the preachers to their circuits.

The effect of a locally practiced discipline emerging through a whole network of leaders loyal to John Wesley and sustained by the same patterns in dozens of societies across England, Scotland, Wales, Ireland, and America, was to create a "collective national identity and loyalty" exceptional for organizations of its time. "English government was local more than national," as Rack described it, "and most churches reflected a similar ethos."[35] Not that the Methodists achieved their purpose—"to reform the nation, particularly the Church."[36] They were never a large organization, after all, by 1800 still with only about 85,000 adherents among a population in England and Wales of over 9.1 million inhabitants (less than 1 percent).[37] But they did accomplish a consciousness of being a movement transcending local and regional boundaries.

Placed in the context of a nascent American society, the Methodist connection flourished. Unlike the traditional societies of Europe, America as a whole had no inherited polity either secular or religious, no established church, no given order of ministry. Forms of church were established in some colonies, to be sure, and many European immigrants brought with them ideas of ecclesiastical order. But in the relative openness of the American context, the Methodist discipline of forming religious societies, sending preachers where needed, and adapting ministry to particular situations was a remarkable fit.

As the American Methodists constituted themselves into a distinct polity, they inevitably developed a system less personally focused on Wesley's practical wisdom. If the American connection before the War of Independence depended on Wesley as "the living bond which held incipient American Methodism together," now they needed a form of organizational discipline that incorporated the democratic spirit and made transitions of leadership possible.[38] Though Wesley personally designated Thomas Coke and Francis Asbury to be superintendents of the Methodist work in America in 1784, Asbury insisted on being elected by the preachers. While Wesley personally directed the conversation at his conferences in Britain, Asbury (or less often Coke) only presided over sometimes contentious debates—even about his own authority—and awaited the conference's vote.

The connection continued to hold the societies to a common pattern of holy living, and to bind together the preachers in an annual conference for examining their ministry. But the spirit of egalitarianism pulled both society and conference toward mutual support and "fraternity" and away from subjection to the judgment of others.[39] The disciplines of mutual accountability that were the heart of the Methodist movement gradually changed toward the easygoing friendliness of Christian fellowship as they were adapted to this new environment.[40]

At the same time, and amid much controversy over its episcopacy, Methodism's system of assigning preachers to travel among circuits of Methodist societies became if anything more rigorous. Asbury and Coke took the title "bishop"—from the New Testament usage of *episkopos* or oversight—and the former especially traveled the entire connection, modeling for the preachers a constancy of purpose in extending the work.

The connection's continuing power to enable people to imagine a movement became a common bond for societies scattered over sparsely settled territories. Its sense of solidarity quickly appealed as well to other immigrant groups such as the German-speaking people gathered in Evangelical and United Brethren societies, and to freed African slaves seeking a unity that transcended the vicissitudes of particular locales. This connectional power was distilled most evidently in the repeated revisions and editions of the *Doctrines and Discipline* of the church.

POLITY AS ECCLESIAL PRACTICE AND PRACTICAL DISCIPLINE

Lines of Political Development

Methodist polity as it evolved under John Wesley's leadership and then in the formative early national period of America was a peculiar synthesis of theological emphases, ecclesiologies, and political practices. Five major streams flowed into this ever-shifting river, though given Wesley's voracious curiosity about ideas and experiences, as well as the burgeoning variety of Christian practices in America, there were countless other influences from the religious world of the time.

Neither Wesley nor later Methodist people attempted to systematize these streams into a single, rational system. Rather, they drew upon various sources to find their unique way through the often divisive disputes over doctrine and practice of their day. To have resolved all the streams into one would have created a very different church. Contemporary United Methodism's identity lies precisely in its participating in the strengths of so many different traditions. But to make such a synthesis work, United Methodist people must know the multiple assumptions and claims of its varied sources.

Pietism and Puritanism

The stream perhaps most noticeable to Wesley's contemporaries was the influence of seventeenth-century continental Pietism and the parallel movement of English Puritanism. The Methodists had in common with Pietists the sense of being an *ecclesiola*—a small church—within the *ecclesia*—the established church. Gatherings of Pietists were small, usually in someone's home, and comprised of scripture reading, prayer, and exhortation to good works. Members of the *ecclesiola* continued to attend their parish for the sacraments and other ministrations of the church.

Wesley soon differentiated himself from the more sectarian continental groups, in particular the Moravians, finding them quietistic even to the point of abstinence from the means of grace in the sacraments.[41] But his movement shared the political arrangement of small group discipline practiced within the existing geographic parishes of the established, national church.

For the practices of discipline in small groups Wesley and his followers turned to a wide array of sources. Spiritual autobiographies of the inner life were especially useful, and Wesley's journal itself might be viewed as a model that continued such an intensity of focus on the state of one's soul. Many Methodist people read John Bunyan's *Pilgrim's Progress* and Richard Baxter's *Call to the Unconverted*. Of course, the older writings were limited, in Methodist eyes, by their Calvinist doctrine and their relationship to Dissent in England—with which Methodist people, Wesley in particular, did not want to be associated.[42]

Wesley conceived of Methodism as a society, an organization with a special purpose auxiliary to the ordinary work of the church through its parishes. Similar voluntary associations, "English counterparts" to the *collegia pietatis* of the Pietists on the continent, had begun in the Church of England as much as seventy years before.[43] Among the best known and most enduring were The Society for Promoting Christian Knowledge (SPCK), founded in 1698 to publish religious literature and encourage personal piety, and The Society for the Propagation of the Gospel in Foreign Parts, which supported mission work beginning in 1701.[44]

Unlike other societies, though, Methodism was built around practices of preaching and pastoral care that clearly overlapped with priestly functions. Wesley was perpetually caught between his need to authorize and control the lay—and in some cases ordained—preachers whom he wanted to encourage, and his insistence on remaining within the Church. Ironically, many of the steps he took in order to strengthen his control over the preachers pushed him farther into a structure differentiated from the Church. His conferences, assignments of preachers to their circuits, detailed descriptions of their responsibilities for the societies under their care, and outpouring of sermons and tracts defining his movement, tended toward separation. But the idea that Methodism might become a mere sect was utterly repellent to his Anglican instincts.[45]

Anglicanism

The second clearly identifiable stream, then, was the continuing if often ambiguous loyalty of Methodists to the Church of England. Wesley was an ordained priest of the Church, licensed as a Fellow of Lincoln College, Oxford. He honored the *Book of Common Prayer* as the basis of Christian worship. He made it a rule of his own life and that of the societies to receive the Lord's Supper regularly in an

Anglican parish. He respected the role of the bishops in ordination and oversight of the church.

Wesley also was steeped in the theological character of Anglicanism, that is, its comprehension of themes from both Catholicism and the Reformation to form a national church. While he began his priesthood with High Church views of the episcopacy, ordination, and sacrament, later in life he adopted positions in common with moderate church opinion—those who wanted the church to encompass a wide breadth of understandings based on a consensus in essentials.[46]

Thus Wesley could argue that no specific church order was prescribed in the New Testament and that Anglican order was only for the well-being *(bene esse)* of the church, not of its essence *(esse)*.[47] He wanted Christian people to focus on their common mission of reformed and sanctified life, not on ecclesiastical quibbles or points of mere opinion.

In his sermon advocating a "Catholic Spirit," he urged that Christians realize their "union in affection" and common ground of love in Christ. "May we not be of one heart, though we are not of one opinion?" he pleaded. Modes of worship, forms of prayer, and ways of administering the sacraments did not touch the essentials of faith:

> Is thy heart right with God? . . . Dost thou believe in the Lord Jesus Christ? . . . Is thy heart right with thy neighbor? . . . Do you show your love by your works? . . . "If it be, give me thy hand."[48]

Wesley's movement itself, however, was in growing tension with the Church. Methodist itinerant preaching ignored parish lines and transgressed the responsibilities of local priests. Field preaching was particularly repugnant to those charged with orderly parish life. Lay preaching without a license from the Church was a violation of canon law.[49] Bishops and priests alike condemned the irregularities of Methodism on these counts.

Yet Wesley fiercely disputed any Methodists who proposed separating from the Church. Only when the American Methodists needed to organize themselves as a church did Wesley consider actions that would separate part of his movement from the Church of England. Even then, he viewed the nascent church as Anglican in essentials, instructing the Americans to organize their ecclesiology around basic elements of the Articles of Religion and the *Book of Common Prayer.* "I think [the Church of England] the best constituted national Church in the world," he wrote the Americans, though he agreed that they should not be entangled in "the English hierarchy." After much agony of conscience, he and other priests ordained Richard Whatcoat and Thomas Vasey as deacons and elders and Thomas Coke—already a priest—to superintendency. They in turn would institute an orderly priesthood in America with ties to the apostolicity (if not to the episcopacy) of Anglican tradition, while "stand[ing] fast in that liberty wherewith God has so strangely made them free."[50]

But Wesley could not really conceive of the complete openness of American society. He wanted Methodist people to be able to receive the sacraments in orderly fashion, but could not even imagine the organizational problems that would have to be resolved in the absence of a parish system. When Asbury and Coke took the name bishop, Wesley was horrified perhaps mainly because he was thinking in an English frame of reference, the bishops being a higher social class with standing in the House of Lords. None of that framework existed in America, and the new bishops—at least Asbury, certainly—took the name as biblical *episkopoi,* overseers of the church's work.[51]

The American Methodists were nevertheless in continuity with much Anglican tradition. Through their episcopal system of oversight and ordination as well as their sacramental ritual they maintained an ecclesiology much in keeping with the Church of England. Their practices perpetuated as well the tensions between society—*ecclesiola*—and church—*ecclesia*—inherent in the Methodist movement in England. The intensity of discipline in small groups continued through Methodist societies in the new nation. The Americans continued the British Methodist habit of calling their buildings chapels, not churches.

Yet the very fact of their continued welcoming of anyone of any persuasion who came seeking salvation, combined with the need now actually to be a church—providing the sacraments under the administration of an ordered ministry and serving the whole community—broadened American Methodism into a comprehensiveness that resonated deeply with its Anglican heritage. No wonder William Williams's recent assessment could call Methodism "a second 'English' church," an evangelical Anglicanism offering an alternative to "the Anglicanism of patriarchy and gentility."[52]

Catholic Tradition

To an already complicated mix of influences must be added the Catholic nature of much Methodist practice. Wesley's opponents were reaching for extremes in labeling him papist or "Popish" in his authority. Yet in both spiritual discipline and organizational style Methodism did have much in common with Catholic traditions.

Wesley and many other eighteenth-century divines were part of a trend toward the classics—a rediscovery of the practices of holiness described by fourth-century Christians such as "Macarius the Egyptian" and Clement of Alexandria. This led Wesley to a fresh claiming of Christian perfection as the goal of a disciplined life. A progressive view of sanctification had been a Catholic teaching across the centuries. Wesley's urging of Methodist people to seek progress in holiness, to be always "going on to perfection," along with his claim that perfection in love was possible in this life, picked up themes of this deeper Catholic heritage.[53]

Moreover, while Wesley was no pope, his organization of preachers had definite overtones of a kind of evangelical preaching and teaching order such as the Dominicans or Jesuits. These latter groups also sprang up from the vision of a particular individual and grew rapidly in their mission. They were comprised of men under vows of celibacy and obedience, free to itinerate wherever they were needed. The Jesuits, begun in 1534 by St. Ignatius of Loyola, even built preaching houses that brought them into conflict with the established church. Eventually both orders were disciplined, reformed, and embraced by the Roman Catholic Church (though they remain fiercely independent in character).

In the early years of American Methodism similar features were quite pronounced. With few exceptions Methodist preachers were male. Less than one fourth were married. They survived on a subsistence income, all receiving the same amount. They had a fraternal sense of mission and willingness to go (not without complaint, of course) where sent. Most preachers were under thirty years of age, and most lasted less than twelve years in the work. Many died young; many others got married and started families. Francis

Asbury bewailed every marriage that took his men away from the rigors of itineracy. Marriage was virtually equivalent to "location"—being unavailable for travel. In Asbury's mind the first loyalty of itinerants was to their conference of "travelling preachers"—their order, one might say—and to locate was to give up one's right to participate.[54]

Thus while Methodism did not share institutional ties in any way with Roman Catholicism, it did continue aspects of Catholic tradition. Like other orders it blossomed as an evangelical movement at first on the fringes of the church. In a sense it remains to be seen how Methodism may eventually—like the earlier orders—bring its unique gifts and experience into broader unity with the larger organic church.

Reformation

Methodism was also deeply influenced by the emphases of the sixteenth-century Reformation. John Wesley's discovery for himself of the profundity of Romans 1:17—the same verse that had called Martin Luther into a new realization of faith—was the spark of his new preaching in the late 1730s. Justification by faith alone connected with Wesley's passionate belief in the all-surrounding power of God's grace. His zeal for the discovery drove him against all his Anglican instincts out into the fields to preach to people who rarely if ever would find their way inside a church.

Likewise Wesley viewed scripture as the primary foundation for this promise of faith, and made "searching the Scriptures" a central activity of his societies. For there God's salvation and God's will were revealed, if people would simply read and meditate upon it. He believed that the Word of God contained all the rules necessary for Christian life, and that Methodism was a plain expression of scriptural Christianity.[55]

Like the Reformers, Wesley was captivated by ideas of the "primitive church," the church as it was originally meant to be. He took this to mean not that there was a specific, authoritative church polity contained in the New Testament, but that the church should be grounded and constructed on the principles and practices of early Christianity. He saw much to protest in the body of canon law and priestly practice that intervened between contemporary Christians and the primitive church.

60

These impulses Wesley expressed mainly through his controversialism in England as he sought to reform "particularly the Church." Only in the case of America did he really see the radical prospect of creating a church based on biblical principles. Of course, he was still confident of Anglican forms. But he told the Americans that they were "now at full liberty simply to follow the Scriptures and the Primitive Church."

Even the basic terminology of his ordinations, while imitating the threefold ministry of the Church of England, reflected an impulse toward fresh translation of New Testament terms. "Deacon," "elder" (sometimes "presbyter"), and "superintendent" were intended to cut back through the Anglican usage of "bishop" and "priest" to the root of the original Greek.[56]

The form of Wesley's ordinations—gathering priests or "presbyters" around himself as priest—connected with Reformed more than Anglican practices. These were certainly presbyterial, not episcopal, ordinations, for which Wesley sought justification in part from the early church at Alexandria which also practiced ordination by a body of presbyters.[57]

Charles Wesley, by now greatly at odds with his brother anyway, in fact complained in the wake of this (to him) shocking event that "the Methodists would become a new sect of Presbyterians."[58] Yet ironically, of course, the very act of ordaining Coke to his post, who in turn ordained Francis Asbury to superintendency as well, eventuated in a Methodist episcopacy to which was delegated the exclusive right of ordination.

Evangelical Revival

If the infusion of Pietist, Anglican, Catholic, and Reformed streams of tradition were not enough already, to them must be added yet a fifth influence, the evangelical revival that swept Britain and America in repeated waves through the eighteenth and nineteenth centuries. From this revival sprang all kinds of practices largely unknown to earlier generations of Christians—outdoor preaching, protracted meetings, mourners' benches, and emotional outbursts of shouting, jerking, and catatonia. The conversions and zeal for the faith that revival methods produced not only brought new energy to existing churches but often fomented rebellion against established authority.

Thus the evangelical revival always stood in ambiguous relation to established ecclesiology. On the one hand, revivals made Christian faith available to many people who would never have entered a church building. George Whitefield, along with Wesley among the best-known preachers in England, argued that his field preaching was for people excluded or alienated from church and that if it produced conversions it surely was the will of God.[59]

As the revival continued, it also served to confirm and deepen the commitment of people already participating in a congregation. In fact, some scholars have argued that pleas for "awakening" in America actually followed rapid expansion of congregations, not the other way around. Revivals helped solidify congregational discipline by drawing newcomers more fully into experiences of Christian life.[60]

On the other hand, American revivals became a democratic force that transgressed all traditional boundaries of ecclesiastical authority. No pastor and certainly no bishop could monitor or control the flights of doctrine expounded from revival and campmeeting pulpits by preachers more famous than they. Indeed, an ordered ministry for which candidates carefully prepared through study and which gave pastors authority of Word and sacrament in their congregations often seemed to be the last interest of Americans influenced by the revivals.

The primary test of ministry was preaching, and the primary criterion for preaching was the ability to sway, convict, and convert an audience. Methodists were especially adept at this rhythm of portraying the horrors of hell, offering God's grace freely given to repentant souls, and painting a picture of the sins to be avoided and the behavior to be rewarded in a sanctified life. A whole folklore grew up around the preachers' depictions of Judgment Day, so vivid as to cause a crowd to scream in terror or rush for the doors in panic.[61] No rhetorical excess that produced converts was too much, and with Bishop Asbury's encouragement Methodists made the early campmeetings their grounds for recruitment.[62]

This privileging of preaching, and particularly its removal from the context of liturgy and sacrament, had deep roots and far-reaching consequences for church polity. Americans have often claimed that the rapid spread of Methodism through scattered frontier settlements necessitated an emphasis on preaching, as the young Methodist preachers rode from place to place organizing and discipling Methodist societies on their far-flung circuits. The movement could not pause properly to ordain enough elders, so that usually the regular visit of the "presiding elder" who oversaw a group of circuits was the only occasion for celebrating the Lord's Supper.

But this argument is hardly sufficient. In fact, Methodism had always privileged preaching. The movement broke into public consciousness because of the boldness of its preachers. Wesley devoted much of his energy to encouraging, cajoling, teaching, and chastising his preachers. The societies gathered to hear preaching, and for that primary purpose built chapels or "preaching houses" in no way subject to the Church.[63]

Wesley defended this from both sides of his mouth, on the one hand insisting that Methodism was not a sectarian split from the Church because after all it only involved preaching—it was not a replacement for the full priesthood—and on the other touting the preaching gift of Methodists in contrast to the failure of priests to preach the gospel and bring people to faith. This he complemented with a distinction between the inner call of the Holy Spirit and the outer call of the church.[64] The former, the call of God, was sufficient authority for preaching, even lay preaching, and for preaching anywhere, regardless of parish lines or canon law regulations. The latter, ordination by the church, was necessary authority for administering the sacrament of the Lord's Supper, which he wanted Methodist people to observe in their parish churches. Methodists increasingly resisted this, in part because Wesley himself had separated the authority to preach from the authority of ordination. Why receive the sacrament from a priest who lacked the inner call of the Holy Spirit or preached doctrines contrary to the Methodist themes of grace and perfection?[65]

As a consequence, in the unstructured context of America, Methodist preachers felt complete freedom to ignore Wesley's Anglican liturgy for Sunday service and to neglect the Lord's Supper as of secondary status. After all, had not Wesley himself argued that preaching was absolutely essential for bringing people to salvation, and the Lord's Supper but one of the means of grace?[66] The circuit riders organized societies, not congregations, and encouraged the people to build chapels, not churches. The preachers itinerated constantly; they were decidedly not resident priests providing pastoral services to a parish. They met annually in conference as an evangelical order of preachers and for generations successfully resisted any structure that would give the laity of local societies representation in that conference. After all, conferences were about itinerant preaching and aggressive organizing in an expanding mission field, not about settled congregations.

This names at least part of the tension often described as Methodism's journey "from society to church."[67] Once an evangelical society within an established church, it had now in America to become itself a church. But the abiding resistance to this shift indicates what is sometimes not fully acknowledged. Methodism as a preaching order and connection of societies was in fact a polity distinct from churchly order. It represented a different ecclesiology.

Early Methodist preachers praised the openness and spontaneity of the revivals, the freedom both preacher and listener felt to know the power of faith. But of course, these occasions were far from unstructured. They were carefully planned and orchestrated events with a distinct order of their own.[68] Likewise, the preachers sang the praises of itinerant preaching and the flexibility of the Methodist movement to go where the people were. What they took for granted and did not articulate were their ecclesiological assumptions around the primacy of preaching that underlay this well-ordered system of polity.

The fruit of a preaching polity was a Methodism that by the end of the nineteenth century had almost completely given up the class meeting structure, relying instead solely on the pulpit for discipline—preachers expounding Christian truth and spurring the conscience of believers.[69] From an ecclesiological standpoint the societies were left as little more than audiences for evangelical preaching, audiences who to be sure responded by organizing a variety of mission activities as any well-tuned American voluntary association would. But they now lacked even the characteristic discipline that had given continuity and consistency to Methodist meetings, a personal constancy borne by the lay participants. The Sunday school took the place of the class meeting, gathering in assembly halls and classrooms that, like the main auditorium, emphasized the speaking of one person while the others listened.[70]

This picture is moderated by the zest with which Methodist people joined in these meetings, their lusty singing and enthusiastic commitment to missions and social activism. But the underlying polity tension remained. Was Methodism becoming a church? Or was it simply evolving from its roots as a voluntary society into an ecclesiology of unselfconscious adaptation to the private individualism and bureaucratic organizational mode of American society and culture?

Wesley's Synthesis in America

Henry Rack has argued that Wesley's eclecticism can hardly be called a theological synthesis, so conflicting and unresolved were its constituent elements.[71] Wesley was a prolific writer, but most often in response to conflicts between Methodist preachers and proponents of other doctrines, or as an advocate of certain ethical concerns. He was not a dogmatic theologian, and his synthesis, such as it was, was elastic and highly personal.[72]

On the other hand, in his outpouring of tracts, sermons, aids to Bible study, letters, and journals, Wesley was a practical theologian *par excellence.* He sought to construct a path between the parties that divided the Christianity of his day. He wanted neither the rational purity of doctrinal propositions nor solely the immediacy of individual felt experience, neither the conformity of established ritual authority nor the quietism of awaiting God's action. He advocated instead "an orientation of the heart . . . a certain pattern of affectivity" that would bring Methodist people to "the love, joy and peace of holiness." He preached an active Christian life, infused with God's love and enacting that love in community with the neighbor.[73]

Certainly in practical terms the system through which Wesley hoped to advance Methodist theological accents, the "connexion," in general arose from conflicts of authority that regularly sent him scrambling to his various sources for confirmation.[74] He was constantly trying to adapt Methodist practice to particular situations and seeking justification for doing so. A prime example was his ordaining preachers not to the church universal, but to certain places in need of priestly functions—particularly America and parts of Scotland.[75]

Such pragmatism was perfectly suited to an unstructured American society just coming into coherent shape in the 1780s. Not burdened with a legacy of fidelity to an established church tradition, yet not having the character of sectarian separation from ordinary society, Methodism could break new ecclesiological ground. Historians have often declared Methodism the most American of denominations, in part because American culture itself was assembled pragmatically from diverse influences that coincided in unsytematic synthesis.

Organized as societies much of the membership of which was recruited from revival meetings; welcoming people to a warm-hearted fellowship of worship and singing; preaching the availability of grace to people of any race, class, or gender who threw themselves on God's mercy; inspiring and providing the leadership for work in education and missions both in the U.S. and other lands; recruiting lay leaders for many important roles such as class leader or exhorter; Methodism was the quintessential American voluntary association.[76] It was hugely influential, with a presence in most American communities and a membership by 1850 comprising over a third of all church members in the U.S.[77]

This astounding expansion provoked sometimes raging debates over polity, often couched in terms of Methodism's fit with democracy. What justified the exclusion of laity from annual conferences? What exactly were the powers of a bishop, and how could these be reconciled with equality of rights (at least for white men)? Why couldn't laity and preachers have the right to turn down a proposed pastoral appointment? What was the authority for Methodist ordination? On what grounds were women not to be admitted as delegates to General Conference? And so the questions continued through the nineteenth and into the twentieth century.

But while these discussions clarified some aspects of polity, Methodism's ecclesiology in general remained anomalous. Indeed, muddied streams from the original influences are still apparent and generally unreconciled in contemporary denominational life.

- The language of "societies" faded away a hundred years ago; but United Methodist churches are still organized and related systemically as local units of a larger connection.

- Class meetings disappeared so completely that their slight comeback recently is not nearly on the original scale; yet in a recent survey of UMC annual conference members, respondents ranked Bible study, evangelism, prayer and spiritual discipline as the highest priorities for the denomination.[78]

- Bishops continue to hold life tenure and final responsibility for ordination and appointment making; yet they have no membership in any body of the church except their own Council, no legislative role, no liturgical function in congregations, and no organic relationship to the laity. Their influence in the denomination derives largely from their preaching and powers of persuasion.

- The itineracy persists, but its qualities as a missionary order of preachers have given way to a more professional model with itinerants less and less able simply to go where sent.

- The laity won their century-long battle to be represented in annual conferences, but they have limited official role in the core functions of polity—ministerial orders, discipline, and appointments.

- Testing and evaluation of candidates for ordained ministry has become increasingly rigorous, setting an ever higher standard for ordination; yet unordained local pastors are still authorized to administer the sacraments in the local church to which they are appointed.

These and other anomalies evidence the many shaping influences of United Methodist polity and practice. The point is not to resolve them all, but to recognize the strengths each brings to the ministry and mission of the church. United Methodists must know well the varied sources of their polity. That knowledge can then inform polity decisions in response to current needs and contexts of ministry.

The vaunted pragmatism of United Methodism's character as an organization is grounded in Wesley's practices and in the ready adaptations of the movement to various world societies. But this freedom to do whatever seems necessary to make Christian faith available to people must not degenerate into simple indifference. Nor will platitudes make it work—as in the immortal words of the American Bishop Charles Henry Fowler (elected in 1884), "Methodism means always doing the best possible thing."[79] If the synthesis is not continually being knit and woven together in the conferences as United Methodists debate what to teach, how to teach, and what to do, it will fray and eventually disintegrate.[80]

United Methodists have always joked that when conflict gets too heated or debate too divisive, everyone stands and sings a hymn. There is great truth in the laughter over this. Especially when the song is "Marching to Zion," United Methodists are continuing a long heritage of appealing to "Zion" as the faithful community that transcends "church" and glosses over human differences.[81] Moreover, song and prayer, scripture and fasting, communing and giving to the poor, are disciplines deeply etched into Methodist character. Returning to them regularly is still the pattern that allows new syntheses to be woven.

CHAPTER 2

Denomination and Polity in America: The Case of United Methodism

The polity of The United Methodist Church is fed by a complex stream of ecclesiological influences first synthesized by John Wesley. Today's polity, however, cannot be interpreted apart from the context of the American society in which it primarily has been generated. Any movement toward becoming a global church of many cultures must take this inheritance into account, for American presuppositions pervade most of the practices that comprise United Methodist polity. And to understand the mutual influence of United Methodism and American culture, we must attend to the form of Protestantism unique to American voluntary society, the denomination. In fact, one can argue, in company with historian of American religion Nathan Hatch, that Methodism "invented the American denomination, making obsolete the European reality of church at the cultural center and sect at the periphery."[1]

Denominations have been the basic form of organization for Protestant Christianity in America ever since the nation's founding. To play on words, the older "denomi-national" groups are national bodies; they are identified with the unfolding of national culture and with national and international mission. Denominations have grown up with the nation, and are an ecclesiological form unique to a society committed to the voluntary exercise of religion without state control. In such a system some form of organized association of like-minded persons has to be created. With constitutions, declarations, and books of law and discipline, denominations have announced their place in American life.

This manner of organizing religion is an innovation that defied older categories of European social theory from which American scholars have so heavily borrowed. The denomination simply does not fit the church—sect—mysticism typology of Ernst Troeltsch and other analysts of religion.[2] A denomination is not a "church" in the European sense. It enjoys no identification with the state; it receives no public funding; it cannot claim to encompass all the population. The local congregations of denominations are not organized as parishes with responsibility for all the citizens of a certain neighborhood. Even the denominations that attempt to organize simply their own adherents into neighborhood parishes have limited success at establishing firm boundaries.

Nor can denominations be considered sectarian, that is, in some way a separate society or counter-culture. In the American religious marketplace the vast majority of congregations strive to attract members on the basis that anyone is welcome, even if a new convert subsequently has to meet rigorous standards of belief and behavior. The rhetoric emitted from pulpits or denominational publications may sound sectarian in the way it attacks the larger culture or calls for specific beliefs that set it apart from secular culture. But the more successful denominations are in disseminating their message, by definition the less sectarian they could be.

No matter what a denomination proclaims, if its adherents constitute a fourth of the population of an entire region, as Southern Baptists do in much of the American South, for example, it can hardly be considered a sect or its views sectarian. It *is* the culture. Similarly, while researchers such as Roger Finke and Rodney Stark have argued that growing denominations advocate beliefs that clearly run against the dominant culture—such as a literal heaven and hell—when a Gallup poll shows that a majority of Americans believe in heaven and hell anyway, such denominations cannot be considered sectarian.[3]

Denominations do not function as mystical cults, either. They may look back to charismatic founding figures as formative influences. An Episcopal church may have a Canterbury Room or a Seabury Hall, and a United Methodist church may have an Epworth Room or a Wesley Library; founder portraits may hang on many walls. But these are artifacts of a broader denominational culture now, not the paraphernalia of a cult centered on one leader.

Yet denominations are churches. Through their congregations they offer the Word and Sacrament that are traditional marks of the church. For the most part they are open (at least as a theological tenet) to receiving new members of any background. They announce their presence in communities and publicize their activities. And in myriad ways they either take responsibility for—or provide a forum in which adherents can take responsibility for—the problems and directions of American society as a whole.

European interpreters have puzzled over this voluntary church at least since the well-known wonderment of Alexis de Tocqueville. Using the term he knew, Tocqueville wrote,

> The sects that exist in the United States are innumerable . . . religion directs the customs of the community, and, by regulating domestic life, it regulates the state . . . [it] takes no direct part in the government of society, but it must be regarded as the first of their political institutions; for if it does not impart a taste for freedom, it facilitates the use of it.[4]

For American Christians this voluntarism remains the given social environment in which their churches take form.

The taken-for-granted character of denominationalism does not always serve American Christians well, however. Particularly in times of severe questioning of denominational structures, members have difficulty articulating what exactly a denomination is, or how it should function. Few people have a sense of how denominations have changed through various historical periods, or what might be distinctive about this era at the turn of the twenty-first century.

Evolving Functions of Denominations

Recent essays by Russell Richey and by Craig Dykstra and James Hudnut-Beumler are helpful in delineating the phases of denominational life in America. Certain predominant denominational functions are associated with each historical period and continue in some form today.

In the colonial and early national period, denominations "responded to the ecclesiastical problems of ministerial succession, guidance, and governance brought on by the fact of America's emergence as a separate nation." They constituted themselves as bodies to provide a framework for supplying trained and tested pastors and for undergirding order and discipline in congregations. Dykstra and Hudnut-Beumler call this the "constitutional confederacy" era of denominationalism, because ecclesiastical bodies beyond the congregation took as virtually their sole purpose the basic functions of church discipline.[5]

In connection with what came to be called the Second Great Awakening of American Protestantism, denominations began to focus on what Richey identifies as their central missionary purpose. With a common rhetoric of Christianizing the land, denominations followed the westward expansion of the European population, preached the gospel to African slaves and Native Americans, educated people through schools, tracts, and class meetings, and advocated such causes as temperance and Sabbath laws.

While much of the organizing energy of mission was channeled into independent voluntary associations, the leaders and participants in those associations were often drawn from the ranks of denominational groups.[6] As historian Conrad Wright put it, the antebellum "benevolent empire" had "the same men . . . serving as trustees or directors in more than one of [the associations], so as to form a sort of loose interlocking directorate." These voluntary societies were largely led by laypeople (and segregated by gender), with businessmen and entrepreneurs bringing bureaucratic skill to the enterprises.[7]

After the Civil War, Protestant denominations went into what Richey calls their "churchly" phase. They became intent on their own organization, building new churches, expanding their Sunday schools and educational literature, and developing associations for women, men, and youth. Denominations began to assume many of the functions of earlier voluntary associations, absorbing and consolidating their programs and reducing the duplication of fundraising and recruitment efforts.[8]

This led to a fourth phase which Dykstra and Hudnut-Beumler name the era of the "corporation." Just as business and government were moving toward large centralized bureaucracies and increasingly rationalized procedures for efficiency, so the denominations built headquarters facilities and centralized functions in national offices. Denominational assemblies began to look something like "stockholders' meetings [as] participants voted on actions prepared between meetings by denominational executives." Giving was unified in centrally managed campaigns, with apportionments or shares of denominational funds bearing some resemblance to the newly instituted federal income tax.[9]

Finally, in response to the human rights revolutions of the 1960s and 1970s, denominations formed new units and wrote new legislation giving them the character of "regulatory agencies." They instituted rules for protecting rights of participation and due process. They enacted their theology of inclusiveness in policies for representation and monitoring functions. As the costs of maintaining a corporate bureaucracy increased, so did measures for adjudicating the distribution of scarce funds.[10]

To this picture Richey adds the observation that denominational agencies, once the expression of a coherent missional purpose enjoying national support, seemed to cast about for a consistent role. They operated at times like grant-making foundations, at other times like franchisers of a specific evangelism or stewardship product line, or at other times like accrediting and credentialing bodies.[11]

Thus over more than two hundred years American denominations have evolved three fundamental functions. Originally and most basically, they provide the credentialed ministerial supply and the congregational discipline necessary to the continuity of the church. Second, they undertake a common mission by coordinating the resources and efforts of their constituent congregations and judicatories. Third, they advocate the inclusion and full participation of all persons who wish to affiliate with them, and to one degree or another put specific structures in place to ensure that inclusion.

As subsequent chapters will show, United Methodist polity both mirrors and further contributes to these historic functions. While the term "constitutional confederacy" describes more accurately the polity of Reformed churches, it does allude to the basic discipline of ministry and membership carried forward by annual conferences from the beginning of American Methodism. Denominational mission was exemplified in the Methodist slogan derived from the English societies under Wesley: "To reform the Continent, and to spread scriptural Holiness over these lands."

Again, while this was not quite the same as the Reformed striving to create "a Christian America," Methodists unquestionably shared a faith that as more people became Christian, American and world civilization would grow more like God's Kingdom.

No denomination was better prepared to enter the post–Civil War era of denominational institution-building, as the Methodist centennial offered the opportunity for constructing hundreds of new local churches—often in grand Victorian style—as well as hospitals, homes, and schools. None undertook more eagerly the rational reorganization of mission into a well-ordered corporate bureaucracy, for many Methodist lay leaders were now the heads of large business enterprises. United Methodism adopted fully the social principles of human rights and progressive justice, and by the 1970s put in place the rubrics for full participation of all persons.

All of these functions are embedded in United Methodist polity. In fact, their complexity accounts for the bulk of the *Discipline.* Yet one could ask whether all these functions are really compatible in one denominational polity, or put excessive strains on organizational structures. How wide a range of activities can participants expect a denomination to carry out? This has been an important question in every period of American denominational history, as it is today when churches stand out in many communities as the associations that enjoy the highest level of participation and public trust.[12]

Perspectives on Denominations

The older mainstream denominations not only have evolved multiple functions over time. Their development is also deeply interwoven with the patterns and changes of American society and culture. Their collective life can be viewed from a variety of perspectives, each of which highlights an aspect of their heterogeneity as institutions.

Denominations as Local

Much writing on denominations focuses on their national (or international) structures. From another perspective, however, one can argue that denominations are primarily local in nature. Congregations of particular affiliations provide a point of entry into the religious and social life of a community. Joining a congregation is one basic way Americans have for belonging and participating in society. Even Muslim and Hindu groups form something like congregations in the U.S., which do not exist as such in most other societies in which their faith is practiced.[13] As William Swatos suggested,

> The essence of denominational religiosity is localism. Denominations fit people into the local community, while providing reference to the larger society. . . . To align with one denomination or another in a community gave one a heritage—practically a family—whose boundaries transcended time and place.[14]

Thus most people's experience of denominations is local. Church members know their own local church. They vary greatly in their degree of realization that their congregation's forms of worship, preaching, education, mission, and discipline are shaped by a particular denomination's heritage. Most members are more immediately (though often unconsciously) aware of the unique character of their own congregation: its location, building, sounds, smells, rituals, language, symbols, stories, activities, fellowship, and ways of doing things.

It is largely futile for pastors or denominational leaders to fret over the average layperson's lack of knowledge of the denomination as a whole. Most people experience a denomination only at their own particular point of entry—in a local congregation of a certain community.

The congregation is the only point at which, for most people, the distinctiveness of a denomination's heritage will really make any difference anyway. That is why the central task of denominations is to provide the resources for practicing Christian faith in congregations: hymnals, Bible translations, educational materials, coordinated mission projects, books of discipline and order, lay training, and of course the credentialing and oversight of clergy leadership.

Thus denominations are a peculiar mix of the national (or global) and local. They have had periods of organizational zeal for converting and transforming society—or all societies—as a whole. They have generated remarkable resources for carrying out national and global programs. But in their most enduring form denominations consist of the local congregations whose discipline and ministries they in some way administer and coordinate.

Denominations as Assembly and Community

As church institutions have developed and programs and financial resources have grown in size and scope over the last century, denominations have found bureaucratized offices more effective and even indispensable for managing ministry and mission. This has always provoked criticism, though, from those who want the church to be more participatory and more local.

Much of the tension over corporate bureaucracy arises from the sense many members have that denominations are first and foremost participatory assemblies. Historically denominations have authorized gatherings in which members could make their voice heard, either in person or through a representative. While such assemblies have been constituted in a variety of ways, participants have expected to play a role in writing legislation, making decisions, and authorizing actions. These roles are essential to the American sense of voluntary association.

Denominational assemblies are not simply legislative, however. They have also been occasions for revival, testimony, covenant-making, and fellowship. Any denominational gathering exhibits the ways in which denominations are human communities woven together from years of personal relationships among colleagues, friends, and family. All the clearly stated doctrines, constitutions, legislative rules, and rational procedures in the world cannot sustain a denomination. Its coherence depends on the mutual respect, caring and support of members and leaders together.

In an essay about Protestant leaders at the turn of this century, William Hutchison showed how many of the key figures in Protestant churches vacationed in the same places, socialized together, and enjoyed the blending of their families through the marriages of their children.[15] For anyone who has ever visited a Montreat, Gulfside, or Junaluska, though, this is common knowledge. The gatherings of members from many congregations create the working relationships and the friendships that make denominational life possible.

When a church like the UMC is formed, one of the least talked about but most critical problems is that people do not know each other. The most poignant lament among Evangelical United Brethren about the union with The Methodist Church in 1968 was that EUB pastors, lay leaders, and denominational executives had known each other for years and learned how to work together. EUBs arriving at the first general conference of the new UMC were overwhelmed by the numbers of new faces and the less tightly knit fellowship of the much larger denomination with which they were uniting.[16]

One of the strengths of United Methodist polity has always been its joining of all the clergy of an annual conference in a covenant fellowship. This model has its drawbacks. Clergy membership in an annual conference makes it a primary locus of their collegiality in a way that laity cannot share. Yet one need only listen to a few clergy retirement speeches in a conference session to know how significant that covenant fellowship is in sustaining a commitment to ministry. And as the laity of a conference come to know each other, they, too, realize ways in which their particular congregation is strengthened by sharing challenges and hopes with other communities of faith in the connection.

The mobility of American society has made continuity in denominational relationships much more difficult. Yet for all the changes of residence and career so typical of restless Americans, it is amazing how many staff have worked in denominational offices for years, or how many clergy have given their lives to the same conference, or how many laity have served on committees and boards regularly for decades.

These relationships are hidden behind printed words of doctrine or polity. But they comprise the community of memory that gives a denomination its peculiar character and bears its unique contribution to the work of the church in the world.[17]

Denominational Culture

As they function over time, all organizations develop a corporate culture consisting of the symbols, stories, language, places, practices, artifacts, and ways of doing things that make each organization distinctly itself. Only recently have the cultures of religious organizations received much attention, and only a beginning can be made here.[18] But certainly no one can understand a denomination without some grasp of its culture.

Names and Identities

At the most basic level of definition, a denomination is literally a name, the denominator, of a group. Such names express something of a common organizational identity. They may be:

- Biblical, taken from a text of scripture—such as Disciples of Christ; Assemblies of God, Church of God (both *ekklesia tou theou* in the New Testament);

- *Personal*, named after a founding or seminal figure—such as Wesleyans, Lutherans, or Mennonites;

- *Theological*, recalling their central theological position—such as Reformed or Evangelical Covenant;

- *Political*, naming the polity by which they govern their organizational life—such as Episcopal or Presbyterian—or stating the political position that brought them into being—such as Free Methodist or Continuing Congregational;

- *Ethnic*, describing the primary racial/ethnic group whom the denomination serves—such as African Methodist Episcopal, Korean Presbyterian, or Swedish Covenant; or

- *Regional*, denoting the geographic area of origin—such as Cumberland Presbyterian, Missouri or Wisconsin Synod Lutheran.

For United Methodists it is important to realize that the UMC belongs to yet another group of names, denominations that represent themselves through a *practice*—Methodist, Baptist, Pentecostal. That is, the distinct identity claimed through the name is a specific way of practicing Christian faith. In the Methodist case this means the methods or disciplines of spirituality and holy living that were refined by John Wesley and taught by generations of preachers and class leaders of Methodist societies.[19]

Logos, Symbols, and Rituals

A name is only one aspect of a whole organizational culture that builds up over time as a denomination carries out its work. The culture also may include a logo, such as the various cross-and-flame designs which now appear on business cards, stationery, bulletins, hymnals, books of discipline, educational materials, signboards, walls of buildings, and countless other places.[20]

Many symbols—an etching of a circuit rider, a globe with the caption "the world is my parish"—evoke a denomination's specific tradition. At the same time, denominational life in its interaction with the wider culture is subject to trends and fads that are never "officially" related to any particular heritage.

Many Protestant churches have "portraits" of Jesus hanging on the walls of their sanctuaries, assembly areas, or classrooms. The art of Werner Sallman became immensely popular in the 1940s and 1950s.[21] Though few people know the artist's name, his imaginative depiction of Jesus became almost like a photograph to those who found it bound in their Revised Standard Version Bibles or saw it every time they went to church. Earlier generations were devoted to stained glass representations of biblical scenes, such as Jesus kneeling at Gethsemane or the women meeting the angel at the empty tomb. Many of these pictures are identical in numerous sanctuaries.

Though never officially advocated by denominational bodies, the "children's sermon" was adopted by many congregations in the 1970s. A whole literature of such sermons was published, but more interestingly, a certain way of doing them spread rapidly through varied churches (a lone adult sitting on the chancel steps surrounded by children about age 10 and under, telling a story or making a point usually as an object lesson with a moral attached). This form stands in a long line of rituals that have come into common practice at various periods of denominational history, such as the use of small plastic or glass cups for communion grape juice or the placement of brass altar crosses, candlesticks, and offering plates.[22]

Surprisingly few of these symbols and rituals are mentioned in official denominational documents. The United Methodist *Discipline* contains virtually no ritual instructions or canons for the use of symbolic objects. *The United Methodist Hymnal* and *Book of Worship* are adopted and endorsed by the General Conference, but they have a more ambiguous legislative status since they are generally understood to be resources for worship, not forms of worship to be rigidly and exclusively followed. As a result, the symbolic and ritual life of the denomination is extremely fluid and often rides the currents of wider trends in church and culture.

Geography

Denominational culture includes significant places of gathering or doing business. As people assemble year after year for conferences, convocations, or simply holidays such locations become magnetic poles of memory, lore, and friendship. The sites of denominational headquarters also have remarkable power to symbolize the organization's center of gravity and cultural identification.

United Methodists who are active to any degree in programs or administrative bodies soon learn the denomination's unique geography. Assembly grounds such as Ocean Grove, New Jersey; Lake Junaluska, North Carolina; Lakeside, Ohio; Mount Sequoyah, Arkansas; and Gulfside, Mississippi, have been familiar places of meetings and vacations for generations. Many annual conferences have met on the same college campus or in the same church building for years.[23]

United Methodists who participate in or observe a General Conference pick up the tradition of remembering those conferences by their place of meeting—Cleveland, Denver, Louisville, St. Louis, Baltimore, Indianapolis, Portland, Atlanta, Dallas, to name just those of the UMC. The place is rotated among the geographic jurisdictional regions in the U.S. so that each region can have a sense of ownership and hospitality for the conference.

United Methodist general agencies are situated in various locations for definite historical reasons retained to one degree or another in the corporate memory. The General Council on Ministries (GCOM) is housed in Dayton, Ohio, in the building that formerly served as headquarters for the EUBC. The General Board of Higher Education and Ministry (GBHEM), General Board of Disciplehip (GBOD), United Methodist Communications (UMCom), and United Methodist Publishing House (UMPH) are located in Nashville, Tennessee, the locus of Methodist Episcopal Church, South (MECS) offices and publishing interests prior to 1939.

Decisions to relocate denominational headquarters have great symbolic significance. The General Board of Global Ministries

(GBGM), for example, has operated for many years out of New York, the leading city of the nineteenth-century belt of northern Methodist strength stretching from New Jersey across to Iowa. Much of the 1992 appeal for moving the Board closer to the continental center of the U.S. was a sense that denominational strength had shifted south. Furthermore, New York had become too diverse and diffuse for some people to identify with it culturally. Even the symbol of the Interchurch Center in which the GBGM has offices—built in 1960 with the help of the Rockefeller family as a locus of Christian unity—was no longer an adequate pull. Other mainstream denominations have left that building in recent years, most United Church of Christ and Presbyterian Church USA offices moving to Cleveland and Louisville, respectively. The GBGM was not moved, however.

In a national and international denomination like United Methodism, a distinct regionalism is almost inescapable. While most apparent in the crisis over slavery and the Civil War in the mid-nineteenth century, the power of regions to shape organizational culture and lifestyles continues to be the source of both humor and tension. The place of the church in society is strikingly different, for example, between the West Coast and the Southeast. United Methodists in the West see themselves as a minority faith and their congregations as mostly invisible leaven in a very large loaf. United Methodists in many areas of the Southeast comprise a tenth of the total population. In a region in which churchgoing is normative, United Methodists feel much at home in practicing their faith.[24]

Subregional environments also have their effects. United Methodists in northern Alabama and southern Tennessee are immersed in a religious culture dominated by the Church of Christ. Because the latter congregations practice weekly communion, so do many United Methodist churches. Similar adaptations in preaching, hymn singing, or revival formats prevail wherever United Methodism finds itself part of a dominant regional style.

These particularities by and large do not find their way into official polity documents. Yet the way basic principles of polity are practiced may vary greatly from region to region. United Methodist bishops in the Southeast walk into a heritage of effusive courtesy and deference, culminating in large gifts and outpourings of honor and affection upon retirement. Traditionally they are ascribed great power and influence not only over clergy appointments but over church decisions more broadly. Bishops in the Northeast or the Plains states may have to introduce themselves and remind people of the powers of episcopacy stated in the *Discipline*. They find church bodies ready to act independently on most matters.

Language and Rhetoric

Another core dimension of organizational culture is language. In fact, some scholars argue that organizations are essentially rhetorical in nature. As George Cheney proposed in a study of the uses of documents in the Roman Catholic Church, "much of what organizations do is rhetorical or persuasive and much of what is rhetorical in contemporary Western society is organized."[25]

From the corporate or collective side, rhetoric enables complex organizations to manage the "multiple identities" of various constituencies or "stakeholders." By developing a corporate "we" that uses a certain grammar and vocabulary, a large organization attempts to demonstrate the common purpose and values of diverse groups within it.

From the individual side, rhetoric enables a person to identify with an organization. Knowing the language not only facilitates participation, but reinforces the individual's identification with the goals and interests of the organization. Certainly in American society, individual identity is much dependent on such identifications. In Cheney's words, drawing on the philosopher Kenneth Burke, "our corporate identities are vital because they grant us personal meaning and because they place us in the matrix of the social order."[26]

Thus denominations have developed a distinctive grammar and lingo of phrases, references, and acronyms that express a corporate identity of shared meaning. Knowledge of the language—much of which is expressed "officially" in books of order, but much of which is an oral tradition—is not only essential for participation in programs or decision-making bodies, but also provides a basis for denominational leaders to appeal to a common cause.

The acronyms of church offices and agencies mystify newcomers, amuse oldtimers, and madden language purists (John Ciardi or William Safire would have a heyday). In the UMC, one must certainly find out soon who the DS is, and may receive mailings from the COM and the CFA. Any quick read of official communications will introduce the reader to GBGM, GBOD, GBCS, GBHEM, GCAH, GCCUIC, GCSRW, and many other cryptic signs.

Fluency in this lingo—or the lack thereof—has the unfortunate effect of creating insiders and outsiders, people with experience "in the know" and people who have not participated as much. But knowing the signs also creates cameraderie among diverse people who are trying to work together and provides shortcuts in discussing, speaking and writing about activities and decisions.

American Methodism has been characterized by varied rhetorics from the beginning. As Russell Richey has shown, the languages of evangelical revival, Wesleyan practice, episcopal heritage, and republican egalitarianism flowed freely through the writing and speech of early Methodists. They came to use the term "Zion" as a vision for community that would transcend ecclesiological and political differences. These languages and the echoes of Zion may still be heard in virtually any annual conference even today.[27]

United Methodists continue to learn this lively, fluid vocabulary much of which has been passed from generation to generation. Appointment, circuit, itineracy (or itinerancy—the spelling is disputed), bishop, ordination, conference—all are terms that have been in currency throughout Methodist history. Society, traveling preacher, temperance, or holiness are terms more associated (for better or ill) with the Methodism of years past. Apportionment and local church are terms that appear to have originated in the "corporation" era of American Methodism. Class meeting, a Methodist original, is making a comeback. And neologisms such as discipleship and spiritual formation continually spring into use as the denomination takes up new interests and directions.

Like all complex organizations, denominations often adopt the rhetoric of other organizations in the society. For a recent study undertaken by the United Methodist General Council on Ministries, as principal researcher I was able to identify nine different rhetorics or pools of language to which church leaders were appealing. Each brought with it certain basic assumptions about the nature of the church. Yet these assumptions are rarely explored, which can make communication much more difficult.

(1) *Marketing:* market, segment, targets, needs, visibility.

(2) *Communications:* technology, information highway, networking, computers, linkages, video.

(3) *Organizational science:* downsize, streamline, decentralize, eliminate overlapping functions, flatten the hierarchy or pyramid, bureaucracy more lean, local control versus top down, flexibility.

(4) *Quality management:* paradigm shift, quest for quality, primary task, core process, learning organization, vision, benchmarks.

(5) *Politics:* power, control, hierarchy, democracy, bloated bureaucracy, not responsive to local needs, distance from local.

(6) *Justice:* inclusiveness, economic disparity, lack of adequate ethnic minority ministries, inclusion of homosexuals, illiteracy, unemployment.

(7) *Theology:* mission, make disciples, Matthew 28:19, ministry of laity, community, Wesleyan heritage, covenant connection, stewardship, servant leadership.

(8) *Demographics:* bilingual, immigrants, ethnic diversity, population shifts, urban, suburban, exurban, rural, aging, generation x, busters, boomers.

(9) *Crisis:* in the UMC—change, loss, decline, shift; in the larger society—values, family, drugs, gambling, children out of wedlock, violence, crime.[28]

Much could be said about each of these forms of rhetoric and what they assume about the nature and purpose of the church as a human organization and as the body of Christ in the world. Is the church like a commercial enterprise with a product to sell in the marketplace of religions? Is the church a sociological entity best described by the demographic variables of its participants? Is the church an organization in need of a new paradigm? Is the church primarily a prophetic community advocating justice? Is the church in a critical state of decline? Such widely varying perpectives inevitably create tension as basic assumptions conflict.

Denominational rhetoric may cluster at the poles of various "parties" within the church. Scholars and leaders have given great attention in this century to differences between so-called "evangelical" and "liberal" viewpoints in the church, each of which has its own pool of language. Evangelism, church growth, soul-winning, conversion, making disciples, and lay witness are among the terms associated with the former. Inclusiveness, diversity, pluralism, multicultural, empowerment, justice, liberation, and transformation are among the words linked with the latter.

Robert Wuthnow has gone so far as to argue that in contemporary Protestantism the evangelical and liberal perspectives are the primary points of affiliation. Denominations have declined in significance enough that evangelicals of various denominations have more in common with each other than with other members of their own denomination—likewise the liberals. Thus the "symbolic boundaries that divide up the social world" have shifted to new alignments as these camps develop their own distinct "discourse, moral obligations, commitments" as well as patterns of social interaction.[29]

This is a troubling argument for those in a complex organization such as United Methodism who do not wish to use language to identify themselves with particular parties within the church. Nor do they wish to have words taken away from them through their use in establishing the boundaries of party viewpoints. Perhaps nothing was more touching, humorous, or indicative of this tension than the rhetoric at recent General Conferences. At times it seemed as if every speaker or group, no matter their persuasion or the substance of their argument, was determined to appeal to John Wesley and the original principles of Methodism. If Wesley was thus stretched into a shapeless mass by the tug and pull of this Leviathan he helped create, at least all parties seemed to be trying for a common ground of appeal.

The use of language in an organization as diverse as United Methodism is critically important in a broader culture of sound bites, tabloid headlines, and talk radio. Hence especially those who use the rhetoric of crisis must be aware of the potential of their words to divide, alienate, and rearrange power as well as to create new understandings. As Cheney put it, "large bureaucratic organizations . . . must be concerned about how to (re)present the organization as a whole *and* how to connect the individual identities of many members to that embracing collective identity."[30] Effective forms of communication—both internal and external—

that establish a common language are essential to the maintenance of shared identity and purpose.

Denominations as Economic Institutions

Whatever else may be said about their theology, practices, or organizational culture, denominations in America are also independent economic institutions that generate an enormous amount of economic activity. As voluntary associations denominations must raise their own funds to maintain or increase their work. Their ability to inspire giving and to manage effectively the funds that accumulate over time determines their economic strength.

Occasionally someone will jest that United Methodism or another denomination will never break up; the pension fund will hold it together. Certainly with about 65,000 participants paying into its pension plan, the assets of which now total over $13 billion, United Methodism has an enormous financial center of gravity managed by its General Board of Pension and Health Benefits in Evanston, Illinois.[31]

But this is only one piece of the economy generated by this organization. The grand total of expenditures in United Methodism in the U.S. is over $4.5 billion annually. Of that total over $1 billion goes toward clergy support (including the superintendency). Benevolences in the U.S., encompassing all gifts for connectional service and mission, come to over $455 million. United Methodist Women (UMW) alone raise over $25 million a year.[32] The buildings, property, parsonages, reserve funds and endowments of the 35,600 local churches in the U.S. are collectively worth over $37 billion. Another $1.9 billion is invested in mortgages or loans to build or improve facilities.[33]

Denominations are the source of economic support for various constituencies. Through their congregations, but often with strong influence from judicatory administrators (such as district superintendents), they provide salaries, health and life insurance coverage, pension contributions, and other benefits for their clergy. They make grants to congregations that qualify for certain programs such as ethnic minority ministries or inner city urban mission. They offer scholarship funds for persons attending colleges, universities, and seminaries. They provide cash subsidies to qualifying congregations that cannot afford the salary and benefit package necessary to employ a pastor.

Because of the scope of their economic activity and its voluntary nature, denominations also generate a lot of tension and conflict over money. Congregations vary wildly in the amount they pay their pastors, salaries mainly (but not exclusively) correlating with church size. Consequent differences in lifestyle, indicated by clothing, type of car, or ability to travel, are evident in any clergy gathering.

Some United Methodists view such differences as an unbiblical detriment to the common work. Appeals for equalization of salaries come regularly to annual conferences, and Americans often look sheepishly to the British Methodist Conference in which all clergy are paid on the same scale in keeping with early Methodist practice.

Economic disparities between racial groups mirror the tensions in American society. United Methodist congregations of predominantly African American heritage on the average have far less financial strength, older and less well-maintained facilities, and fewer full-time pastors, than predominantly white congregations. Denominational efforts to redistribute funds from more to less affluent sectors of the church have had limited success.

Tensions also increase in all church units beyond the congregation as funds for denominational service and mission decrease or fail to keep pace with inflation. In United Methodism and other mainstream denominations, general agencies continue to reduce budgets and eliminate staff positions while being forced to compete more vigorously for diminishing funds. Subunits are merged, meetings are canceled, programs are not carried out. Annual conferences are reducing their budgets by as much as 15 percent, reorganizing and eliminating staff positions, and putting responsibility for such funds as health insurance back to congregations as direct bills.[34]

Many people suppose that the economic problems of denominations will be solved by greater emphasis on financial stewardship—the responsibility of a faithful disciple of Jesus Christ to give a regular percentage of income to the church. But recent studies of denominational giving in the U.S. offer little empirical support for this hope.

Unless a major change of attitudes and motivations occurs (and I do not doubt the power of the Holy Spirit to make this possible) it will remain true that as a rule about 20 percent of church givers contribute about 75 percent of the money given. It will also be true on the whole that people who attend church more often are more generous givers, and that people who are active in other community organizations as well as the church tend to donate more of their money and time. People who plan their giving (through pledges, for example) will give more than spontaneous donors. People of lower or middle income will give a higher percentage of their income than high income persons, with the exception of high income persons of particularly strong (usually "conservative") convictions.

Data clearly show that the denominations making the most demands of their members and holding most strictly to their doctrines and practices generate the highest levels of giving. Thus groups such as the Latter Day Saints (Mormons) and Assemblies of God rank much higher than mainstream groups such as Presbyterians (PCUSA) and United Methodists.

Dividing total annual expenditures of the UMC by the number of members gives a figure of about $543 per member. Discounting endowments and other sources of income, this figure may be a bit high to be considered the average annual gift. But clearly United Methodists on average give less than 2 percent of their income to the church. One study shows that United Methodist average giving is a third that of Mormons and about half that of Southern Baptists.[35]

Given that these patterns are unlikely to change significantly, denominational leaders are considering new strategies for interpreting financial needs and raising funds. Common sense and experience show that when American Protestants can see an immediate need, such as the suffering caused by natural disaster or war, they will respond generously. Likewise they are more willing to pay for resources—in worship, education, evangelism, and the like—which they can put to immediate use.

Denominational bodies cannot count on simple loyalty to the organization to provide a sure base of support. But then they never have had that luxury. The interpretation of causes beyond the local congregation has always required major effort. In every historical period leaders have wrestled with how to enable local church members to identify with work going on through denominational headquarters or through local churches and conferences in other places.[36]

These efforts have been phenomenally successful in retrospect. Mainstream denominations have developed or sponsored an enormous capital of service through hospitals, homes, schools, colleges, community centers, missions, and countless other institutions. Many have now been spun off to be self-sustaining. Others continue to rely on church funding. In any case, it remains for each generation to articulate its own vision for ministry and raise the money to put it into practice.

Denominations and Social Location

Americans have always known that denominations correlate in various ways with social class and ethnicity. Jokes and folklore about these differences abound in popular culture (a Methodist is a Baptist with a college degree, a Presbyterian is a Methodist with a Ph.D., and so forth). Current studies suggest that the older social boundaries among mainstream denominations, and between mainstream and other denominations, endure though they are gradually changing. Race continues as a consistent, definite dividing line.

By most social status indicators, such as income, education, and occupational prestige, the denominations with colonial roots— Unitarian-Universalist, Presbyterian, Episcopalian, and United Church of Christ—along with Jews, continue to hold the highest ranks. They are disproportionately represented in leadership positions such as the U.S. Congress and governing bodies of major institutions.

Methodists, Lutherans, and Disciples of Christ have long held the middle ranks. But over the last forty years they have been joined by Roman Catholics, Mormons, and many new evangelical groups who have moved into white collar employment and mainstream enterprise. Meanwhile such groups as Pentecostals, Assemblies of God, most Baptists, and all black denominations occupy the lowest status indicator ranking.[37]

Upward social mobility has correlated strongly with denominations in two ways. Entire groups have risen in social status over time, the Methodists being a good example. In the early nineteenth century, Methodist people were mainly farm and working families, especially in frontier settlements. By the late nineteenth century, Methodists included many people of wealth and a rising middle class of merchant and professional occupations. By the mid-twentieth century, Methodists were enjoying new levels of education, moving more broadly into professional positions, and riding the post-war economic escalator to an unprecedented standard of living.

Second, individuals switch denominations according to their self-perceived social status. It remains true that a major cause of switching is movement, say, from Methodism to Episcopalianism as persons rise in income and occupational prestige.[38]

Ethnicity also remains a factor in denominational affiliation. Immigrant groups have usually established their own congregations and denominational connections in the U.S. But the general pattern has been for first generation immigrants to find in the church a place of continuity in language and culture, the second generation to be restless with those limitations as they learn English language and receive an American education, and the third generation to move fully into the mainstream of society even if reaching back to retain valued customs and memories of their culture of origin. One might demonstrate this pattern with the merger of predominantly German EUBs with the more mainstream Methodists, or the union of predominantly German Evangelical and Reformed congregations with the more mainstream Congregationalists (forming the United Church of Christ), or the forming of the Evangelical Lutheran Church in America to finally unite Lutherans of many northern European ethnic backgrounds.

Today's immigrants are founding their own congregations and working out ways to relate to denominations. In United Methodism, for example, a number of Korean congregations are meeting in the facilities of predominantly white local churches or in their own buildings. They are led by Korean pastors appointed by United Methodist bishops. They conduct services and use educational materials in the Korean language. A question before the UMC now is whether to organize Korean congregations into a separate Missionary Conference or to continue the model of gradually absorbing ethnic congregations into the denominational mainstream. An additional question is how United Methodism should relate to congregations of the Korean Methodist Church, an autonomous body headquartered in Seoul but conducting mission work in the U.S.

Denominationalism and Race

The persistent factor of race continues to cause tremendous pain in denominational life even while racial groups strive to appreciate each other's forms of worship and ways of being church. It remains true that the most segregated hour of the week in American life is when particularly blacks and whites but increasingly also Hispanics, Asians, and others, go to their respective churches. Even in congregations that make an effort to include members of another race, the latter usually comprise only a very small percentage of the membership.

Some African Americans have experienced upward mobility in the years since civil rights laws were passed to ensure access to public facilities, education, and jobs. Many black congregations are struggling to hold the interest and participation of a new generation of educated, professional young adults. But the upward mobility of blacks does not usually lead across racial lines dividing institutions.

The story of the African American struggle for full participation in Methodism has been told in several studies.[39] They all conclude that the injustices of white racism continue to impede the kind of mutual respect and Christian love that would make the "United" in United Methodism truly meaningful. As Peter Paris has argued eloquently, the fundamental ethical tenet of black Protestant Christianity in America has been the "brotherhood of man and the fatherhood of God," in the traditional language. Black congregations on principle have opened their doors to all persons. They have preached the new birth into a gospel community that overcomes racial difference. But this openness has not often been reciprocated by whites.[40]

As a consequence of the failure of majority white Methodists to welcome partnership with blacks in denominational life, there are today three major denominations of black Methodists. The African Methodist Episcopal Church (AME) and African Methodist Episcopal Zion Church (AMEZ) were founded in the early nineteenth century in response to direct efforts of white church members to exclude blacks from full participation in worship or congregational life. Both denominations are rooted in Methodist discipline, polity and practice, and in their perpetuation of terms and practices such as stewards and class meetings are much closer to the Methodist original than is contemporary United Methodism.

The Christian Methodist Episcopal Church (CME) consists historically of black congregations mainly in the South that were organized into a separate denomination after the Civil War in 1870. The white MECS looked upon these congregations of former slaves as their special mission and continued to provide financial support for them right up to the time of Methodist union in 1939. But the whites could not conceive of integrated conferences or activities, and thus encouraged blacks to form their own denomination. Originally called the "Colored" Methodist Episcopal Church, the denomination changed its name in 1954.

A fourth black Methodist group consists of the approximately 384,000 African American members and 1500 predominantly black congregations of The United Methodist Church.[41] These black Methodists came into the dnomination mainly through the congregations and missions of the former Methodist Episcopal Church (MEC), the main northern branch of Methodism from 1844 to 1939.

When the MECS and MEC, along with Methodist Protestants (MP), began to talk about reuniting, the place of blacks in a new denomination was a prominent issue. The solution—both for southern whites who still could not conceive of integrated conferences or itineracy, and for northern whites who had carefully helped blacks organize and maintain separate annual conferences—was to create a nonregional Central Jurisdiction. This anomalous unit of the denomination would have the power to elect its own bishops and coordinate its own annual conferences.

The story of the Central Jurisdiction is largely hidden from contemporary readers of the *Discipline,* but its effects remain. Not only is it a jarring example of how church polity is sometimes worked out on the backs of the voiceless. It is also a scar on the body of Christ that continues to ache with the church's failure at true fellowship. James P. Brawley recalled the scene at the Uniting Conference in Kansas City in 1939, as quoted in Bishop James S. Thomas's account:

> It was the hope of the Negro membership of the Methodist Episcopal Church that his status would be improved in the new United Church and that no structural organization would set him apart and give him less dignity and recognition than he already had. . . . He therefore rejected the Plan of Union. . . . This was a stigma too humiliating to accept.

Bishop Thomas continues:

> The rejection was decisive. Of the forty-seven African-American delegates to the General Conference, thirty-six voted against the Plan of Union and eleven abstained . . . when the General Conference rose to sing "We Are Marching to Zion," the African-American delegates remained seated and some of them wept.[42]

Throughout the 1950s and early 1960s the General Conference of The Methodist Church (MC) looked for ways to correct the injustice of segregating its black members. Amendment IX to the Constitution, passed in 1956, created a voluntary system through which local churches and entire annual conferences could be transferred from one jurisdiction to another. Finally in 1968, as the EUBC and MC united, the Central Jurisdiction was abolished.

Such a constitutional act, while critical to the identity of the new denomination, could not in itself bring about a united church. Four more years were required finally to merge the last separate black and white annual conferences in the Deep South (South Carolina, Georgia, Alabama, Mississippi, Louisiana, and Arkansas). The General Commission on Religion and Race (GCRR) was created in 1968 to continue to advocate racial justice and monitor racial inclusiveness in the new denomination. The "ethnic minority local church" was made a denominational priority for funding and programming from 1976 to 1984. Many black leaders joined forces in a caucus group called "Black Methodists for Church Renewal," also founded in 1968, which has continued to press for racial justice in United Methodism from outside the official church structures.

Even with all these efforts, glaring racial issues remain. The economic inequities between black and white churches mentioned above, so reflective of the larger pattern of race in the American economy, persist in spite of efforts to redress them. From one point of view, local churches may be considered independent economic units parallel to small businesses competing freely in the marketplace of religion. Thus this inequity simply reflects the relative income of church members and is just part of life in a market society. From another viewpoint, the church is a community set apart with an ideal of mutuality and justice named in Acts 2 and 4, and this inequity is an injustice and a mark of the church's continuing sinfulness.

Open itineracy is still not widely practiced, though significant cross-racial appointments have certainly been made. Black clergy tend to circulate among black congregations—among the larger black congregations often moving between annual conferences—thus functioning more as if black congregations and clergy together constituted a national church within the church. The lack of interracial participation in most congregations means that clergy and lay leaders must make continual efforts to create special occasions for United Methodists of different races to worship and work together. The UMC has found somewhat readier avenues to inclusiveness in connectional offices, for example, electing seven African Americans among thirteen new bishops in 2000, including three African American women.

United Methodism offers an unusual opportunity for blacks and whites to know each other and to work in ministry and mission together. Many lasting friendships have developed over the years. Given the new surges of white racism and racial tensions in American society today, however, the church is challenged more than ever to respond by modeling a community of mutual appreciation and justice.

This story of black Methodism indicates why Lawrence Jones could write in an essay about black Protestantism more broadly, that "unconditional loyalty to a particular denomination has never been a realistic option for African-American Christians . . . they rarely have had the experience of being fully incorporated into the institution's life." Moreover, the black church has been the central institution of black society within the dominant white society. Churches have been places of gathering, organizing, fund-raising, and mutual support, as well as places of worship. Because of their social location, black religious groups have come to "share a single religious tradition which they have labeled with names derived from the larger religious culture [but they all] exhibit a distinctive spirituality which is a response to the experience of being black in this society and a consciousness of having 'no other helper' but God." While Jones may gloss over here the significant variety of religious expression in black Protestantism, there is a deep element of truth in his generalization.[43]

Sixty-five years ago H. Richard Niebuhr spoke passionately of the collusion of denominationalism with social status and racial boundaries in America. "Denominationalism in the Christian church is such an unacknowledged hypocrisy," he wrote.

> It represents the accommodation of Christianity to the caste-system . . . of national, racial, and economic groups. It draws the color line in the church of God . . . it seats the rich and poor apart at the table of the Lord.

Niebuhr argued that denominations allowed the ethics of the social classes of which they were an expression to dominate over Christian ethics. "Each religious group gives expression to that code which forms the morale of the political or economic class it represents." Therefore denominations were a moral failure to the extent that they ignored the "ethics of brotherhood."[44]

Niebuhr's words jolt the injustices of American society to the surface and continue to challenge Protestants to connect their professed faith and their social attitudes. Yet in recent years scholars and leaders of the churches have sought a new perspective on the enduring ethnic and cultural diversity of American society. The older appeal to "the brotherhood of man" not only evokes a social world in which male leadership predominated. It recalls a kind of "melting pot" ideal in which ethnic identities would be blended together and much of their distinctiveness lost in a stew flavored predominantly by white Protestant ideals of Christian civilization. Since many Americans today resist absorption and claim the cultural memories and practices of their ethnic heritage, the challenge has been to find ways to celebrate this rich diversity and to offer all groups equal access to the means of expressing their uniqueness.[45]

For denominations this new ethnicity represents a fresh challenge. Churches do indeed bear the distinctives of various cultural traditions. The persistent question is how to encourage this diversity in the context of a vital and mutually supportive unity. In United Methodism one can see numerous efforts to become a community of cultures. The 1989 *United Methodist Hymnal*, for example, includes songs of many cultures and languages. Special funds and program priorities have put emphasis on work among ethnic groups that are in the minority in United Methodism and the U.S. Native Americans, Hispanics, and others have organized caucus groups to advocate their interests. A number of congregations have taken as their specific mission to become fellowships that incorporate members of many ethnic and cultural backgrounds.

But the denomination will have to seek a new rhetoric for these efforts. The language of "ethnic minority," for example, which came into currency in the 1970s, has settled into a syndrome of assumptions that the ethnic groups whom it is supposed to represent are always somehow lesser or in the "down" position. In some circles this label for nonwhite people has been replaced by the 1980s term "racial/ethnic." The problem with that language is that it clearly assumes that white persons are neither racial nor ethnic, but just "human" (or something).

Until white people recognize their own ethnicity, they will continue to be trapped in a taken-for-granted world in which they think of their own ways as normative and everyone else as an aberration. They thus will have no perspective from which to tell their own story or name their own cultural strengths and needs. This unreflective condition not only drains away the vitality of their congregational life, it also makes them poor partners in imagining and constructing a church that truly incorporates the whole human family.[46]

Denominations, Gender, and Sexuality

Gender and sexual orientation have been highy visible issues in denominations, the former for well over a hundred years, the latter more recently. The roles and relationships of women and men in the church have generally reflected trends of American society. Mirroring what Jean Miller Schmidt called "the rigid Victorian gender ideology of separate male and female spheres," nineteenth-century denominations encouraged women into service roles and associations for education and missions.[47] Men were recruited and supported for public leadership roles as pastors, agency executives, and leaders of capital fund drives and building programs. Assumptions growing out of this division carried over well into the post–World War II era through such patterns as the denial of ordination to women until 1956 in The Methodist Church, and the exclusive use of male pronouns in the Disciplinary language about offices and leadership positions until 1972.[48]

The strong connections between churches and Victorian family life were evident in the way congregational work was organized.

The men's association would meet for dinner, with their wives doing all the cooking and cleanup. Women did most of the Sunday school teaching for children, men most of the teaching of adults. Women oversaw the classrooms, kitchen, worship flowers, and other decorations. Men served as trustees and financial officers, overseeing the budget, making repairs to the building, and keeping the grounds. Some of these patterns, of course, remain intact in the church as they do in many families.

Women's associations had a strength that male leaders generally did not know quite what to make of. When the Women's Christian Temperance Union, for example, produced a leader of national stature in Frances Willard, male denominational leaders were pleased—until she began to campaign for able and duly elected women to be seated as delegates in the 1888 MEC General Conference. At that point James M. Buckley (a major commentator on MEC polity) and other male leaders took it upon themselves to remind women of their appropriate spheres of work.[49]

Women have raised their own funds and administered their own mission programs for generations. The Woman's Foreign Missionary Society, Women's Society of Christian Service, and since 1972 the United Methodist Women (UMW) developed a whole range of missionary enterprises and institutions. Their mission education materials hold the field in United Methodism, and active UMW members are certainly the best informed laity regarding the conditions and activities of mission work in the U.S. and around the world.

But the independence of women's organizations within denominations has been a continual source of conflict. A hundred years ago "women had to battle their parent mission boards for the right to raise and disburse their own funds."[50] More recently women had to negotiate wisely in order to retain autonomy as a "Women's Division" of the GBGM, to continue to own and operate institutions and to avoid dominance by male clergy executives.

Thus the exclusion of women from leadership roles for the denomination as a whole led to their creating spheres in which their gifts could be utilized. But their very competence in organizing and fund-raising in their own associations put them in competition with the denomination-wide programs designed, voted into place, and administered by men.[51]

Gender roles in denominations today are in as much flux as in society at large. Women have moved into traditionally male leadership positions in congregations as well as denominational units, serving as lay leaders, chairs of boards, moderators, and executives. Women have entered seminaries in increasing numbers since the late 1960s, comprising half or more of the enrollment in some schools. Over 7200 women are ordained clergy in the UMC, making up about 16 percent of the total active clergy. Over one hundred clergy women presently serve as district superintendents and fourteen women have been elected to the episcopacy since the first female bishop, Marjorie Swank Matthews, in 1980.[52]

Many women who attend seminary are never ordained, though, and may become active in other ministries such as chaplaincy or spiritual formation. Many women of all (or no) denominational backgrounds are choosing to worship together in "women church" groups, though it is striking that women have not formed their own publicly visible American denomination in the traditional sense.[53]

Meanwhile single sex associations such as UMW and United Methodist Men (UMM) are struggling to interest new generations in their style of work. Since many younger people do not divide gender roles by the Victorian model, these organizations have had to find new flexibility to accommodate, for example, women who cannot meet on weekdays because of their employment or men who cannot meet on weeknights because of their childcare responsibilities.

Moreover, men's organizations seem to have thrived in the past "when large numbers of men perceived a direct connection between the mission of the church and broader social and political issues facing the nation as a whole."[54] In an era when broad consensus on these issues is lacking, men's associations must find other connections such as mission projects or groups for support and spiritual growth.

Thus while women and men have reached a greater balance in rights of participation in denominational life over the last thirty years, their respective roles in church authority, leadership, and influence are unsettled. The instability of their relationships in church life is evidenced by controversies over the efforts of some women and men to create new language and imagery for expressing Christian faith in a way that more fully includes women's experience.

Moreover, women are bringing increasing numbers of complaints, charges, and civil suits against male clergy, staff, and laity on grounds of sexual harassment and misconduct. This previously "behind closed doors" subject is increasingly in the public eye. Every United Methodist annual conference has witnessed the exit of male clergy under the cloud of such complaints. Jury awards to women who take their cases to civil court have created the urgent necessity for bishops and boards of ordained ministry to keep better records and take more decisive action against inappropriate behavior.

In response to changing gender relationships and the desire of women to take more leadership in the church, the 1976 General Conference authorized a standing General Commission on the Status and Role of Women (GCSRW), with parallel units in annual conferences and local churches.[55] Like the General Commission on Religion and Race, GCSRW exists to advocate justice and to monitor church activities to ensure their inclusiveness. With the ever-present signs of male violence against women in the larger society, such as the high incidence of rape, abuse, and harassment, the church has been committed to speaking out for the empowerment of women and for a model of church based on equality and mutuality.

Tension over varied understandings of gender and sexuality in the church is reflected in another obvious way in the denominations' preoccupation with homosexuality. While gay and lesbian people always have participated in church life, only in recent years have they been more outspoken about their lives and their desire for full acceptance in the church.

American society is struggling with how to protect the civil rights of homosexuals in the face of many groups who publicly proclaim their desire that homosexuals be excluded from participation. At such points as the enlistment of gays and lesbians in the military, or the hiring of gay and lesbian teachers in public schools, the impassioned disagreements of American citizens have flared out.

Denominations have experienced similar ambiguity and tension. The United Methodist Social Principles attempt to hold a middle ground, difficult in a society so polarized over the issue. Placing virtually opposite sentences side by side, the UMC declares itself in full support of homosexual civil rights and participation in congregational life. At the same time, the UMC states that homosexual behavior is "incompatible with Christian teaching" and not to be condoned (¶161.G, ¶162.H).

Likewise, the UMC attempts to exclude homosexuals from ordination into the ministry by declaring that "self-avowed practicing homosexuals" are not to be accepted into candidacy, ordination, or itineracy (¶304.3). Since an undetermined number of homosexuals are already ordained, of course, or are graduating from seminaries, denominations have to come to terms with what such language really means. Many church people do not wish to investigate the sexual practices of clergy as long as those practices are not harassing or abusive of other persons. Many people are more comfortable with the U.S. military's solution of "don't ask, don't tell." On the other hand, many church members would not accept a gay or lesbian pastor living openly in the church parsonage with a same-sex partner.

The widespread occurrence of AIDS among gay men has only exacerbated these tensions. While many mainstream Protestants have responded to the crisis of this virulent disease with ministries of compassion and comfort, many others have kept their distance. Some have connected the disease with what they consider sinful behavior and found in AIDS one more reason to exclude gay people from the church.

Some mainstream congregations have made public their welcoming of gays and lesbians into full participation. The Reconciling Congregations Program now includes over 160 United Methodist local churches. The growing numbers of those congregations only increases tensions, of course, over how to interpret the conflicting statements of the Social Principles. And at each General Conference proposals are made to make the language more accepting, from the one side, or more exclusive, from the other.

An additional complicating factor in gender and sexuality issues is that an international denomination such as United Methodism has not only the conflicts of U.S. society to contend with, but also the differing opinions and traditions of other cultures. Many societies are far less accepting of homosexuality than is the U.S. Women have yet to achieve leadership roles in most societies. This puts American Christians in a real dilemma. Should they advocate the gender and sexuality mores of a constantly changing U.S. culture, thus becoming a revolutionary influence in traditional cultures? Or should they respect the cultures of other lands and allow churches there to exclude the very persons whose rights the American church has tried to protect? As the number of delegates from non-U.S. parts of United Methodism to General Conference continues to increase, divisions over gender and sexual orientation will become sharper and require far greater efforts at reconciliation.

Theology and Practices of Faith

Many people assume that what gives a denomination its distinctive identity is its doctrine and theology. Certainly the traditions represented by contemporary mainstream denominations have been born from theological ferment and the desire either to represent a definite doctrinal stance or to perpetuate the teachings and practices of a founding figure. It is striking, however, how many of those founding figures—John Wesley among them—did not envision and only reluctantly agreed to the organization of their followers into a separate polity.

Denominations grounded themselves in certain creeds or confessions, to be sure. But such statements of faith were widely shared, and not exclusive to the denomination. Obviously the ancient creeds of the Apostles and of Nicea were common to the whole Western tradition. Even the Heidelberg or Westminster Confessions, or the Articles of Religion of the Church of England, were embraced by various groups.

Generally, mainstream denominations as corporate bodies have been reluctant to try to further condense their teachings into concise statements of doctrine. When they have written their theology down, it has been stated in broad terms that would keep the boundaries open for further insight and for wide participation by adherents of various understandings of those terms.

On the other hand, denominations have expressed certain theological accents or typical concerns. Only recently United Methodism has attempted to record this officially. The Disciplinary document on "Our Doctrinal Heritage" puts forward the distinct emphases of Wesleyan theology on God's all-surrounding grace and humanity's grateful response in holy living (pp. 45-48). This captures the character not only of typical United Methodist preaching, but also

101

practices such as open communion, regular invitations to membership, formation of class meetings, and action for social justice,
through which United Methodist people have tried to live their
theology.

Not surprisingly, then, most Americans have come to identify
mainstream denominations by their practices, not by their creeds.
Despite the efforts of those who advocate a clear verbal declaration
of belief, these denominations are for the most part known for the
way their congregations practice the faith. The hymns, prayers,
liturgical order, conduct of the sacraments, language, and symbols
of congregational worship are distinctive signs of denominational
difference. Ways of making decisions, ordaining leadership, calling
or receiving pastors, and organizing for ministry are notable as distinguishing marks of the various traditions.

Far from implying that "theology" is not important to denominational identity, this perception only suggests that what is available for reflection and dialogue is mainly the lived and practiced
theology of a denomination's adherents as they worship and work
together in congregations, councils, missions, and manifold other
forms of church. Practices express theological stances deeply rooted
in a denomination's heritage of being church. When a Presbyterian
church holds a meeting of all members to elect elders from among
the laity to govern the ministries of that congregation, they are
carrying forward a belief in the intentional, covenantal responsibility of each congregation to care for its own life and the life of its
community. When an Episcopal church installs a priest, they are
continuing an understanding that a priest represents the bishop in
a definite geographical parish and is pastor for the people of that
place—the ritual does not limit priestly duties to Episcopalian
"members."[56]

In recent years denominations have tended to structure their
doctrinal statements around methods for theological reflection on
Christian practices. United Methodism is exemplary of this trend,
even naming its 1988 statement "Our Theological Task." That is,
the statement is about a task, method, or theological practice, not
about doctrines the church teaches.

The task is "both critical and constructive . . . individual and
communal . . . contextual and incarnational . . . [and] essentially
practical." The statement then names the "sources and criteria" for

faithful theological work, beginning with scripture, and including tradition, experience, and reason (¶104).

Some United Methodists have advocated clearer doctrinal statements or the naming of fundamental doctrines without which the church cannot be an authentic witness to Jesus Christ. To date, however, the UMC has not exhibited much consensus around such a task. Perhaps the primary reason for this is United Methodism's characteristic preoccupation with practices of education, service, and mission, that is, practices that arise from the meeting of gospel and world.

Contemporary Ecclesiological Issues

The interaction of the church as a community of witness to the gospel with human needs and world crises is the source of most theological reflection today. At the beginning of the twenty-first century theological attention is focused on several large questions of enormous import for the living of Christian faith, and more particularly for this discussion, the denominational manner of being the church.[57]

The issue that has always packed the most punch for schism is the ground of authority for Christian faith. The place of scripture is especially critical, as methods for exploring the literary and historical context of biblical writings have proliferated. Are Jesus' words as recorded in the Gospels able to bear the weight of inquiry? Are the proclamations of scripture concerning Jesus' crucifixion and resurrection trustworthy? Does the Bible endorse any particular ecclesiology? Is the authority of leaders in the church dependent on their adherence to and ability to interpret certain scriptural declarations about Jesus Christ?

The sensitivity of these and like questions has made for denominational language about scripture in which every word counts. Assertions about the truth of the Bible—and what words are necessary to make a particular assertion—have become magnetic poles for theological parties within the churches that are perhaps more virulent now than at any time since the denominational schisms over slavery. Then as now, denominations were split over how literally to carry on practices advocated in scripture,

[handwritten margin note: The Bible and authority]

especially opinions of the apostle Paul. Then as now, denominations were torn between those who argued for the Lordship of Christ in a Kingdom to come and those who argued for the ways of the Kingdom to be practiced first and foremost in today's society.

These tensions shake the authority structure of the denominations themselves to the very foundations. Since denominations are also voluntary associations, their forms of inherited or ascriptive authority are relatively weak. As open national organizations occupying a middle ground ideologically, they are vulnerable to uprisings of well-organized parties of any persuasion. In an episcopal polity, some people insist that the bishop must act according to their views if they are to respect his or her authority. In presbyterial or synodical polities, some congregations send word that if decisions do not go their way, they may have to consider withholding funds or withdrawing altogether. The message is clear: the authority of the denomination extends only to points with which "I"—or "we"—can agree. This kind of autonomy and individualism, while very American in style, itself undermines the very authority that would come from a faith commonly held.

A second question of critical importance to the ecclesiology of denominations is the meaning of Jesus Christ. Who is Jesus Christ and what is the place of Christian claims about Jesus Christ as Savior in a world of many religions? If Christians do not insist on Jesus Christ as the only path to salvation, will there be any further motivation for mission?

These questions are basic to denominational life, because as seen above in the historical survey, American denominations grew up around mission ideals. Much of the impetus for congregations pooling their resources, and for their members joining national associations for particular causes, was the drive to make America a Christian land and the world a Christian civilization.

This cause shared so widely among the denominations corresponded with the institution-building era of American society. Churches were instrumental in founding the schools, hospitals, homes, lyceums, and more largely the public life of newly formed towns and cities across the land. In their zeal for these ideals of education, family, health, and work the denominations carried the mission to many parts of the globe with the same hopes for building Christian societies.

In the early-twenty-first century world, though, claims about Jesus Christ do not seem to translate so readily into unambiguous action. Christians are far more aware of the history and integrity of other world religions. Missionaries have had to seek new language for proclaiming the gospel in ways that invite faith, not threaten potential converts with exclusion. Moreover, the vast expansion of world markets has made clear that the benefits of Western life are available without the specifically Christian values that were once thought to be their necessary complement. Denominations have had to find a new institutional niche in responding to the crises of inhumanity that accompany the breakdown of societies—war, hunger, and oppression—while trying to assist indigenous peoples in building the institutions they need to sustain basic justice.

A third critical ecclesiological issue for denominations concerns the nature and purpose of the church. Contemporary Western societies pose the question of why Christian faith cannot be practiced in the privacy of one's own home or daily routine. Is joining a congregation or being part of a community of believers really necessary?

Denominations were originally created to provide order and discipline for ministry in and through congregations. Yet congregational life is under tremendous stress today. Communications technology and the pace of everyday life combine to make people treasure the privacy of their homes. Today's Americans do not join anything in nearly the numbers of earlier generations—political parties, parent associations, lodges, fraternities and sororities, or churches. When people do participate in congregations, they bring with them all the tensions of family and community that they live with every day. Some also bring expectations that the church will provide religious services to them, rather than calling them to serve others.

Denominations have not been accustomed to trying to articulate the purpose of Christian community or the inherently social nature of Christian faith. For years, of course, they have mounted membership drives and harangued members about "going to church." But these efforts were set within a world of assumptions that people who thought of themselves as good citizens could be motivated to get involved in a congregation.

United Methodism has never developed much of an ecclesiology for congregations—or more broadly, for the practice of Christian faith in community. The bishops' foundation document on *Vital Congregations—Faithful Disciples* (1990) is one of few such efforts. Thus United Methodism is confronted with a multifaceted task of articulating its understanding of congregations and also its commitment to a connection of congregations, members, and leaders as the embodiment of church.

A fourth issue of vital importance to the future of the denominational form of church is the message of Christianity in a world of continual war, famine, overpopulation, gender and racial injustice, ethnic conflict, and ecological disaster. Is there any hope? How can the church express hope in a way that makes God's biblical promises real, that enables trust? What kind of church can make that hope tangible through its practices?

Much of what goes on in denominations does not reflect hope. Resources are scarce. Conferences cut back on staff and program. Constituencies are split over the church's way of addressing social issues.

Denominations face the question of what form of church can express Christian hope. No ecclesiology can be embodied in anything more than a clay vessel. No church can eliminate conflict, produce only cordial relationships, or reach instant consensus on actions and directions. Christians have to put Christian hope into practice with courage, determination, and perseverance.

This is not the same as the bland face of American cultural optimism. This is hope grounded in the proclamation of Jesus Christ and the promise of God's Reign in the world. People possessed by this hope will not be content with any polity that is inadequate to express new ways of living in hope.

Finally, what are the distinctive contributions of particular traditions as frameworks for responding to these large questions confronting all expressions of Christianity? What does each denomination offer in language and perspective and practice to dialogue around these questions? Is there a peculiarly United Methodist way of living into these issues?

Many consultants in church growth and other observers have argued that denominations are losing their distinctiveness and that people do not really care any more about the traditions represented by denominations. The pews are full of people who know little of the denominational heritage of their congregation.

Marriages across denominational or faith lines are much more common today. Far more people base their church membership solely on what a particular congregation offers them or how it fits their personal style than on the affiliation named on the sign out front. Many people learn of their congregation's polity only when the pastor announces that the bishop has asked her or him to go to another church, or when they are invited to stay after worship to elect new deacons.

Just as pastors struggle with whether to teach new members what is distinctive about Presbyterianism or United Methodism, so in every arena of their ministry denominations are wrestling with whether and how to articulate the way of being church that arises from their traditions. Books of discipline and order are a central place in which the distinctive character of traditions is recorded. Here again, though, there has been little consensus around really giving attention to such writings as a profound expression of a denomination's characteristic ways.

I would argue that whatever pundits may say about the loss of distinctives, denominational ways are not only noticeable, but critically important contributions to a full ecclesiology. That is, each tradition brings strengths and truths to the daunting challenge of trying to be the church today. To ignore them is to lose a living heritage and the wisdom of generations of believers. To build on them is to undertake a generative task of theological practice grounded in past experience and hopeful about the church's faithfulness in the future.

Polity

The preceding sections begin to demonstrate how complex the phenomenon of denominations really is. Part of the ambiguity of many discussions of contemporary denominationalism is that participants bring so many different perspectives to them. An institution that is at once a profound source of communal memory, an economic system, a many-layered culture, and the location or occasion for people's religious experience cannot easily be grasped, much less managed or steered in certain directions.

Yet arguably what gives denominations their coherence in the most comprehensive sense is their polity. Their forms of authority, governance, order, and decision making constitute the covenant that binds them into institutions. Polity is not sufficient to make a denomination; moments of assembly, networks of friendship, and the energy of shared purpose are among many critical factors. But polity is certainly a necessary condition if denominations are to have continuity and endurance.

Polity is among the most neglected subjects in the literature on mainstream denominations. Interpretive handbooks such as Bishop Jack M. Tuell's *Organization of The United Methodist Church* or Robert L. Wilson and Steven Harper's *Faith and Form* have been helpful teaching tools. But no full-length scholarly study of United Methodist polity has been published since Bishop Nolan B. Harmon's *Organization of The Methodist Church*, last edited in 1962. Some of the most useful resources for understanding United Methodist polity date to the turn of the twentieth century, especially the work of Bishop John J. Tigert.[58]

Little has been written, either, about the church as an organization. The distinctiveness of particular ecclesiologies and their expression in denominational forms of governance has been only sparsely explored. Emerging theories of organizations, such as efforts to understand organizational culture or the nature of modern institutions, have been little used in denominational studies.[59]

Polity, in short, has been part of a taken-for-granted world. Church leaders and members know it mainly in the immediacy of decision making. Scholars have overlooked it as both a historical and contemporary window into the richness of denominational life. The current ferment over change in the church, however, promises to awaken new interest in foundational questions about what denominations really are and what they are for.

American denominations have worked out their polities in the ever-changing context of a society coming into being, a nation still little over two hundred years old. Neither churches in the European sense—a unitary expression of national culture coinciding with the authority of the state—nor sectarian communities living apart from mainstream society, denominations have had to create their peculiar forms of being church. They have written constitutions in order to constitute themselves as distinct, self-perpetuating bodies.

Through their books of order and discipline they have set out the authority and organization of ministry, and established the standards and responsibilities of membership.

The denominations translated from European polities varied elements of congregational, pastoral, and episcopal practice. But always these have been adapted to the realities of the American context. In a society largely lacking in inherited forms of authority and governance, but in which authority was to a great extent conferred by the governed, the denominations refused much of the formality and ceremony accompanying European traditions. For example, the newly elected Bishop Francis Asbury tried the episcopal garb suited to England, discovered that it was totally impractical for riding horseback, and never wore it again.[60]

To the basic polity of ordination, ministry, and congregational discipline the denominations gradually added the legislative by-laws necessary to govern their expanding mission in America and other lands. As their enterprises grew, so did their provisions for governing and funding them. And to that legislation was added even more regulatory language as the churches sought to establish their ministries more permanently and to be more comprehensive and inclusive in their connectional and cooperative work.

Today's books of polity thus are a great deal longer than their early nineteenth-century antecedents. They reflect the denominations' efforts to respond to an increasingly complex society. Through their paragraphs are interwoven the wider realities of culture, economics, and society that denominations both mirror and affect through their actions. Even so, books of order record only the bare outline of the church's action. The responsibilities of church councils, bishops, and pastors cover multiple pages, but do not begin to describe the actual day-to-day work of those assigned to carry them out. Moreover, the issues to which polity documents often allude are intertwined with denominational life in a far more complex way than could ever be put on paper.

To understand fully a denomination's polity is not only to know its book of order, then, but also to study the changes and tensions out of which the book is born. A sentence can evoke a whole history. Paragraph 365.2 says simply that "both men and women are included in all provisions of the *Discipline* that refer to the ordained ministry." But well over a hundred years of conflict, pain, breakthrough, and continuing struggle for mutuality and acceptance are stirring behind those words.

A provision that names something fundamental to the polity normally does not even touch on the context within which it must be carried out. "All elders in full connection who are in good standing in an annual conference shall be continued under appointment by the bishop," says ¶328.1. But all the sleepless nights for bishops and district superintendents trying to fit pastors and places, and all the career, marriage, family, and personal issues that confront pastors in accepting an appointment, are present only in the experience of trying to be faithful to this basic tenet of United Methodism.

Thus denominational polity is both a written text and a lived practice. The early circuit riders used to say that all they carried in their saddlebags was a Bible, a hymnbook, and a *Book of Discipline.* Like scripture, books of discipline proclaimed many truths about the Methodist, Evangelical, or United Brethren way of being church. For a rapidly expanding movement under orders "to reform the continent and spread scriptural holiness over these lands," the *Discipline* was another Gospel. But like the hymnbook, the *Discipline* was basically a practice, meaningful only as it was lived through the actions and relationships of Methodist, Evangelical, and United Brethren people. It only distilled on paper an oral tradition shared through the common experiences of its adherents.

Denominational polity in word and practice weaves together the functions and contexts of the church's ministry in immensely complex patterns. This complexity reflects the varied dimensions of denominations as cultural, economic, social, and theological institutions. Because they have grown up with American society, mainstream denominations generally reflect the social changes and cultural trends of the nation. Because they have expressed a world mission and are joined with like denominational bodies in many lands, they increasingly mirror the tensions of cross-cultural relationships. Because their adherents are also full participants in the wider culture, they adopt in various ways the rhetoric and styles used in many organizations—especially in a commercial culture like America, the rhetoric of business and the marketplace.

No single text could adequately describe the density or subtlety of these relationships of denomination and culture. But as this particular study of United Methodist polity moves along the outlines of the *Discipline*, we will note how the context is always present in the language, the choice of legislative provisions, and the attention given to particular issues. There will be points to ask as well whether certain ways of defining the church's practices are really adequate to the challenge presented by the contemporary world.

The Book of Discipline *Today*

The *Book of Discipline* is the only polity document that United Methodists have in common across the whole connection. The *Discipline* has been in continuous revision and publication for over two hundred years, and contains within it the cultural and ecclesial influences identified above and many others besides. It is itself an exercise in practical theology, demonstrating how the church has responded to changing contexts and situations.

Thus the *Discipline* is necessarily the focus of this book and of any detailed discussion of United Methodist polity and organization. The *Discipline* does not begin to capture the richness and complexity of practice in varied situations around the globe. This is borne in oral tradition sustained by networks of collegiality and friendship and passed from generation to generation. But the *Discipline* remains the distillation of practical wisdom in written form and comprises the only law the church has. Every word of it has passed—albeit fleetingly at times—under the eyes of General Conference. Whether it is used or not is, of course, up to the laity and clergy to whose hands it is entrusted.

Some voices suggest that the *Discipline* is much too long and full of unnecessary regulation. Bishop Roy H. Short argued over twenty years ago that

> United Methodists for some reason have persisted in going into great detail in writing church law. At this point they are scarcely paralleled by any other great ecclesiastical body. It seems to be a favorite sport among United Methodists for everyone to attempt to get his particular pet ideas embodied into church law, thus making them obligatory for everyone else. . . . There are, however, those United Methodists who feel that we go into too great detail in writing church law and that something would be gained

if general directions and warrants of power were given without superimposing a large amount of carefully spelled-out, legal directions.[61]

It is true enough that many paragraphs of the *Discipline* go into great detail. It has grown longer in recent years as more and more descriptions and regulations have been added. This only promises to increase, for example, with the need for more attention to processes that can help the church in legal proceedings.

Yet what is striking about the *Discipline* on the whole is not its length or detail, but its unevenness and inconsistency. Long paragraphs have been inserted to cover special situations that involve relatively few local churches. Yet paragraphs providing an ecclesiological foundation for ministry and mission are slim or nonexistent. By far the weightiest section of the book is chapter five, over 200 pages on the general agencies, titled "Administrative Order." This is the only document where the basic legislation for these organizations can logically be placed since they are distinctively connectional in nature. Yet the section on the ministry of the laity, which has the potential to be instructive about the discipline and vocation United Methodism expects of its participants, is only six pages long.

The episcopal address introducing the 1939 *Discipline* of the new Methodist Church probably explains this situation best:

> The Methodist Discipline is a growth rather than a purposive creation. The founders of Methodism did not work with a set plan, as to details. They dealt with conditions as they arose. . . . In such a process of adjustment, the Discipline became not a book of definite rules, nor yet a formal code, but rather a record of the successive stages of spiritual insight attained by Methodists under the grace of Christ. We have, therefore, expected that the Discipline would be administered, not merely as a legal document, but as a revelation of the Holy Spirit working in and through our people. We reverently insist that a fundamental aim of Methodism is to make her organization an instrument for the development of spiritual life.[62]

It is possible to be in sympathy with this episcopal explanation and still note the consequences of a book that is a growth. For one thing, the *Discipline* contains no record of how it has grown. No paragraphs or provisions have any annotation whatsoever to indi-cate when they were added or under what circumstances. As Robert Emory complained in 1844,

> When a young Methodist preacher enters, in accordance with the direction of his church, upon the study of its Discipline, he is curi-ous to know when and by whom that Discipline was framed. . . . There is internal evidence that the present Discipline was not all composed at one time. At what periods then were its several parts introduced, and what modifications have they undergone? These are points not only of curious inquiry, but essential often to right interpretation. But they are points on which students generally can obtain no satisfactory information. . . . the Discipline, as revised at each General Conference, being in itself complete, sup-plants all that had gone before it, and the previous editions are cast aside as of no further use.[63]

This is still the case, even with the Constitution. Amendments are not listed separately, but simply incorporated into the present body of the document. No reader can find out how it has been revised without referring to all *Disciplines* since 1968.

Moreover, the *Discipline* as published is the work of a committee charged with the daunting responsibility for "mak[ing] changes in phraseology as may be necessary to harmonize legislation without changing its substance" (p. ii). They also check the consistency of paragraph numbering, a task which has often led to confusion because numbers change as legislation is added (or more rarely deleted).[64]

To these perennial difficulties must be added the problem that the General Conference gives no one in the church responsibility for considering the book as a whole—how it is organized, which sec-tions need strengthening or fuller rationale, points of conflicting mandates, or even the format in which it is printed. The 2000 episcopal greeting insists that "communication is essential for understanding what the Church is and does" (p. vi). But one could legitimately ask whether the current published form of the *Discipline* really communicates with the audience for whom it is intended, or enhances communication between various entities of the church.[65]

In any case, what the church has in the *Discipline* is "the most current statement of how United Methodists agree to live their lives together" (p. v). In that sense it must be taken with utmost seriousness, not just because it is the book of church law, but because it is the record of practices the church intends. It is a book of accountability for the discipline United Methodists profess. It provides the structures and procedures that can put that discipline into practice.

Finally, the *Discipline* is the product of Christian conference—the elemental form of Methodist life. As United Methodist people continue to live together, to seek the fullness of God's love in community, and to fulfill God's mission as one connection, they must do so in conference. Here all the streams of political influences—along with the languages and concerns of contemporary cultures—flow together. Here United Methodist people must discern together the direction the Spirit is leading.

In this practice, United Methodists inherit a living tradition. They can look back to one of the most intriguing characters in Christian history, John Wesley, not so much for answers as for provocative and pragmatic ways of living the way toward the Reign of God. They can draw as well upon the experience of United Methodist people across the generations who also sought authentic ways to be the church in their own times and places.

CHAPTER 3

The Constitution of United Methodism

From an ecclesiological standpoint, a formal constitution for a church body seems an oddity. How strange to think of the Body of Christ in the world needing a constitution. The church just *is*, after all, and not by human invention. As the United Methodist baptismal ritual declares, "the Church is of God, and will be preserved to the end of time."

Through baptism the people of God are "incorporated by the Holy Spirit into God's new creation," the present manifestation of which is to be "initiated into Christ's holy Church."[1] The church is called into being by the Holy Spirit in the new reality of the resurrection. The Spirit charges the church with carrying on Christ's ministry of witness and service to the Reign of God, and provides all the gifts necessary for this task.

The church is a living body of traditions originating in the apostolic era, formed in councils for doctrine and polity, and shaped by faithful women and men of every time and place. Christ has promised to be present in any gathering in the name of the Lord, bringing all such gatherings into unity. So what could it possibly mean for a church to have a constitution?

The Constitution of the UMC, devised and adopted respectively by The Methodist Church and The Evangelical United Brethren Church General Conferences in 1966 and put into effect at the Uniting Conference of 1968, begins at this broadest ecclesiological vista. "The Church is a community of all true believers under the Lordship of Christ," the Preamble declares. Word and sacrament are definitive for this community, and all expressions of ministry and mission—fellowship, worship, edification, and redemption—follow from them "under the discipline [N.B.] of the Holy Spirit" (pp. 21-22).

Thus far comes the basic definition. But then there is a cloud on the horizon. The capital-C Church of the first sentence turns out in the realities of the world to be divided into parts. There is more than one church in the Church. In fact, the Preamble continues, the purpose of the negotiations behind this document is to bring about a union of churches as "an expression of the oneness of Christ's people." And because the churches have been distinct bodies, a statement is needed in order to make their unity "actual in organization and administration in the United States of America and throughout the world."

A constitution, then, is necessary to constitute—to create, establish, or bring into being—a new ecclesial entity, in particular in the context of a free society of diverse religious practices. As an organization, the church must be constituted by certain fundamental principles and organic units that together give it its substantive nature. Unlike an individual person, the church cannot exist in itself; its associative being has to be constituted.[2]

The Commission on the Constitution of the MEC, which worked from 1888 to 1900 to formalize a constitution for the church for the first time, defined their object this way:

> A constitution is an instrument containing a recital of principles of organization and of declarations of power, permissions, and limitations which cannot be taken from, added to, or changed in any particular without the consent of the power which originally created the instrument, or by the legal process determined by the body possessing original power.[3]

Therefore in Division One of the 1968 Constitution, the general provisions for the church first name the originating bodies of this Constitution by declaring the union of The Evangelical United Brethren Church and The Methodist Church (Art. I). The articles go on to give the new entity a name, The United Methodist Church (Art. II), specify continuity of doctrine with the bodies now joining (Art. III), and claim the physical assets through which the church expresses its ministries (Art. VI). They also make explicit the fundamental nature of the church as an open community striving toward "unity at all levels of church life" (Art. IV, V). This nature resonates with the principle of a free society in which "all persons, without regard to race, color, national origin, status, or economic

116

condition" are "eligible" to participate (Art. IV; notice it does not say "welcome" to participate—here the language is of human rights, not hospitality).

To this point the Constitution has basically named the being of this corporate body. The name itself is profoundly significant. The Methodist Church was far the larger entity in this union, and the Evangelical United Brethren needed some indication of their place in this new body. The word "United" not only echoed a word in the EUB name, but indicated a distinctively new church that was committed to a dynamic process of growth toward broader unity in the churches (Art. V). This unity was manifested in the continuity of doctrinal agreement, the merging of properties, and the free and open participation of all persons.[4]

In the subsequent two divisions come the elements that constitute the body. The first of these, Division Two, is titled "organization" but actually is entirely about conferences and how they are constituted. The second, Division Three, is titled "episcopal supervision" and describes how bishops are constituted.

The last two divisions of the Constitution create a process through which it can be adjudicated or amended. Division Four constitutes a Judicial Council to make final determination of "the constitutionality of any act of the General Conference" and to review and "pass upon decisions of law made by bishops in annual conferences" (¶54). These functions belonged to the General Conference or the bishops until the creation of a separate judicial body in the MC in 1939 (following a procedure developed in 1934 in the MECS).

A separate judiciary helps to balance the powers of United Methodism's two basic constitutive entities. Judicial Council rulings limit the powers of General Conference, which cannot judge the constitutionality of its own acts. Judicial Council review is a check on the episcopal powers over decisions of church law. As in civil polity, of course, judicial powers fully exercised do become constructive interventions in the government of the body. The opinions of the Judicial Council can force the General Conference to make new and clearer laws and annual conferences to redefine and revise policies. The Council can overrule bishops and force them to weigh decisions by new or different criteria. The very act of interpreting church law also contributes to the church's self-understanding and certainly affects its practices. But the judiciary is still not a constituting entity in quite the originative sense of the conferences or the episcopacy.

Division Five simply provides a method for amending the Constitution. Amendments may originate in either the General Conference or the Annual Conferences, but must be passed by a two-thirds majority (three-fourths in some cases) of both the General Conference and the "aggregate number of members of the several Annual Conferences present and voting." The Council of Bishops certifies the vote (¶¶57, 58).

Two Constitutive Principles

Thus if one were to ask what constitutes The United Methodist Church, one would take up Divisions Two and Three on the conferences and the episcopacy, respectively. These indeed have been the constitutive elements from the beginning of Methodism. As the constitutional historian of an earlier period, John J. Tigert, wrote,

> Since 1744 the two constant factors of Methodist polity, (1) a superintending and appointing power, and (2) a consulting body called the Conference, have been continuously operative. These two factors are constitutional or elemental in the government of Methodism . . . the former chiefly executive and the latter chiefly legislative.[5]

Much of the tension, both creative and distracting, that has driven Methodist churches through the years is contained in the dynamics of these two original elements.

The Principle of Conference

To state the case more broadly, United Methodism is comprised of an unsettled, often unreflective, yet remarkably creative blending of two constitutive principles. First, the principle of democratic representation essential to free republics and voluntary associations has been constitutive of United Methodism most visibly through its conferences. While these meetings have their origin in the organization of Methodism as a voluntary society in the

Church of England, they took on a distinctly American form in parallel with the legislative assemblies and political conventions of the emerging U.S. in the nineteenth century.

Wesley gathered conferences of Methodist preachers to consult with him, but they were never decision-making bodies. In the American context, however, from the moment they voted to accept Francis Asbury and Thomas Coke as their general superintendents in 1784, the preachers collectively became the fundamental legislative body of the new church.

In fact, one could argue, with the weight of constitutional opinion in the late nineteenth century, that "the body of traveling elders," that is, all the ordained preachers collectively, were the "original or primary constituency" that brought the Methodist Episcopal Church into being. They elected their general superintendents at their constituting "Christmas conference" in 1784, voted on changes to the *Discipline* each year in annual conference, created a quadrennial general conference of all ordained preachers in 1792, and in 1808 made it a delegated General Conference with restrictions on its powers. In a genealogical sense, then, both the conference system and the episcopacy hold their charter from this original body—the "traveling preachers" of this one unbroken "traveling Connection."

Nearly a hundred years passed before laity had any representation in the conferences at all, and fifty more years before it became equal participation. It was still this primal body of ordained preachers who had to vote to amend the constitution on behalf of lay representation. This expanded and continuous body of all clergy in full connection and corresponding lay members of all annual conferences collectively is today the fundamental body—the Connection as a whole—that must vote on any amendments to the Constitution (though amendments must also be passed by the General Conference, ¶57).[6]

The conference system is not fully democratic, of course. Unlike such ecclesiastical bodies as the Southern Baptist Convention, conferences are not open to all laity sent by congregations. In fact, the system is not even based on delegated representation of all laity. The conferences began as gatherings of the preachers, and all preachers are members of annual conferences. Laypersons, on the other hand, are members of annual conference on the basis of one

119

lay member per pastor of a charge, without regard to the size of congregation or other constituency from which any one lay member comes. They are not really "representatives" of a larger lay body, since their membership in annual conference is based on the pastoral charge, not on the membership of a congregation (¶30).

The annual conferences then elect delegates to the Jurisdictional and General Conferences on a basis set out in the Constitution (¶¶12-14). These bodies are also equally lay and clergy, with the laity and clergy voting separately for their own delegates. But since the basis of representation is already skewed toward the clergy in the annual conferences, the delegated bodies can hardly be called fully representative either.[7]

General Conference

The General Conference comprised of these delegates from annual conferences is the only body in the UMC with legislative powers over the connection as a whole. It defines and fixes the powers of all other units, including the bishops, clergy, laity, annual conferences, and "connectional enterprises of the Church" in missions, education, and other ministries (¶15). It is given powers even over the annual conferences which collectively first created it (though annual conference members collectively can still vote down constitutional amendments passed by General Conference).

These powers are not unlimited, however. Beginning in 1808 the MEC built in certain checks on the delegated body it was creating. The "restrictive rules" have continued in force in mainly the same form ever since (¶¶16-20). In The United Methodist Church the rules protect the Articles of Religion (as originally adopted in the MEC), the Confession of Faith (from the EUBC), and unspecified "established standards of doctrine" from alteration except by an overwhelming majority (three-fourths) of all annual conference members (¶¶16, 57). The rules prevent any facile change of the General Rules that originated in the early Methodist societies (¶19). The right to trial of both ministers and members is protected, and the net income of the publishing house is designated exclusively for aiding preachers and their families (¶¶18, 20).

Most important from a polity standpoint, the restrictive rules also prevent the General Conference from taking any action "to do away with episcopacy or destroy the plan of our itinerant general superintendency" (¶17). This general language has been hotly disputed at times. It became a central issue in the split of northern and southern branches of episcopal Methodism in the 1840s. The northern church viewed bishops as elected by and amenable to the General Conference. The southern church viewed the restrictive rule as giving bishops a place alongside General Conference. As the MECS General Conference of 1844 put it, the bishop was "not a mere creature" or in any "permanent sense an officer of the general conference," but rather "a co-ordinate branch, the executive department proper of the government."[8]

The issue arose again when the MEC General Conference made provision for the election of missionary bishops in 1856, and race and language bishops in 1912, whose jurisdictions were limited to their own ethnic or language group—thus excluding them from the "itinerant general superintendency."[9] While this provision was ruled unconstitutional in the MC in 1939—thus reinforcing the historic "plan" of episcopacy—only in 1960 were all bishops of Central (i.e., non-U.S.) Conferences fully included as members of the Council of Bishops.[10]

Similarly, the creation of the MC Jurisdictional Conferences in 1939 decidedly modified the general superintendency. Mainly in order to prevent black bishops from presiding over white conferences, the Constitution restricted bishops' powers of "residential and presidential supervision" to their own Jurisdiction—five of which were regional and one racial. The restriction remains, even in the absence of the racial jurisdiction (¶47).

The Jurisdictional Conference Anomaly

The Jurisdictional Conference remains a constitutional anomaly originally invented to accommodate a social and cultural difference. All the duties assigned to it by the Constitution historically belonged to the General Conference. The basis of representation by annual conference delegates is set by General Conference, and in legislative ¶513 is designated as simply a doubling of whatever number of delegates has been determined for General Conference. An annual conference's General Conference delegates are included in that number and serve in the Jurisdictional Conference as well (¶32). In short, Jurisdictional Conferences are simply regional derivatives of the General Conference and do not have a fundamental role in constituting the UMC.

This is not in any way to dismiss the primary political function of Jurisdictional Conferences—the electing and consecrating of bishops—only to make clear that the function derives from the General Conference. The episcopacy in the U.S. is constituted by the Jurisdictional Conferences—to echo the original language of the 1787 *Discipline*: "Section IV. On the constituting of Bishops, and their Duty"—that is, their election by the conference and their consecration by the laying on of hands. But the number of bishops is determined on "a uniform basis" set by General Conference (¶15.10), and once bishops are elected their membership resides in the Council of Bishops.

"Jurisdiction" is both a regional and a legal term. As a name for a geographic area it carries with it the intention of adapting United Methodism to regional cultures and allowing for practices that best fit and express regional ways. In this sense it served well to enable the MECS to sustain many of its customs and relationships after union with the larger, more centralized, and more national MEC.

As a legal term "jurisdiction" indicates the limits of power of various agents. The Jurisdictional Conference has various legal and covenantal relationships with the educational and mission institutions within its boundaries. The bishops elected by a Jurisdictional Conference have "residential and presidential supervision" in the annual conferences within the bounds of that Jurisdiction.

The designers of this system intended it to create a balance or distribution of powers throughout the connection. Membership of the general boards and agencies would be elected by jurisdictions. The work of general boards and agencies would be complemented by jurisdictional auxiliaries. Jurisdictional Conferences would have power to determine the boundaries of the annual conferences within their own territory. John M. Moore, the MECS bishop who worked tirelessly for this plan, put the argument best in 1943:

> The Jurisdictional Conference is the essential, vital, and principal administrative and promotional unit of the Church, with legislative power limited to regulations on regional affairs . . . [it] is the key and core of the entire system . . . The Plan of Union [1939] sets up a commonwealth of balancing bodies wherein no one shall be supreme, except in its own field.[11]

122

A survey of current Jurisdictional Conference journals, however, shows clearly that these hopes were never realized.[12] Only the Southeastern Jurisdiction—the region of the old MECS—has any significant level of staff and budget for program.

Moreover, the jurisdictional structure as originally constituted embodied the fatal flaw of an apartheid system, segregating African American churches into a separate, nonregional "church within a church." In the thirty-year period of its existence, the Central Jurisdiction did provide a coherent organization for supporting African American institutions and developing lay and clergy leadership. But much of the energy of all six of the original jurisdictions was diverted to the political task of achieving racial unity—a task completed legally in the 1968–1972 quadrennium but yet to be fulfilled in many ways today.[13]

In sum, jurisdictional powers are exercised on behalf of the church as a whole, not as a region. Trustees of church-related institutions may be elected by the Jurisdictional Conferences, but there is little reason from the institutions' standpoint why those elections—or the relationship they express—would have to be or even ought to be regionally based. Membership on general boards and agencies is selected from a pool that originates in the annual conferences, not the Jurisdictional Conference. The bishops practice their superintendency within the whole connection, not just the jurisdiction of their election.

The Constitution simply does not make jurisdictions in any way fundamental or constitutive—except for their role in constituting bishops. Little wonder, then, that the real agenda and only excitement when these conferences gather surrounds the episcopal elections. In an ironic twist on the regionalism that originally made jurisdictions seem necessary, they now serve mainly as political bases for ensuring balance in the election of bishops from distinct regions of the church.

Central Conferences

Central Conferences have powers and duties parallel to the jurisdictions, but in a distinctive context that makes them in practice much more constitutive of the church in their regions. The Central Conference as an entity originated over a hundred years ago based on reasons well expressed by Bishop James M. Thoburn:

[The General Conference] with its immense responsibilities and limited time, would never be able to legislate for a church spread out over the whole globe. There must be a legislative body, with carefully defined powers, in each separate nationality.[14]

Central Conferences have not always followed national lines. But they have enabled United Methodism to develop a distinct identity related to the culture of various regions of the globe. To them is granted not only the power "to make such rules and regulations for the administration of the work within their boundaries"—this in common with Jurisdictional Conferences—but also the power to make "such changes and adaptations of the General Discipline as the conditions in the respective areas may require" (¶29.5).

Central Conferences may not make changes "contrary to the Constitution and the General Rules of The United Methodist Church" (¶537.9). But this still leaves wide range for encouraging local churches and annual conferences to organize in the most suitable fashion, and for churches of a region to adapt their ministry, worship, and other practices to the local or national context.

The seven current Central Conferences organize United Methodist work in twenty-two nations. Each of them has the power to set the boundaries of the annual conferences within its bounds, and to elect bishops to preside over them. While the General Conference retains the power to determine how many bishops may be elected, the Central Conference fixes the limit on episcopal tenure, usually requiring reelection every four years (¶537.3). Central Conferences have full representation in General Conference and general boards and agencies, and their bishops are full members of the Council of Bishops.

The Principle of Episcopacy

The second principle that constitutes United Methodism is episcopacy. But because of its synthesis of varying polities, one could certainly agree with Bishop John L. Nuelsen that United Methodism has "an episcopacy that the Christian church ha[s] not yet seen."[15] United Methodist bishops are elected to office by lay and clergy delegates in Jurisdictional or Central Conferences, and their presidential duties are limited to those conferences. Yet they are to practice a general superintendency. The bishops in Council are charged by the Constitution with planning "for the general oversight and promotion of the temporal and spiritual interests of the entire Church" (¶45).

The Constitution further grants bishops the power to appoint ministers to the charges in consultation with the district superintendents, who are extensions of the episcopal office (¶52). The Constitution also gives bishops life tenure. These are both features associated ecclesiologically with a monarchical episcopacy, that is, an episcopacy understood as rule by divine right and succession with an essential difference of order from the body of clergy. In these features United Methodist episcopacy is kin to earlier Anglican and Roman Catholic forebears.

Yet while United Methodist episcopacy was initiated by Wesley, Coke, and others steeped in the Anglican heritage, it is significantly different. In Anglican ecclesiology, the bishop is the unit of church and presides over a diocese. Parishes are local expressions of the episcopal diocese. Clergy are the expressions or extensions of the bishop in a local place, and a parish receives the clergy as a representative of the bishop. The bishop visits each parish to perform confirmations, because all parishioners are members of the bishop's extended congregation.

Little of this applies in United Methodist episcopacy. Oddly, the Constitution fails to specify even that a United Methodist bishop has authority to ordain the clergy—this is listed as one of the "presidential duties" in legislative ¶415—much less other aspects of an Anglican model such as the authority to confirm new members. The sacraments are not mentioned either, which means that in United Methodism episcopacy is not understood as a distinct order retaining sacramental authority which is then delegated to clergy-persons as extensions of the bishop when they are ordained elders.[16]

This leads to the conclusion of Bishop Jack Tuell that "the episcopacy is a constitutional office, rather than monarchical in character."[17] United Methodist episcopacy does not constitute the church in the traditional sense either from Ignatius in the second century—"where the bishop is, there is the church"—or from the monarchical or organic understanding of the succession of bishops providing the church's fundamental continuity from the apostles.

United Methodist bishops are elected and consecrated to office, not ordained to office. Though the Constitution does not state this explicitly, legislative ¶¶403-4 make clear that bishops remain part of the body of elders (a translation of *presbyteros* in the New Testament), functioning as *primus inter pares*.[18] In the absence of a bishop, an annual conference elects "a president pro tempore from among the traveling elders" (¶603.6).[19] Bishops remain part of the itineracy, receiving their assignments from the Jurisdictional Conference via the Jurisdictional Committee on Episcopacy (¶48). In short, as Nuelsen had it, Methodism has "an episcopal form grafted into a presbyterian stem."[20]

Thus United Methodist episcopacy constitutes the church through the bishops' active role of oversight and superintendency practiced from its American beginnings, coincident with the conferences of the preachers. This superintendency, including the authority to ordain, is essentially a practice that embodies an ever-changing ecclesiological understanding, rather than a fixed ecclesiological principle that issues in well-defined practices. In Bishop James Mathews's words, United Methodist episcopacy is "flexible, experimental, pragmatic, and functional . . . what the people, under God's guidance and in response to the demands of history, determine it shall be."[21]

Indeed, for all the lack of traditional warrants in the Constitution, bishops have enormous influence in United Methodism. They represent the connection. The first pages of the *Discipline* contain a list of their names in the order of their election since 1784. Bishops of Methodist, EUB, and Central Conference heritages are listed together as an unmistakable sign of the church's unity.

Bishops are called to a broad mandate of oversight. In one of the *Discipline's* simplest and most compelling phrases, they are asked "to lead"—"to lead and oversee the spiritual and temporal affairs of The United Methodist Church" (¶414.1). The generality of this duty is also its strength. Bishops are given wide latitude to speak, intervene, encourage, preach, evangelize, to put themselves on the line. As it was with their ancestor Asbury, their constant travel and omnipresence makes the connection tangible.

The conferences—fleeting moments of assembly—would never be enough to sustain the connection without the itinerant superintendency. Little wonder, then, that many voices in United

126

Methodism today call for stronger episcopal leadership—not authoritarianism or autocracy, much less monarchy—but a leadership of presence and vision that will give the connection its coherence for the future.

In a charge added in 1992, the *Discipline* gives bishops the responsibility "to guard, transmit, teach, and proclaim, corporately and individually, the apostolic faith" as well as "to teach and uphold the theological traditions of The United Methodist Church" (¶414.3, .5). Especially since the 1980s, United Methodist bishops have sought new ways to practice their teaching role, not as an authoritative magisterium in the Roman Catholic sense but as a council of wisdom. (Only the General Conference could make any doctrinal statements for United Methodism, and those might well require constitutional amendment). This task supplements or even regularizes the evangelistic emphasis on preaching that traditionally has made many bishops among the most popular preachers in the connection.

The bishops have also had wide influence in the missional activism of United Methodism. They serve on and preside over general boards and agencies and boards of trustees of church-related institutions. Their energy and experience are in such demand that they have had to be wary of becoming mere program promoters and "sales managers," in the words of one.[22]

But the persistent ecclesiological question is in what sense the tasks of teaching, evangelism and mission constitute "church." The traditional Methodist privileging of preaching and mission activism over sacramental order results in enduring ambiguities for the *episkopoi* of this church. The episcopacy is a constitutive principle of United Methodism by traditional practice, influence, and attributed authority far more than by organic law. The Restrictive Rule protects "the *plan* of our itinerant general superintendency" (emphasis mine)—that is, its role in advancing the church's mission—more than any inherent authority.

The episcopal prerogatives of appointment-making and life tenure have been challenged repeatedly—in the 1820s, 1890s, and 1970s. The word "episcopal" was dropped from the denominational name when The Methodist Church was formed in 1939, in part to make the Methodist Protestant partners to the union more comfortable in accepting ecclesial life with bishops, whose appointive authority had been one source of their protest in the 1820s. Moreover, many twentieth-century United Methodists have complained of the association of episcopacy with patriarchy and an outmoded culture of deference and gentility.

All this unrest indicates that for lack of a firm ecclesiological basis, the functions of United Methodist bishops depend far more on "the consent of the governed," so to speak, than on organic roots in the traditional understanding of episcopacy. At the same time, it must be said that the UMC continues to depend on the episcopacy for much of its coherence and continuity.

The Meeting of Principles

The two constitutive principles of conference and episcopacy meet most visibly when conferences are actually in session. But their interaction is subtle and complex, and may lead to great confusion.

Bishops preside in all General, Jurisdictional, Central, and Annual Conferences, as they have done from the beginning— though the Constitution designates the presidential duties in General Conference under the powers of General Conference, not the bishops (¶15.11). Presiding conveys authority and power, to be sure, as bishops maneuver through often complex parliamentary procedures. But the presidential role is not to be confused with executive power as it is exercised, for example, in state or national government. The description of bishops as "the executive branch" of church government—a common comparison throughout Methodist history in America—can be quite misleading.

Unlike the President of the United States or a governor of a state, the bishops individually or collectively do not make any legislative or budgetary proposals. Even as a Council they do not constitute a prelatical House of Bishops for either executive or legislative purposes.[23]

Bishops do not manage departments charged with carrying out legislation, nor do they have an exclusive role in appointing executives for such departments (i.e., councils, boards or agencies). The bishops are amenable to the General Conference for "carrying into effect the rules, regulations, and responsibilities prescribed and enjoined by the General Conference" (¶45). But they are not employees of any conference and do not manage any programs.

Moreover, bishops participate in no committee work or debates, and do not vote in conference. Their only membership in the church is in their own Council; they are not members of any conference. When General Conference is in session, all the bishops are seated on the stage facing the delegates; but they have no right to speak unless it is specifically granted by the body. Nor as presiding officers, of course, do they have any standing to comment on legislation that is before the body.

Yet the bishops' presence is an essential, visible sign of the continuity of the church. After all, in a real sense none of the conferences exist except when they are in session. No session of a conference can bind the next one. Conferences have no continuing executive bodies to sustain them and no executive officers designated or employed to carry on their work between their gatherings. Conferences do, of course, authorize various agencies to carry out the actions and programs they adopt, but no one of them holds executive authority on behalf of the conference as a whole.

As William F. Warren lamented in 1894, General Conference delegates have no tenure of office after serving in a particular session (except that they may serve again if a special session is called before the next quadrennial meeting). "Instead of being a perpetually living corporation for the execution of a perpetual trust," the General Conference is only "a quadrennial convention."

> Accordingly, through forty-seven of every forty-eight months the Church has no supreme governing body, and even in an emergency would have to stop to create one . . . each General Conference has a life of from twenty to thirty days only [now it is only eleven days] . . . no completed action of one General Conference legally binds another.[24]

Some United Methodists have been confused about the role of Councils on Ministries, thinking that they somehow provide executive management of the conferences. But nothing in the *Discipline* grants them such powers, and of course there are entire areas of church life that are outside their purview. The General Council on Ministries is charged only with "facilitat[ing] the Church's program life as determined by the General Conference" (¶904). The Council of Bishops and the General Council on Finance and Administration are completely separate. In parallel fashion, an annual conference Council on Ministries has nothing legally to do with the Board of Ordained Ministry, the Cabinet, or the Council on Finance and Administration—though cooperation is essential to the conference's functioning.

The Constitutional Place of the Annual Conference

Beginning in 1939 in the MC *Discipline* and carrying over to the present Constitution, the annual conference is described as "the basic body *in* the church" (¶31). There is some variation of prepositions, though, which gives pause. Annual conferences are also named "as the fundamental bodies *of* the Church" (¶10), which might lead to the conclusion that this unit, too, is a constitutive element in United Methodism (emphasis mine).

The most basic, historically grounded way in which this might be true is that annual conferences are the locus of membership of the clergy. United Methodist clergy do not hold membership in a congregation, but rather in an annual conference to which they are amenable for their ministry. The Constitution grants to annual conferences "the right to vote . . . on all matters relating to the character and conference relations of its clergy members, and on the ordination of clergy" (¶31). This core function of discipline has been practiced in annual conferences from their beginnings as gatherings of the preachers.

Laity are now members of annual conferences as well, but not on the same basis. Their church membership remains in their congregation, and they still are excluded from the core function. "Lay members [except lay members of a Board of Ordained Ministry] may not vote on matters of ordination, character, and conference relations of ministers." So it is not, after all, the "annual conference" that votes "on all matters relating . . . to ministerial members," but only the clergy members of the annual conference—or as a subtext, the "real" members of conference (¶31).

From a polity standpoint, an annual conference is primarily a covenant association of clergy. Because it alone has the power to admit clergy to the ordained ministry, it alone is the "covenant community" for the two Orders (¶311). Clergy are amenable to this covenant body for their conduct and effectiveness. More particularly, the covenant of elders means that each agrees to serve where sent by the bishop (with consultation) and to abide by the *Discipline*, in return for being guaranteed an appointment (¶¶328, 329).

The annual conference normally also develops initiatives in program and mission and budgets to pay for ministerial and program support. Its sessions may even turn into a revival meeting to celebrate a common faith and spirit. But at its core, an annual conference is the home base of its clergy, to which they are accountable and from which they receive an appointment to their work.

The bishop presiding over an annual conference is most directly related to this clergy function. A bishop has general oversight but no executive management responsibility for a conference budget or program. A bishop's most immediate duty is to preside over the business sessions of the conference and to appoint the clergy, the latter entailing close work with the Board of Ordained Ministry regarding conference relations and the Cabinet regarding appointments.

The appointment process requires consultation with local church congregations (¶431) and certainly works best when the bishop and district superintendents know well the congregations they are superintending. Congregations have a voice in interpreting their ministry needs to the bishop and cabinet. They also have a voice through the lay member of annual conference in the program and budget of which the congregation will carry an apportioned share.

But nothing in the *Discipline* indicates in any way that the annual conference as presently constituted may be understood as a covenant body of congregations. Pastoral charges, not congregations, are granted a lay member to conference, one per clergy. Lay members attend conference thinking of themselves as representing "the folks back home," to be sure. But in fact, there is no formula for democratic representation of the body of laity. Thus the laity have little substantive connection with the annual conference and may with good reason wonder why they are there. As Bishop James Straughn complained in 1958, "it is difficult to get leading laymen [sic] to attend the conference . . . there is nothing for them to do except to sit on hard benches and have no really decisive voice or influence in the direction of conference affairs."[25] While many annual conferences are seeking creative ways to involve laity, the fundamental polity of United Methodism remains unchanged.

For that matter, in terms of constitutional polity, laity also have little relationship with the bishop. Oddly—in light of their exclusion from considering the conference relations of clergy—lay delegates to Jurisdictional Conferences do vote for bishops and serve on the Committee on Episcopacy that recommends the assignments of bishops to their residences. They come to know and respect their bishops through their preaching and through mission activities. But laity are not confirmed into the church by the bishop; they rarely if ever receive the sacrament from the bishop; and they have only a consultative role in the bishop's task of making appointments.

The Constitution suggests that annual conferences are the basic body *in* the church also because they vote on constitutional amendments. But as we have seen, it is the whole connectional body of all clergy and lay members together whose vote is decisive on amendments, and has been so since 1828 in the MEC. As Tigert put it, after the clarification of wording by the 1828 General Conference, "the Annual Conference rightfully ceased to be in any sense a connectional unit."

From a constitutional standpoint, annual conferences are derivative from the whole connectional body. They are not self-constituted entities which join together to form United Methodism. This is another point on which American Methodists drawing parallels with state and federal government have often become confused. Nobody is more lucid on this than Tigert:

> The truth is that the several Annual Conferences bear no such relation to the Connection as the several states bear to the general government of the Union. The number and extent of the Annual Conferences is a mere accident, mutable at the will of any General Conference. The Church was not formed by their amalgamation; but they were hewn out of the territory and the ministry of the Church.[26]

Yet despite all these caveats and constitutional lacunae duly noted, it remains true in practice that annual conferences are the basic bodies at least *in,* if not *of,* the UMC. This is largely true because of their organizational culture developed over time.

Annual conferences have been greatly reduced in number over the last thirty years. In 1960 the MC had 94 conferences, with some bishops presiding over as many as five. At the time of merger in 1968 the EUBC had 32 conferences.[27] The tendency since has been to merge conferences and increase the number of bishops. As of 2000 there were 65 annual conferences in the US and 50 bishops. Through mergers, U.S. annual conferences have come more than ever to parallel the boundaries of American civil states. Political geography more than settlement or culture shapes the design of conferences; longitude and latitude, or occasionally a river, designate the boundaries. Cities or traditional sites of gathering or exchange have little or nothing to do with this rational civic pattern (in contrast with ancient Christendom in Europe and the Mediterranean world).

Political geography is mirrored as well in the boundaries of Jurisdictional Conferences in the U.S. The civil states comprising each Jurisdictional Conference are named in the Constitution (¶35). This apparently means that if General Conference wanted to exercise its authority to change a boundary (¶37) it would have to do so by constitutional amendment. More significantly, Jurisdictional Conferences are not defined by episcopal areas or annual conferences of the church. They follow civil, not ecclesiastical, politics.

This dependence on civil states creates many unfortunate divisions in church life and administration. Prime examples are Washington, D.C., seat of the U.S. government, a metropolitan area divided by the states of Maryland and Virginia and the District itself into separate annual conferences and jurisdictions, and the St. Louis metropolitan area, a settlement of three million people spread over several counties in the states of Missouri and Illinois, divided not only into two annual conferences, but two different jurisdictions.

But civil politics have also become one point of identity for many annual conferences. Since conferences really only exist when they are meeting, a corporate sense of continuity is difficult to maintain. Conferences need cultural icons of some sort. These might include loyalty to state culture—even the state university athletic team—symbolized through flags, mascots, or visits from state politicians; or a place of meeting such as an assembly ground or denominational college understood to be serving primarily that state. As evangelistic and preaching assemblies conferences have relied on long-time song leaders, a conference lay leader (or even a "political machine") in place for forty years or more, and particular styles of doing conference business such as a bell for the call to order or a certain ceremony for recognizing clergy retirements. In many ways, conferences resemble state political conventions as they pass resolutions (platforms), negotiate coalitions of various interest groups, nominate candidates for the episcopacy, and provide a place for networking, patronage, and general schmoozing.[28]

Annual conferences are expressions of civic culture also in their use of parliamentary procedure. James M. Buckley once described Methodism as "an unparalleled free school of parliamentary law" in which hundreds of conferences are held over a quadrennium, each "presided over by expert parliamentarians."[29] While there is much discussion today about finding ways to make decisions in the church without voting—which tends to create winners and losers, majorities and minorities—United Methodist conferences and congregations remain places in which participants learn about the civility necessary for being citizens of free societies.

Finally, because of their critical role as the locus of membership for clergy, annual conferences become a peculiar blend of covenant community and regional labor union. Most clergy give their entire careers to one conference, and hence remain in one civil state. Many clergy would argue that to be forced to move to another state would bring additional hardships: relicensing cars, new certifications for a spouse who works in teaching or medicine, writing a new will under the new state's inheritance laws, and so on.

The effect, however, is that annual conferences come to resemble regional unions or state merit systems. Clergy tend to think of existing local churches within their conference—and thus within their civil state—as their rightful turf. They inevitably expect unwritten laws of seniority to advance them to larger congregations and higher salaries within those bounds. A legislative declaration such as ¶430.2, that "appointment-making across conference lines shall be encouraged," is sailing into a strong wind. It is certainly debatable how many United Methodist preachers view themselves as part of one unbroken "traveling Connection" embracing the U.S. and the globe.

Consequently, despite Tigert's argument that annual conferences are "a mere accident" of pragmatic circumstance, the psychology of annual conferences has gravitated toward a sense that United

Methodism is indeed an association of these regional organizations, each of which has the right to a certain number of delegates to the (inter)national meeting every four years. Thus denominational politics come to mirror national politics; the civic political forces wanting to reduce the size of federal government and give more power to the states are paralleled in the church by groups wanting to reduce the centralized bureaucracy for denominational mission and strengthen annual conference units that can better serve the local church's initiatives. The national body is the "They" or "Them" of "bloated bureaucracy" that has lost touch with "Us"— "the silent majority." The well-being of local communities must come first, and so "we" want to keep "our" money closer to home.

The issue, of course, is not which view is right, but rather how the church can maintain a healthy balance. Just as the nation (and globe) needs government for the common good of all the states (or nations), so the church needs a connectional government in order to support the ministry and mission of its local churches throughout the world.

The Constitutional Place of the Local Church

A critical issue as denominational culture has become less ascriptive is whether United Methodism ought now to move toward a more self-consciously democratic principle. General Conference has legislated more and more rules of participation to ensure balance of gender, ethnicity, lay or clergy status, and other categories. The next step might be to find ways in which congregations can become decisive units of United Methodist polity. This would move United Methodism in a more fully "federal" direction with self-constituted assemblies for the local, regional, national, and global church.

Certainly an alternative constitutive principle for a denomination could be the congregation, which some United Methodists advocate in one form or another and many United Methodists worry about a lot. There is much de facto "congregationalism" in practice, but whatever may exist is not evident in written polity. In the Constitution nothing is said even about what would constitute a local church as an independent entity, much less how congregations in covenant would constitute a larger body.

135

That congregations are not a constitutive element of the UMC connection is clear from the preference for the term "local church" over "congregation" in the *Discipline*. That is, a local church—known through much Methodist history as a local society—is the manifestation of the whole United Methodist connection in a particular place.[30]

Local churches in United Methodism clearly are not self-constituted. They are governed not by annual meetings, but by a charge conference—known historically as a quarterly conference—called and presided over by the district superintendent. Thus their organizational business is conducted for the connection by a representative of the connection. They do not own their property outright, but hold it in trust for the connection (¶2503).

A charge is defined not in the Constitution but in legislative ¶205 as a church or churches to which a pastor is appointed. A charge conference is organized around the pastoral appointment. The Constitution authorizes a charge conference "for" each church or charge (¶11) or "in" each charge (¶41)—not *of* each church. Likewise legislation authorizes a charge conference "within the pastoral charge" (¶245). All these prepositions demonstrate clearly that a charge conference is a local expression of the connection called and conducted by the district superintendent, not by the congregation itself.

The Constitution does refer to "the congregational meeting" (¶39) as necessary for transfer of a local church from one annual conference to another, but this meeting—its name taken over from EUB tradition[31]—is nowhere described nor its organization specifically authorized. A legislative paragraph offers the option of convening a charge conference as a church conference authorized by the district superintendent in which all members may attend and vote (¶247), but with no powers other than those of a charge conference. The only circumstance under which such a church conference is mandated is for approval of a building project (¶2543.6). Similarly, a "church local conference" is authorized in multiple-church charges for the oversight of a specific local church's property (¶2526), so that the charge conference does not have supervision and control of the property. But no other powers are given this local conference.[32]

So one might well ask, what constitutes a local United Methodist church? The United Methodist term "local church" means not as in Roman Catholic tradition all the Christians of a city or defined region, but rather a specific "society of believers" (¶203) in a certain place who follow United Methodist practices in connection with other United Methodists. United Methodism was originally constituted by a wealth of such societies for mutual upbuilding in the faith.

Today's local churches may have societies or class meetings in the Wesleyan mode functioning within them, but the churches themselves are open to all persons in their communities regardless of their willingness to join in a specific disciplined life. Thus the "General Rules of Our United Societies" can hardly be said to be constitutive of local churches any longer.

At the same time, the practice of discipline "in society" did not provide an ecclesiology to replace the practices of "church" in the organic, traditional sense. The United Methodist liturgical heritage is widely varying informal, pragmatic, and adapted to local culture. As a result, despite the 1989 *Hymnal, Book of Worship,* and official liturgies approved by General Conference, worship and sacrament do not establish a constituting center for local churches, either.

Further, a United Methodist local church is an assembly without its own covenant. It has no local constitution, but takes its rules of organization from the common *Discipline.* As noted above, a local church has no constitutive or substantive link with either the bishop or the annual conference. The local church receives a pastor from the available pool of clergy in the conference; the clergyperson represents the conference in a local place as a "missionary" sent out by the itinerant system. The bishop is responsible for "fixing" this assignment (¶430.1). The district superintendent, an extension of the superintendency in a smaller region, is usually the face of this deployment in the local church's eyes.

Thus in United Methodism there is a clergy covenant within the Annual Conference, and an individual believer's covenant with God—often renewed through Wesley's covenant service. But United Methodism has no middle level covenant either in the congregation or among the congregations as mediating local assemblies or institutions. United Methodist congregations remain essentially as audiences to hear and respond to the proclamation of the preachers, associations for educational and missional purposes,

this is a weaknesses

137

and sponsors of disciplined formation in the Christian life. Neither a rational-political covenant, nor a constant and disciplined practice of piety, nor an organic-liturgical tradition is available to give United Methodist local churches constitutional coherence. They exist as mission outposts, formed by a connection reaching into every human settlement, led by a representative of the missionary order of preachers, and directed toward a mission of reforming their communities, continents, and world.

What the Constitution Is and Is Not

Finally, one ought to take note of what is not in the Constitution.

There is no constitutional provision for clergy and no positing of ordination as that which constitutes a deacon or elder. The only reference to itineracy is contained in a simple statement of episcopal duties: "The bishops shall appoint, after consultation with the district superintendents, ministers to the charges" (¶52).

As noted above, the authority of bishops to ordain the clergy is not mentioned.

The sacraments are considered a mark of the church in the Preamble but are not named or described elsewhere.

No essential ministry or mission of the church is specified other than the most general phrases of the Preamble—"the maintenance of worship, the edification of believers, and the redemption of the world."

Entities that one might assume were constitutional are also not mentioned. Episcopal areas through which the bishops carry out their superintendency are nowhere constituted (in fact, they are not defined or described anywhere in the *Discipline*). The General Conference is given the authority "to provide boards" for "connectional enterprises" (¶15.8) but there is no mention of any specific "enterprises" or general agencies or commissions designated "for their promotion and administration"—legislation for which takes up by far the largest section of the *Discipline*.

Many people (including the bishops in their Greeting, p. v) consider that United Methodism has moved toward a "conciliar" principle by placing four councils—Ministries, Finance and Administration, Bishops, and Judicial—at the connectional center

138

of the church. But the only ones in the Constitution are the Council of Bishops—the principle of episcopacy—and the Judicial Council, neither of which are parallel to the other two, as indicated by their names. The Council "of" Bishops—not "on" bishops (as in the other conciliar terms)—and the Judicial Council represent offices, not functions.

In short, what the Constitution names are those basic elements that constitute the UMC in its nature as a connectional body. These fundamental principles and organs of government are also what make United Methodism a distinctive ecclesiastical body within the Church universal. Perhaps because of that sense of being only part of a greater whole, or certainly also because of the Methodist heritage as an *ecclesiola* within the *ecclesia*, the Constitution does not attempt to say what constitutes the UMC as the fullness of Church.

The Constitution also exhibits the distinctiveness of the UMC as an organization. Especially in the nineteenth century but also today it has been popular to draw parallels between United Methodism and the three branches of government in the U.S. Many church leaders and scholars have wanted to legitimize the church as an authentically "American" institution and show the contribution Methodism was making to the emergence of the U.S.'s form of democratic government. This is a misconceived comparison, however, not only because United Methodism is an international church, but because such comparison blurs the ecclesiological uniqueness of the UMC.

Conferences are not parallel to the legislative branch. They do not represent the population of United Methodists, but rather the way the church's mission is organized through pastoral appointments to charges. Bishops are not an executive branch of government. They do exercise the power of appointing clergy to advance the church's mission, but they have no control over whom the conference selects to serve as clergy. They cannot propose or advance legislation, they do not manage any programs, and they have no single office with powers concentrated in any way parallel to the U.S. presidency. The Judicial Council bears a distant resemblance to the Supreme Court of the U.S. in its powers of ruling on constitutionality and its status as the final court of appeal. But it is part of no system of continuous lower courts (church trials are strictly *ad hoc*) and as part of a voluntary association its opinions, like all

139

church actions, must find acceptance in some broader consensus across the connection.

Neither is the UMC like a business corporation. Again, many leaders and interpreters draw parallels between the church and business practices, trying to apply management theories or techniques of sales and public relations to church practices. Unlike a corporation, however, the church has no board of directors and no chief executive officer. Decisions are made in conference and carried out largely by volunteers who cannot normally be sanctioned or fired. Units of the denomination such as local churches, conferences, and agencies may be incorporated as nonprofit organizations for the purpose of holding property and employing staff. But the *Discipline* is at pains to establish that The United Methodist Church as a whole does *not* exist as a legal entity (¶139). The UMC is a connectional mission, not a single corporation.[33]

Both the principle of representative democracy as expressed in conferences and the episcopal principle have a central place in defining what constitutes United Methodism. Their conjunction is what gives the UMC its ecclesiological uniqueness. But their exact relationship is not—and probably never could be—clearly delineated. After all, the church is a living cultural tradition that endures because people are loyal to it, not because it has a precise Constitution. The interaction of the two principles in practice creates an ever-changing chemistry of understanding and consensus. That United Methodism has been able to build on the practices and traditions of both unquestionably has been one source of the church's effectiveness in mission. The conferences have drawn United Methodist people and local churches into connection. The episcopacy has called to the forefront gifted leaders to help articulate the connectional mission. Yet one must still say that many explicit and nascent conflicts and misunderstandings in the church may be laid at the door of this constitutional synthesis.[34]

CHAPTER 4

History, Theology, and the *Discipline*

United Methodists have not exhibited great interest in writing down their theological doctrines. One cannot help but reach this general conclusion upon studying Parts II and IV of the *Discipline*—"Doctrinal Standards and Our Theological Task" and the Social Principles—along with prefatory material including the Episcopal Greetings, list of bishops, and Historical Statement. United Methodists show considerably more interest in the story of their mission.

The whole section and the documents within it illustrate this tendency. The *Discipline* devotes many pages to historical accounts or narrative descriptions of United Methodist practices and activities. The long statement on "Our Theological Task" that has dominated General Conference discussion for over twenty years is centrally concerned with theological method and consensual sources of authority, not doctrinal content. Even some of the oldest sources— the General Rules, along with Wesley's *Sermons* and *Notes* (the latter not actually printed in the book)—are essentially practical or pedagogical in nature.

A Narrative Disposition

Two characteristic features of United Methodism help account for this relative lack of published doctrine. First, United Methodists and their predecessors in Wesleyan tradition have always had a predilection for narrative—explaining themselves historically more than doctrinally. The earliest Disciplines adopted the pattern of Wesley's Large Minutes, placing first a section titled "Of the Rise of Methodism (so-called) in Europe and America." This brief account soon became a separate historical preface that remained intact for 150 years. Its form and much of its content was the same in all books of discipline within the larger family of Methodist denominations.

The statement served mainly to make two theological claims: that "the great revival of religion" brought about by Methodism was an expression of the providence of God, and that therefore Methodist episcopacy and ordination were justified.[1] As Russell Richey has noted, neither Episcopalians nor Presbyterians, as two examples, undertook such narratives. Neither required history to assure their legitimacy. The former simply considered themselves to be in continuity with the organic church from apostolic times. The latter took Scripture as their sole basis of authority.[2]

The Methodists, however, viewed themselves as a movement the legitimacy of which would derive from its effectiveness in bringing people into Christian faith and life. And the only way to judge that was to tell the story.

When the MC was formed in 1939, the historical preface was modified to a descriptive statement of institutional events leading to the union. It was completely rewritten for the 1968 union of the MC and the EUBC and has been expanded since then. No longer making theological claims about providence, the statement now legitimates the church primarily by providing information, with an explicit effort to be sure that all streams of tradition within United Methodism are included (pp. 9-20). It continues as strictly prefatory material, lacking a paragraph number and being placed even before the Constitution.

The list of bishops plays a similar role as descriptive and integrative history. First created in 1964 at the request of the Council of Bishops in the MC, the list originally was alphabetical by year of election. Now the bishops are named in the order of their election. The list includes names from all the Central Conferences and from all bodies that united to form the UMC.

Thus the list serves to weave together varying strands of United Methodist expression over two centuries by reciting the elected episcopal leaders of the churches. The placement of the list immediately after the Contents suggests the primary role of episcopacy in giving continuity and coherence to the UMC. By contrast, for example, general secretaries of general boards and agencies, members of the Judicial Council, or lay leaders of annual conferences are not listed here. There is no list of current annual conferences, nor of the dates and places of General Conferences. The bishops hold prior place as a constitutive office in the church.

United Methodist doctrine and theology has depended for coherence, then, first and foremost on the telling and retelling of narratives of the movement. The stories of people finding new life in Christ, of new societies (later "local churches") springing up across the land, of the movement's spread into nations around the world, and of the church's dynamic, popular leaders, have been much more compelling for United Methodists than dogmatic statements. United Methodists have traditionally done theology more by appealing to people to join in the challenge of a continuing mission than by setting up doctrinal criteria as the basis of consistent authority.

Pragmatic Authority

United Methodism's narrative disposition thus leads to a second feature of United Methodist theological character: a fluid, pragmatic sense of authority that grows out of a continually changing theological practice and consensus.[3] At its worst, of course, pragmatism can degenerate into mere expediency or simplistic adaptation to culture. At its best, though, pragmatism names the self-conscious practice of ecclesial action and theological reflection that is central to Wesleyan tradition. Pragmatism keeps the church focused less on the rational coherence of doctrinal propositions and more on the embodiment of faith claims in the forms and actions of church life.[4]

The Episcopal Greetings illustrate the fluid authority that derives from a pragmatic approach. Bishops have been writing a brief statement like this continuously since 1790, and their Greetings have always come first in the *Discipline* as a whole, placed even before the Contents (pp. v-vi). Whoever serves as president of the Council of Bishops at the time a new *Discipline* is printed joins the secretary in introducing the book and their understanding of its purpose and role in the church.

The current Greetings make certain claims about the *Discipline*. It is a "book of law" but also a "book of covenant." It is not

> sancrosanct or infallible, but we do consider it a document suitable to our heritage. It is the most current statement of how United Methodists agree to live their lives together.

While the bishops insist that the *Discipline* "remains constant" over time, the inherent flexibility of United Methodist ecclesiology is apparent here. No polity or plan of order is carved on stone tablets. United Methodism is primarily a practice of ministry and mission which the *Discipline* reflects and reinforces. Therefore authority derives not from the book, but from accordance with United Methodist practices as they have evolved.

This indicates a strongly consensual model of authority. For example, the bishops state that the covenant community of United Methodists affirms inclusiveness, "the conciliar principle and connectionalism," and the global and ecumenical character of the church. These practices enjoy broad consensus, the bishops claim by their Greetings. Therefore the authority of church law and leadership derives from their accordance with the character of the church produced by these (and other) practices.

Doctrinal Standards

All this is not to say that United Methodists lack doctrine. While the title of *The Book of Discipline* has been shortened from the original "doctrines and disciplines of the ___ Church," it still contains statements adopted by the General Conference comprising basic doctrines of the UMC. Certain of these statements are held to be doctrinal standards which the *Discipline* protects from simple alteration by the General Conference. But the fact that there is some dispute today over what counts as such a standard reflects how United Methodism's narrative consensus has been strained in recent years.

The doctrinal documents in the *Discipline* are significant for polity for two reasons. First, they are the product of United Methodist polity in action. Each has been adopted under certain political circumstances to meet a specific ecclesial need. The more contemporary statements have been created by groups of scholars and leaders commissioned by General Conferences. Each topic, paragraph, and phrase has been examined word for word in study commissions and debated and approved by General Conferences. In every case, the choices of subjects for discussion and the language used to develop them reveals much about the theological nature of United Methodism in its changing social and cultural context.

Second, the content and character of these statements clearly exhibits the United Methodist understanding of ecclesial authority. United Methodism originated as a missionary order of preachers who organized lay societies for spiritual discipline. The movement assumed as foundations already in place the basic propositions of Christian doctrine contained in the Anglican Articles of Religion (reduced and modified) or in Reformation confessions of faith. Methodists as well as Evangelicals and United Brethren were more intent on the practices of Christian life—on preaching and holy living—than on formulations of doctrine.

Only two documents put forward doctrinal propositions. The Articles of Religion originated in the Church of England in the sixteenth century, with slight modifications in later years. John Wesley revised them by removing articles on works, predestination, and other items that he found unnecessary or repugnant, reducing the number from thirty-nine to twenty-four.[5] He then sent them along with revised liturgies to the American Methodists in 1784.

The Confession of Faith was originally adopted by the EUBC in 1962. It represented an effort to unite and harmonize the previous United Brethren Confession and the Evangelical Articles of Faith which had remained intact since the merger of the two groups in 1946. The new Confession retained the substance of earlier statements, "but every endeavor was made to clarify and to find living language to match convictions."[6]

Both of these "confessional" documents specify basic doctrines regarding the Trinity, order of salvation, canon of Scripture, purpose of the church, and nature and number of the sacraments. Both reflect the Reformation doctrine of justification by faith alone. Neither of them, however, specifically incorporates distinctively Wesleyan, Methodist, or EUB teachings or emphases—with the possible exception of Article XI in the Confession asserting "entire sanctification."

For content specific to United Methodist tradition, one must go to documents that are not considered doctrinal standards even though they have been placed in the *Discipline* by the General Conference, namely, the paragraphs on "Our Doctrinal Heritage" and "Our Doctrinal History" (¶¶101, 102). The central theme of these sections is that a "recovery of interest in Wesley" promises to help United Methodists "reclaim and renew the distinctive United Methodist doctrinal heritage" (p. 55). As Richard Heitzenrater, one of its principal authors, described it, the statements reflect a desire for continuity with the past as well as naming common grounds for a new consensus to guide United Methodist teaching.[7]

In the service of that effort, the subsection that specifically describes "Our Distinctive Heritage as United Methodists" is almost entirely dependent on the theology of John Wesley. As Russell Richey has pointed out, every paragraph has reference to Wesley's writings. Methodist experience since Wesley is not described. Theological themes that have arisen more specifically in the American or other national and cultural contexts are not named here.[8] (They do appear in a sense in the Social Principles.) This is an appeal, then, to a consensus around origins—critically important for a narrative tradition like United Methodism.

The "Heritage" section puts forward a number of theological claims about what United Methodists "share," "confess," "assert," "hold," or "emphasize." It cites the original Methodist declaration of purpose commonly printed in earlier Disciplines: "to reform the nation, particularly the Church, and to spread scriptural holiness over the land." The statement goes on to name "Wesleyan Emphases" such as the pervasiveness of grace in awakening, justifying, and perfecting the faith of a Christian. It continues with two subsections on mission, the first viewing mission as an expression of scriptural holiness, the second emphasizing the social and communal forms of mission carried forward by the Church. The "Heritage" section concludes that "devising formal definitions of doctrine has been less pressing for United Methodists than summoning people to faith and nurturing them in the knowledge and love of God" (p. 50). But that leaves unclear the doctrinal status of the whole statement.

"Our Doctrinal History" (¶102) attempts to clarify disputes about what exactly counts as the doctrinal standards of United

Methodism. Disagreements arise from the vague wording of the First Restrictive Rule, originally written in 1808 (¶16):

> The General Conference shall not revoke, alter, or change our Articles of Religion or establish any new standards or rules of doctrine contrary to our present existing and established standards of doctrine.

Along with the Second Restrictive Rule protecting the Confession of Faith, this provision at the least prevents facile changes in the Articles and Confession. Not only the General Conference, but three-fourths of the collective annual conference members present and voting would have to agree to any change (¶57).

What is less clear is exactly which documents are included as "present existing and established standards of doctrine." "Our Doctrinal History" addresses particularly the issue of whether Wesley's *Standard Sermons* and *Explanatory Notes on the New Testament* were also protected by the First Restrictive Rule. Generally, the statement suggests that the *Sermons* and *Notes* were "the traditional standard exposition of distinctive Methodist teaching" most useful in giving guidance to Methodist preaching. But it also argues that only the Articles of Religion were explicitly protected by the First Restrictive Rule, with other writings carrying "the weight of tradition rather than the force of law" (pp. 53-54).

This argument—specifically that of the scholars who drafted this material for the General Conference, Richard Heitzenrater and Thomas Ogletree—attempts to accommodate the position of other United Methodist theologians such as Thomas Oden, who have insisted that the *Sermons* and *Notes* be adequately represented as doctrinal standards.[9] According to Oden's counter-argument, Methodists always understood the *Sermons* and *Notes* to be included under "present existing and established standards of doctrine," even if they were not explicitly named. As the statement indicates, the Plan of Union for the UMC (1966) asserted that the *Sermons* and *Notes* were specifically included (p. 58).

In any case, by the arrangement of materials in Part II the *Discipline* appears to present the *Sermons* and *Notes* as doctrinal standards (they are listed under that heading). At the same time, they are not actually printed in the *Discipline* and the Articles and

Confession alone are footnoted as protected by restrictive rules. Ogletree explained this arrangement by distinguishing between

> *formal* doctrinal standards, which enjoy constitutional protection, i.e., the Articles of Religion and the Confession of Faith, and traditional doctrinal standards, which have their authority by their constant usage as major resources in doctrinal instruction, in particular Wesley's *Sermons* and *Notes*.[10]

Heitzenrater supported that distinction by arguing that the *Sermons* and *Notes* "do not lend themselves to juridical enforcement."[11] They are not systematic, yet they do put forward a model of Christian formation. Certainly this suits Methodism's heritage as a lay movement preaching the wonders of God's grace and the believer's growth in love. United Methodists generally have much preferred a persuasive, pastoral style of discipline to a legal one.

Theological Method

All the statements in Part II must be understood within the context of United Methodism's characteristically practical theology and consensual ground of authority. The statement of "Our Theological Task" adopted by the 1972 General Conference and thoroughly revised by the 1988 General Conference is most explicit in this regard (¶104). That is, the statement emphasizes not doctrinal content but the method by which United Methodists reflect and explore theologically.

United Methodists do theology "to reflect upon God's gracious action in our lives" and to prepare people "to participate in God's work in the world" (p. 74). The theological task is "both individual and communal"—directed toward "conciliar and representative forms of decision-making" (pp. 75-76). The task "is essentially practical" as opposed to "theoretical" (p. 76). Theology is itself a practice and inseparably bound up with practices.[12]

Therefore United Methodist doctrine, while honored historically and protected constitutionally, consists of "affirmations" that mark "a central feature of [the Church's] identity" (p. 75). Doctrine does not constitute the UMC. Doctrinal standards are not set up as criteria for admission to the church or as laws for testing decisions. They do "assist us in the discernment of Christian truth" (p. 75).

Scripture holds "primacy for faith and practice" (p. 82), yet it is not reduced to particular doctrines or set schemes of interpretation. Scripture is "the primary source and criterion for Christian doctrine," the statement asserts, but no specific criterion or doctrine is named in this connection (p. 78). The "faithful reading of Scripture" cannot stand apart from "the believing community" or from the sources available in tradition, experience, and reason (p. 78).

The precise relationship and interaction of these four "sources and criteria" for theological affirmation and reflection has stirred heated discussion ever since the 1972 statement was approved. The four immediately became known in United Methodist lingo as "the Wesleyan quadrilateral," an immensely popular and widespread term for interpreting the contemporary United Methodist theological stance. Ted Campbell has shown how this phrase originated from the pen of Albert Outler, principal author of the 1972 statement. Most likely he borrowed it from ecumenical discussions, in particular the "Lambeth Quadrilateral" of 1888 which laid out "four essential conditions for a reunited Christian Church."

Indeed, its comprehensive and unifying character was unquestionably part of the "quadrilateral's" appeal in the newly united denomination. The term did not actually appear in the 1972 document, nor has anyone successfully established that Wesley himself would have thought in terms of a "quadrilateral." Yet the device provided much-needed grounds for building consensus in the church. It opened the way for new voices to be heard, especially those of women and of ethnic groups in the minority in the church. It offered the kind of public criteria needed for legitimizing new points of view in a rapidly changing culture.

In particular, the "quadrilateral" helped United Methodists steer clear of the schisms over biblical literalism that were tearing apart the Southern Baptist Convention and other denominations in the 1970s and 1980s. Many United Methodists thought it went too far as stated—to use Timothy Smith's word, constructing an "equilateral" that put Scripture on a par with the other three. Indeed, the term itself seemed to point interpreters to conceiving of theological method in the figure of a square with four equal sides. Some thought this opened the door to a kind of indifferentism in which all opinions and experiences were valid.[13]

Thus the 1988 revision was a carefully crafted effort to affirm Scripture as "primary source and criterion" while also asserting that "our attempts to grasp its meaning always involve tradition, experience, and reason" (p. 79). The basic character of "our theological task" as a broad method for bringing people of varying convictions into consensus remains, however. The very fact of the statement being written in first person plural is indicative of that intention.

Moreover, the statement rises to a concluding assertion that "Christian unity is not an option; it is a gift to be received and expressed" (p. 84). United Methodists will continue to rely on a way of doing theology that is most promising for bringing Christians "to the highest possible level of human fellowship and understanding" (p. 85). In this sense contemporary United Methodist theological method is most in keeping with the "Catholic spirit" Wesley advocated: not that everyone should surrender their distinctive emphases and practices to a blurred lowest common denominator, but that each tradition in its uniqueness can join with others on a common ground of essential affirmations of faith. The irenic generosity of spirit of this method may be United Methodism's distinct contribution to ecumenical consensus and the emergence of a newly catholic, reformed, and evangelical church.

The Primacy of Mission

What is one to make of this juxtaposition of strongly Wesleyan theological teachings, followed by sixteenth-century Anglican Articles of Religion and a relatively contemporary EUB Confession of Faith, then reference to Wesley's *Sermons* and *Notes* and a full printing of Wesley's General Rules, and then a statement of a broad method of communal, conciliar, and consensual theological reflection? Is the method dependent upon or organized around Wesleyan teachings, Anglican doctrines, and EUB Confession? Or are the latter only part of what the method refers to as Tradition, one component in a larger task?[14]

What is the status of the "re-" language in "Our Doctrinal History," stressing the re-covery and re-affirmation of Wesleyan and evangelical heritages (p. 55)? Is it meant to suggest that the UMC has lost its center theologically, that a re-turn to Wesley will re-store focus? When did that center hold more definitely? Evidently the voices heard in these sections—along with the listless final paragraphs of the Historical Statement (pp. 19-20)—view recent history as a decline.[15] Nowhere is it stated what the earlier condition was from which the church has declined, or when and where it existed. Nor do the statements clarify what the place of the historical doctrines now re-asserted is to be.

Part II as a whole reflects the nature of a church that has become increasingly diverse ethnically, culturally, and globally. The immediate and all-consuming task for United Methodists has been to learn to live and work together in one faith communion and one polity. This requires a great deal more intentionality than in the days of complete dominance by relatively uniform cultural norms of Anglo Americans. Even the recording of recent history as well as the interpretation of current events has become far more sensitive and complex.

As a result United Methodists show little energy for the immense undertaking of writing a new confession of faith. Yet they regularly point to Wesley's teachings and discipline as a source for what everyone can hold in common. These latter may well provide the beginning points for a new consensus, as the authors of the heritage and history sections hoped. Indeed, the very disputes over interpreting Wesley, American doctrinal standards, and other aspects of history only show how eagerly United Methodists look to the Wesleyan past for outlines of the authority of an emerging consensus. But this project will take time, and in the end, agreement on how to understand the past is less likely to produce consensus than is a compelling mission in the crises of contemporary societies.

Scriptural Holiness

United Methodism and predecessor bodies have often sought theological focus through an emphasis on personal and social holiness. The theme of holy living runs deep in Methodist, Evangelical, and United Brethren traditions. Holiness was the guiding discipline for the first Methodist societies in England. The General Rules for those societies, somewhat modified to suit the American context, are printed in full in the *Discipline* (pp. 71-74).

The General Rules made participation in Methodism contingent not on doctrinal agreement or confessional acquiescence, but simply a "desire of salvation" to which holy living was a witness. They encompassed not beliefs per se but dispositions and actions—both those to be avoided and those to be practiced. Methodist people were to cultivate giving glory to God as their fundamental disposition. Consequently they would avoid such evils as drunkenness, fighting, wearing "costly apparel," and all forms of self-indulgence. They would practice doing good "by giving food to the hungry, by clothing the naked, by visiting or helping them that are sick or in prison." They would nurture this disposition through regular practices of worship, sacrament, prayer, "searching the Scriptures," and "fasting or abstinence."

While the General Rules enjoy the specific protection of the Fifth Restrictive Rule (¶19) and have a central historical place, they have fallen into disuse as a framework of disciplined participation in United Methodist churches. As Bishop Jack Tuell pointed out, in the Constitution the General Rules are referred to in their original form—"of Our United Societies" (¶19). The heading (p. 71) calls them the rules of "The Methodist Church." Neither one refers to them as rules of the contemporary UMC.[16] Those in the ordained ministry are asked if they know and will keep the General Rules. But even here the section containing those questions is headed "Historic Examination for Admission," as if it were not quite the contemporary examination (¶321.4.d.). Laity are not required to know the rules, and many have never heard of them. The class meeting is enjoying a revival as an optional program in many churches, but is nowhere mandated.

United Methodism's primary expression of holiness today is the Social Principles document, which is much more visible than the General Rules in practice and has received regular attention from General Conferences (Part IV, ¶¶160-66). The denominations that united to form United Methodism each had statements on social issues. The current Principles absorb many of those earlier emphases, greatly expanded and reorganized. They were approved for the united church in 1972 and have been revised and updated since then.

Three aspects of the Social Principles are notable for United Methodist polity. First, they are comprehensive statements encompassing many dimensions of human life—natural, personal, social, economic, political, and global. Some United Methodists have criticized the church's effort to address such a broad range of issues intelligently and faithfully. Yet the Principles implicitly claim that no area of life is outside God's care and therefore none is outside the church's witness to God's intentions for the world. This places the church fully in contact with the "common life and work" of human beings everywhere (p. 96).

Second, the Social Principles are written from a social and cultural point of view. Despite their first person plural voice—representing the consensual voice of United Methodist people—they are American in orientation. They refer to "society" in the singular, meaning the society of the U.S. They assume a free society that recognizes the validity of human rights. While American United Methodists can glibly nod acceptance of such statements, United Methodists in more traditional societies have much more of a struggle to put the principles into practice.

Moreover, the human rights section is particularly striking in its listing of rights for every group except those persons—in America—whose rights are taken for granted. "Ethnic" persons, religious minorities, children, youth, aging persons, women, and persons with handicapping conditions all are addressed. White men of middling age are not. Particularly poignant is the section on "racial and ethnic persons," which seems to assume that white persons are neither, and in which the "we" seems to refer to the white majority. ("We assert the obligation of society... to... redress long-standing systemic social deprivation of racial and ethnic people" [¶162.A]—implying that white society is not ethnic but normative, though in need of reform.)

Third, the Social Principles reflect and reinforce the United Methodist effort to hold the middle ground on social issues. This stance sometimes requires taking virtually opposite positions on the same issue. Thus in ¶161.G, homosexuality is considered a "practice incompatible with Christian teaching," while homosexual

persons are of "sacred worth" and "need the ministry and guidance of the church. . . . We commit ourselves to be in ministry for
and with all persons." In ¶161.J, the church recognizes "tragic conflicts of life with life that may justify abortion" and calls for ministry for "persons who terminate a pregnancy" as well as "to those
who give birth." In ¶164.G, "we support and extend the ministry
of the Church to those persons who conscientiously oppose all war,
or any particular war" as well as "those persons who conscientiously choose to serve in the armed forces."

United Methodist positions on many other social issues are advocated, not as part of the Social Principles, but as resolutions of the
General Conference. These are contained in the quadrennially published *Book of Resolutions*, which is organized around the same
dimensions of human community that guide the Social Principles:
natural, personal, social, economic, political, and global. Unlike the
Social Principles, however, *The Book of Resolutions* is not a foundation document of the church. Resolutions are not legislative; they
expire when the concern they addressed has been resolved; they are
official positions but not a part of permanent church law (¶510.2).

Thus as is characteristic of United Methodist polity more generally, the Social Principles (and resolutions) address an enormous
range of issues confronting a global church, yet are predominantly
American in orientation, and reflect a variety of theological and
political influences. Together with the General Rules they constitute a disciplined pattern of life that witnesses to a vision of justice
and wholeness reflecting the Reign of God in which United
Methodists put their faith.

At the same time, the church's neglect of the General Rules shows
that for a century or more personal piety has become increasingly
private, a matter of individual conscience. Meanwhile, as Randy
Maddox pointed out, the church's judgment on social issues has
been addressed not so much to church members, but to the larger
society or government. This mirrors an assumption—typical of the
nineteenth century—that United Methodism is influential in
American society, that the public and particularly public officials
care about the church's stand. The issue today is whether the real
challenge to the church is in trying to influence the larger society, or
in developing patterns of disciplined formation in which its own
members model the just society envisioned by the church—or both.[17]

154

Tests of Consensus

The vulnerability of a theological stance dependent on broad consensus expressed through mission is most exposed on occasions of church trials or property disputes that originate over doctrinal differences. One of the "chargeable offenses" that may result in a trial of either ordained or laypersons is "dissemination of doctrines contrary to the established standards of doctrine of the Church" (¶2702.1). But to borrow Thomas Langford's image, "doctrine is like a house that a religious communion already inhabits."[18] In United Methodism's case, it is an expansive house usually taken for granted. United Methodists generally are reluctant to throw anyone out unless the offender tries to force on everyone else views not reflecting a broader consensus.

Similarly, the real estate premises for United Methodist worship and clergy housing are held in trust for the denomination, "subject to the Discipline, usage, and ministerial appointments of said church" (¶2503). This legal claim continues a tradition from John Wesley's Model Deed, issued in England as early as 1746. The Model Deed ensured that in Methodist chapels preachers would expound "no other doctrine than is contained in Mr. Wesley's *Notes Upon the New Testament* and four volumes of *Sermons.*"[19]

Being "subject to the Discipline" certainly includes being subject to the doctrinal standards. But the status of these as historical and contemporary standards governing the use of property is itself in some dispute.[20] Again, believing so strongly in a free pulpit, United Methodists are reluctant to monitor preaching so long as a preacher is not advocating withdrawal from the household.

Thus the polity through which the UMC lives its doctrinal teachings is weakest in its mechanisms for excluding voices that disrupt the church's consensus. There are no clear and absolute tests of orthodoxy. The polity is strongest as a continually renewing movement of mission, drawing in the gifts and commitments of new persons, and reaching into new areas of need.

Such an evolving consensual model requires constant attention and care. It puts a premium on clean, clear communication of perspectives and experiences. The social changes sweeping the globe in the twentieth century have pushed this model hard. Until the 1960s United Methodism's theological consensus was simply too

155

much intertwined with an American cultural consensus dominated by white Protestant views. When the latter moved toward more secular diversity, United Methodism had once more to seek an authentic theological voice.

But despite radical shifts in American culture and the expansion of United Methodism around the globe, a strong consensus about theological method remains intact. There is little in the *Discipline* to indicate that United Methodist people are ready to give up their characteristic reliance on narrative and practice as the heart of Christian theology.

Toward Ecumenical Consensus

The practical openness of this method is unquestionably United Methodism's gift to the ecumenical church. As Albert Outler suggested,

> Methodism's unique ecclesiological pattern was really designed to function best *within* an encompassing environment of *catholicity* (by which I mean what the word meant originally: the effectual and universal Christian *community*). We don't do as well by our lonesome. . . . We need a catholic church within which to function as a proper evangelical order of witness and worship, discipline and nurture.[21]

Methodism was a movement *ad interim*, for the time being, that existed for the sake of mission. The "marks of the church" for Methodists were to be found in an evangelical focus on witness, evangelism, mission, discipline, and nurture—in short, on the actions of bringing people to faith. This gave the movement a *"functional* doctrine of the church," in Outler's words, but a "theological apparatus . . . assembled from many quarters."[22]

If one views the continuing journey toward Christian unity as the hope of a new catholicity—a new church universal that both incorporates and supersedes contemporary forms—then United Methodism certainly has a contribution to make. As a church continually on the way, living its narrative, driven by its mission, not preoccupied with the fine points of doctrine or ecclesiology, United Methodism has been able to be something of a gadfly in ecumenical dialogues. Its acceptance of the baptisms and ordinations of other Christians; its open communion table; its synthesis of a variety of theologies and polities—all make it a friend to almost every other tradition, if a maddeningly elusive one at that since it can be very difficult for others to know what exactly a United Methodist is.[23]

In any case, United Methodism knows about being a church on the way to becoming a church. In its statement of "Our Theological Task" the church commits itself to "the theological, biblical, and practical mandates for Christian unity" (p. 84). A primary expression of that commitment is the denomination's full participation in the Consultation on Church Union. COCU represents a conversation that has continued in one form or another for fifty years among the Christian Church (Disciples of Christ), Episcopalians, Presbyterians, Community Churches, United Church of Christ, and major members of the Methodist communion—African Methodist Episcopal (AME), African Methodist Episcopal Zion (AMEZ), Christian Methodist Episcopal (CME), and the UMC. The General Conference has committed the UMC to the covenanting process of Churches Uniting in Christ. In COCU the denominations will enter into a covenant communion which entails mutual recognition of members and ministries, as well as joint mission.

Meanwhile, the Methodist members of COCU—AME, AMEZ, CME, and UMC—continue to explore the possibility of a pan-Methodist union. This would bring together churches that share polity and practice but historically were divided over race.

Whatever the outcome of these discussions, though, questions persist. Is United Methodism still essentially a mission movement? Should United Methodism proceed toward becoming more of a distinct church with clear, contemporary doctrinal confessions? In either case, is there a theological consensus sufficient to move the church toward its ecumenical vocation?

For these questions, the *Discipline* can serve as only a cross-section of a continually flowing stream at one moment in time—the last General Conference. The answers are "out there" in the practices of United Methodists everywhere.

CHAPTER 5

The Ministry of All Christians

One of the clearest accents of Christian ecclesiology in the twentieth century is the ministry of the *laos*, the people of God. The theme resounded deeply in the Protestant Reformation, to be sure. The very definition of the church in the Articles of Religion (XIII) expressed it clearly:

> The visible Church of Christ is a congregation of faithful men in which the pure Word of God is preached, and the Sacraments duly administered according to Christ's ordinance, in all those things that of necessity are requisite to the same.

The congregation, translating the New Testament Greek *ekklesia*, was the primary gathering of the faithful. The assembly, not the hierarchy of offices and orders, constituted the church. Offices and orders were created to assure the integrity and order of Word and Sacrament, but the gathered congregation remained primary.

No single polity followed from this ecclesial understanding. On one side of the spectrum, Congregationalists and Baptists argued that the primacy of the congregation meant laity themselves must assume the task of calling and ordaining pastors. On the other side, Anglicans held that the hierarchy of clergy was necessary for the continuity and good order of Word and Sacrament as practiced in congregations. For Presbyterians and Methodists somewhere in the middle, a connectional system that would balance the faithful responsibilities of laity and clergy was desirable.

Movements influenced by Wesleyan Methodism were organized, of course, around groups of laity seeking to learn scriptural faith more deeply and practice it more thoroughly in their lives. Laity were for many years excluded from the clergy deliberations that guided the course of the various connections of societies. Yet the movements existed first and foremost to encourage the lay practice of piety in everyday life, as well as lay leadership in education, social reform, and mission.

As the missionary expansion of Christianity through America and other lands continued into the nineteenth century, laity were increasingly caught up in the activities of myriad associations for mission and benevolence. Ecclesial life was still centered in Word and sacrament (though mainly Word in much of Protestantism), but from the common ground of witness and service blossomed many new forms of ministry carried out by laypersons.

An Emerging Ecumenical Consensus

By the mid-twentieth century Christians of many persuasions were seeking new ways to articulate the ministry of the *laos*, the whole people of God. World events of war, economic depression, and the technology revolution were disrupting forms of church, society, and culture long taken for granted. The churches were realizing that an effective Christian witness in the world was possible only if every Christian acknowledged and carried out a call to be in ministry.

The documents of the Second Vatican Council represented a breakthrough in a new way of thinking about the *laos*. The main organic tradition of Western Christianity, Roman Catholicism, was known most to Protestants for its episcopal and clerical hierarchy. But now in its Dogmatic Constitution on the Church *(Lumen Gentium)* promulgated in 1964 the Council brought the people of God to the forefront of ecclesiology.

All the "holy people of God" share in Christ's priestly, prophetic, and kingly offices, the Constitution declared.[1] All are called to spiritual worship and active witness to the Kingdom of God proclaimed by Jesus Christ. While some are in holy orders or religious life (e.g., monastic orders), the people are mainly comprised of laity charged with their own "apostolate." The laity "make up the Body of Christ" and participate "in the salvific mission of the Church itself."

> Now the laity are called in a special way to make the Church present and operative in those places and circumstances where only through them can it become the salt of the earth. Thus every

layman [sic], in virtue of the very gifts bestowed upon him, is at the same time a witness and a living instrument of the mission of the Church itself "according to the measure of Christ's bestowal."[2]

Roman Catholicism affirmed its view of clerical orders as different from lay status "in essence and not only in degree"[3] and continued to assert the primacy of the bishop of Rome as the spiritual shepherd of the people of God. But these were understood to be among "a variety of ministries, which work for the good of the whole body." Instituted by Christ, the various ministries have their own distinct spheres of vocation, purpose, and authority. The ministry of the laity is specifically to "seek the kingdom of God by engaging in temporal affairs and by ordering them according to the plan of God . . . for the sanctification of the world from within as a leaven."[4]

A similar ecclesial logic that begins from the ministry of the whole people of God and proceeds to particular ministries was expressed in the *Baptism, Eucharist, and Ministry* document of the World Council of Churches (1982). Here the role of the Holy Spirit in building up the church was especially emphasized.

> The Holy Spirit unites in a single body those who follow Jesus Christ and sends them as witnesses into the world. . . . The Spirit calls people to faith, sanctifies them through many gifts, gives them strength to witness to the Gospel, and empowers them to serve in hope and love. . . . The Holy Spirit bestows on the community diverse and complementary gifts. These are for the common good of the whole people and are manifested in acts of service within the community and to the world.[5]

The Faith and Order discussions that produced this document included representatives of a wide ecumenical range of polities, including Methodism. Acknowledging that "there are differences concerning the place and forms of the ordained ministry," the document still declared that

> As they engage in the effort to overcome these differences, the churches need to work from the perspective of the calling of the whole people of God.[6]

Ordained and lay ministries in the church were understood to be complementary, both arising from the call to ministry of all the people, and each needing the other in order to fulfill the vocation given by the Spirit. In particular, the ordained are responsible "to assemble and build up the Body of Christ" through Word, Sacrament, and "by guiding the life of the community in its worship, its mission and its caring ministry."[7]

The *Consensus* document of the Church of Christ Uniting (Consultation on Church Union, or COCU) reflects a similar ecumenical concern for building up the ministry of the *laos*.

> The ordained and lay ministries of the Church are differing forms of the one ministry of Christ that is shared by the whole People of God. Because they are forms of one ministry, they complement one another. Thus, they must be ordered in relation to one another in the life of the Church.

The document notes the confusion that results from "laity" being derived from *laos*. The *laos* is the whole body, lay and ordained. Within the *laos*, "lay persons are called by their Baptism and membership in the Church to manifest and bear witness to Christ's presence in the world in all their activities." Ordained persons have particular roles within the whole ministry, namely, responsibility for Word and sacrament. Even here, however, "faithful[ly] hearing and proclaiming God's Word . . . rightly administering and receiving the sacraments . . . are actions of the entire People of God."[8]

Lay and Specialized Ministries

Part III of the *Discipline* was added in 1976 as a product of a General Conference quadrennial Commission to Study the Ministry. Entitled "The Ministry of All Christians," it reflects and reinforces a broad ecumenical consensus about the genesis of ministry. Inserted immediately after the church's foundation documents, these paragraphs lay the groundwork for the succeeding chapters on the local church, ministry, superintendency, conferences, and general church agencies—all of which exist primarily to build up the people of God in fulfilling their vocation individually and as a community of faith.

The section is subtitled "The Mission and Ministry of The Church" and begins with a general preface added by the 1996

General Conference. The focus here is on a definition of the church's mission as "disciple-making," based on "Jesus' words in Matthew 28:19-20." Making disciples is described as a continuous systemic process of seeking persons, leading them "to commit their lives to God through baptism and profession of faith in Jesus Christ," forming them in Christian nurture and service, and gathering yet more persons "into the community of the Body of Christ" (¶¶120-122).

This statement retains in a sentence or two at least the sense of a Mission Statement previously located in Part II (1992 *Discipline*, ¶69). "This mission is our grace-filled response to the Reign of God in the world," the new wording puts it (¶121). But the thoroughgoing emphasis on grace before, during, and after human action, so clear in the earlier statement—"the people of God are wholly dependent on God's grace," "mission is witness to the God of grace"—is now reframed as the basis for a systemic process for which the church is responsible—"We make disciples" (¶122). This language comes from a different source, the church growth movement of the 1980s. It reflects the desire of many United Methodists to follow a mandate that provides "a clear sense of mission . . . in order to be truly alive" (¶121). Yet an approach that hinges on a single (and much-disputed) passage of scripture to define mission and that emphasizes what "we" in the church do, with the metaphor of "making" (like a product or output, in systems terms), will probably not hold sway among United Methodists with, for example, a more sacramental view of church.[9]

In the context of this definition of mission, Part III moves on to a statement of "The Ministry of All Christians" that almost completely retains the wording adopted in 1976 (¶¶125-129). "All Christians are called through their baptism to this ministry of servanthood in the world," the *Discipline* declares, for it continues "Christ's ministry of outreaching love" (¶125). The Church as the "community of the new covenant" (¶126) places "the claim to ministry in Christ" upon everyone who is baptized. Through baptism and confirmation, Christians are called, gifted, and nurtured for any of a "variety of services" that is both their "gift" and "task" (¶127).

This places full responsibility on the visible people of God in the world. In some of those rare Disciplinary words that really sing, the text insists that it is they who "must convince the world of the reality of the gospel or leave it unconvinced."

> There can be no evasion or delegation of this responsibility; the Church is either faithful as a witnessing and serving community, or it loses its vitality and its impact on an unbelieving world [¶128].

As the logic of this understanding of ministry unfolds, then, within the people of God there are those called to "specialized ministries among the people of God." Further,

> Within these specialized ministries, deacons are called to ministries of Word and Service, and elders are called to ministries of Service, Word, Sacrament, and Order [¶137].

All ministries, while distinct and diverse, are one in Christ. This seems to be the point of the 2000 *Discipline's* awkward declaration, condensed from previous *Disciplines*, that "the ministry of all Christians in The United Methodist Church is complementary"— oddly omitting to say what is complementary to what. The jarring note of tension remains; "no ministry is subservient to another" (¶129). This sounds more like the protest of laity against clergy (or vice versa?) than a positive statement of the distinctive and essential roles of particular ministries in the community of faith.

The 1976 ministry paragraphs, in place for twenty years, attempted a foray into ecumenical ecclesiology by referring to diaconal and ordained ministries not only as "specialized," but as "representative." The latter term was not explicated in the text; in fact, it was not explained anywhere else in the *Discipline*. Yet it picked up a crucial ecumenical theme for understanding ordained ministries from both the COCU *Consensus* document and the WCC's *Baptism, Eucharist, and Ministry* document. In the former, ordained ministries are said to

> share in the ministry of Christ by representing in and for the Church its dependence on and its identity in, the Word of God . . . they symbolize and focus the ministry of Christ and the apostles as well as the ministry of the whole Church . . . [they] represent to the Church its own identity and mission in Jesus Christ.[10]

164

The *B.E.M.* document names "ordained ministers [as] representatives of Jesus Christ to the community," a ministry that is "constitutive for the life and witness of the Church."[11]

As the *Discipline* interpreted it from 1976 to 1996, there appeared to be two sides to the mirror of this representativeness. On the one side, diaconal and ordained persons re-presented or reflected back to the people of God the ministries to which all the people are called. This was stated most clearly regarding diaconal ministry, which

> exists to intensify and make more effective the self-understanding of the whole people of God as servants in Christ's name [1992 *Discipline*, ¶109, repeated in ¶301].

Similarly, "the ordained ministry is defined by its intentionally representative character" (1992 *Discipline*, ¶110), which presumably meant that the people of God could look to their ordained ministers to see their own ministries of witness, care, and service focused and exemplified (to borrow a term explaining diaconal ministry in 1992 *Discipline*, ¶302).

On the other side, specialized ministries were representative in the way they mirrored the gospel. Here again, this dimension was clearer elsewhere, as in ¶430 (1992 *Discipline*) the ordained were said to be "conscious representatives of the whole gospel." Through their ministry of service (a redundant phrase, to be sure, since *diakonia* can be translated both "ministry" and "service" in English), diaconal ministers (also a redundant phrase) represented and "symboliz[ed]" "Christ's service to humankind" (1992 *Discipline*, ¶109). Likewise, through their proclamation of the Word, administration of the sacraments, and pastoral leadership, the ordained carried on Christ's ministry in a manner that particularly represented the gospel.

Both aspects of this representativeness came into play in the fundamental purpose of these specialized ministries in the community of faith: "the upbuilding of the general ministry" (1992 *Discipline*, ¶110). That is, representative ministries existed not as a substitute or displacement of the ministry to which all Christians are called, but rather for the sake of focusing and ordering the ministry of the whole people of God.

Thus "representative ministry" was a flexible term that could be taken in a range of interpretations. It could mean that the ordained represented Christ through their ordination by a bishop who carried forward the apostolic ministry in succession from earliest times—a more "priestly" and hierarchical view. Or it could mean that the ordained simply represented the church's call to persons who were gifted to lead the community of faith—a more "presidential" or democratic model.

The description of ordained ministries adopted by the 1996 General Conference appeared to move more toward the latter view. "The Church's ministry of service" is said to be generally "a primary representation of God's love" (¶303). The ministry of the ordained "exemplifies and leads the Church" in its service of God (¶310). Deacons (a new order discussed more fully in chapter 7) are ordained to "embody, articulate, and lead the whole people of God in its servant ministry" (¶319). Elders are authorized "to order the life of the Church for mission and ministry" by "leading the people of God"—though elders are not said to "embody" the ministry of the whole people of God (¶323). This hesitation may arise from United Methodism's ambiguous understanding of the place of Holy Communion. Only elders are specifically ordained to administration of this sacrament, echoing the priestly understanding from Anglicanism and Catholicism. Yet United Methodism also permits a host of nonordained persons—local pastors under appointment to a charge—to administer communion in their charges. This leads to a more presidential or pastoral understanding, that the pastor presides for the sake of the good order of the community of faith and thus is acting on behalf of the whole people of God.

The flexibility of all this terminology mirrors United Methodism's middling ecclesiological view of ministry. The ordained are set apart for a specialized ministry, but remain part of the people of God. They must be ordained by a bishop, but not for the sake of apostolic succession, only for the sake of good order. Even bishops have oversight for the sake of good order, not because they are essentially different from the rest of the clergy in either status or capacity to represent Christ to the people. In common with all the people of God, "specialized" ministers have a calling by the power of the Holy Spirit. That call must be confirmed by the community of faith.

The ecumenical ecclesiology for forms of ministry has now been displaced, however, by language that as it stands will surely increase the ambivalence and lack of clarity in United Methodism about the respective roles of lay and ordained ministry. The 1996 effort to describe the basis of ministry relies on the contemporary term "servant leadership," which certainly is unobjectionable as an ideal type for "embody[ing] the teachings of Jesus" (¶131). The breadth of the term appears intended to appeal to laity as well as clergy—all the baptized people of God—to exercise leadership of the church's ministries and mission.

The term presents two difficulties, however. First, it is not a phrase particular to ecclesiology; it has been widely used in recent years in American management literature as a name for an ideal executive role in all kinds of organizations, particularly nonprofit institutions or voluntary associations that exist to serve society. It can be defined many different ways, depending on the organization, the leadership style desired, and the persons doing the defining. The *Discipline* provides no further definition here of what the term means in the context of the church.

Thus, second, the term is not specifically connected with the church's historic manner of ordering its communal life, namely, the language of offices. Later paragraphs defining ordination rely heavily on "servant leadership" as an identifying mark of the call to ordained ministry. Candidates for ordained ministry heed "the call to servant leadership" when they enter the candidacy process (¶306). Deacons must seek an appointment in which they can exercise "servant leadership" in a way that clearly distinguishes "between the work to which all Christians are called and the work for which deacons in full connection are appropriately prepared and authorized" (¶322.6.b.). Elders are to practice "servant leadership" in leading the people of God (¶323), as do bishops in their ministry of oversight and supervision (¶404).

While these usages would seem to identify those who are "set apart" by ordination (¶302), "servant leadership" is also applied to laypersons. United Methodism has always recognized, states the *Discipline*, that "laypersons as well as ordained persons" are called to lead the church. "The servant leadership of these persons is essential" (¶132). The *Discipline* goes on to apply "servant leadership" to both "lay and ordained" ministries, both of which are said

167

to be callings that "are evidenced by special gifts" (¶136). As the text proceeds to adapt language of inner and outer call historically used to interpret ordination (as in Wesley's understanding), the reader is left unclear what, then, constitutes ordination. The lack of definition of "servant leadership" reduces its capacity for distinguishing a "set apart" ministry from the "general ministry of all baptized Christians" (¶310).

The only apparent distinction between lay and ordained appears to lie in the call of the ordained to "a lifetime of servant leadership" devoted "wholly to the work of the Church." In a sense this wording may refer subtly to those employed full time by the church; in another way, though, these terms fail as well to make a clear distinction of roles since presumably all Christians (or is it only some, those with "special gifts"?) are called to "a lifetime of servant leadership" in one form or another (¶137). What exactly is special about the "specialized ministries" of the ordained remains ambiguous and largely undefined.

The actual ministry of the laity is stated only in the most general terms as well. New paragraphs entitled "Servant Ministry" (¶¶133-135) assert "God's call to holy living in the world." Later paragraphs on church membership (¶¶217-220) couch lay ministry broadly as an "obligation to participate in the corporate life of the congregation" and "to be a servant of Christ on mission in the local and worldwide community." The responsibility of local churches for identifying, calling out, training, and bringing into service the gifts of the laity is not clearly developed. No reference is made to church traditions, such as the ways laity may share in Christ's offices (as described in *Lumen Gentium*). What United Methodism expects of its laity in concrete terms of discipline, practice, or action in church and world is left to the discernment of believers and the activities and emphases of particular local churches.

The Unity of Ministry

The *Discipline* seeks to establish the unity of United Methodist mission and ministry in four ways. First, the unity in United Methodism is reinforced through a section entitled "Called to Inclusiveness." Added in 1992, this section appeals for unity directly by defining the inclusiveness assured in the Constitution. "Inclusiveness means openness, acceptance, and support." Addressing the issue of "freedom for the total involvement of all persons" in the church, ¶138 asserts that United Methodists are "a diverse people of God who bring special gifts and evidence of God's grace to the unity of the Church and to society." Therefore all persons "who meet the requirements of The United Methodist *Book of Discipline*" should be enabled "to participate in the life of the Church."

Second, the *Discipline* invokes the principle of connectionalism as the "vital web of interactive relationships" that weaves a global church into unity. Strands of this web include a common basis in doctrine and the General Rules, a shared polity and superintendency, a common mission expressed through conferences, and an "ethos which characterizes our distinctive way of doing things" (¶130).

This paragraph, while still titled "The Journey of a Connectional People," vastly compresses a much longer, rambling discourse on connectionalism that originated in discussions in the General Council on Ministries and was added to the *Discipline* in 1988. The impetus for its inclusion was clearest in a paragraph called "affirmation and stress" (1992 *Discipline*, ¶112.4). Here the document acknowledged that "connectionalism has served us well," but that stresses around such functions as itineracy and apportionments indicated a need for flexibility. In a sentence odd for its personalizing of an abstract principle, the paragraph concluded that "it is important for connectionalism to bend, to *have tolerance* in a changing world, *to be able to live*...with freshness and new *commitment*" (emphasis mine). Who exactly was being addressed here, or who was supposed to take what action, was not explained. Instead, the next paragraph simply asserted that "we have a special opportunity" (what made it special was not spelled out) to make connectionalism work. Therefore it "should be interpreted to all our people in new and fresh ways" (1992 *Discipline*, ¶112.5).

The poignant self-examination of this section was typically Methodist in tone. Here the tradition looked at the state of its own soul (though one still wants to know exactly who was looking at what). The whole of the statement was narrative in structure. Emphasizing the story or "journey" in its title, it began with John

A style of relationship

Wesley, recalled "covenant-making events" (strikingly by quoting one specific individual, Bishop Paul Washburn originally of the EUB tradition), and rooted it all in scripture. It appealed for connectionalism as "a style of relationship rather than simply an organizational or structural framework" (1992 *Discipline*, ¶112.1-2).

This thought was reinforced by the assertion that while connectionalism was "the basic form of our polity," it was still "in essence a network of interdependent relationships among persons and groups" (1992 *Discipline*, ¶112.3). It was a community of shared vision and memory, living under discipline, and providing leadership, mobilization of resources, and "gathering points" to confer about strategy.

In short, the whole United Methodist connection was a class meeting writ large. In the connection, United Methodist people collectively continued their narrative of faith under the disciplines of study, prayer, and action. The forms of conference and conversation were essential to this way of being the church. By assembling and conferring regularly in conversation about how it is with one another, United Methodist people built each other up in ministry. The particular organizational structures of the church were incidental to this larger purpose of mutual witness and service.

The newly condensed paragraph on connectionalism, while still naming a "Journey," lacks the narrative, self-examining quality of the earlier version. It does continue the church's seeming resistance to defining exactly what the connection is. It provides no structural or constitutional explanation, and does not elaborate on what appear to be critical elements of doctrine, polity, and ethos that hold the connection together.

At least one reason for the church's hesitation to define connectionalism may be found in a statement with the ambiguous title of "The Fulfillment of Ministry Through The United Methodist Church" (¶139). Here the *Discipline* is at pains to place in the forefront of the book a definition of the church for legal purposes. At first glance the paragraph appears to be a third way of furthering the unity of mission and ministry by defining more closely what the terms "The United Methodist Church," the "general Church," the "entire Church," and "the Church" really mean. This promising foray into ecclesiology turns out, however, to have a legal purpose in civil procedure.

In light of the stirring testimonies of previous paragraphs, the *Discipline's* statement here that the connection does not exist—at least in the eyes of the law—is a paradox. " 'The United Methodist Church' as a denominational whole is not an entity, nor does it possess legal capacities and attributes." Therefore it is not a body that can sue or be sued. The connection is "spiritual" in nature, a "relation and identity" but not a legal corporate person.[12]

This puts an intriguing twist on the unity of ministry in United Methodism. That ministry is spiritual—a gift of the Spirit—clearly accords with the United Methodist understanding of baptism (¶127). That ministry is relational—part of one whole body of persons called—accords with the United Methodist understanding of unity and connection (¶¶129, 130). But that it is not actually embodied corporately—at least not in the most general sense, and for legal purposes—stirs questions worth reflecting on.

What really does constitute the connection in United Methodism? What actual forms embody United Methodist ministry as a whole people of God? Originally the connection was among Wesley and his preachers, and later among bishops and the preachers in covenant under their appointment. This interpretation is reinforced by the *Discipline's* fourth address of the issue of unity of ministries added in 1996. Here the "employment status of clergy" is clarified by a declaration that, while government may require clergy to be classified as employees of entities such as local churches, the church's polity still holds: "historic covenants . . . bind annual conferences, clergy and congregations, episcopal appointive powers and procedures" (¶141).

But the connection has become more than a clergy connection. At least, the increasing articulation of a ministry of the laity would seem to press for a broader definition. Does the term today encompass local churches, laity, general agencies, and denominational funding? What corporate forms are appropriate for such a broader connection? If nothing else, such questions point to the elusiveness and fragility of the unity of the church. They are a reminder that the ministry of all Christians can be a pleasant ideal, but that only through visible, concrete actions can Christians "convince the world of the reality of the gospel" (¶128).

CHAPTER 6

The Local Church in United Methodism

The local church has been moving to the forefront of the *Discipline* through much of the last century. It now comes first in the "Organization and Administration" division (Part V). The legislative chapter governing it has grown to seventy paragraphs spanning over fifty pages. United Methodism would seem to be focused increasingly on the ministry and mission of the local church, and on the local church as the primary expression of the whole church's mission.

Yet the complex and often contradictory United Methodist understanding of the local church in terms of constitution, organization, mission, and even terminology, is apparent in the Disciplinary provisions. In ¶¶201-4, for example, a local church is described successively as

- "the most significant arena through which disciple-making occurs," the rhetoric of later 1900s church growth literature (echoing the mission statement of ¶¶120-122);

- "a community of true believers . . . a redemptive fellowship," the rhetoric of classical Protestantism;

- "a strategic base from which Christians move out to the structures of society," the rhetoric of 1960s social activism;

- "a connectional society of persons who have professed their faith in Christ," the rhetoric of Wesleyan Methodism; and

- a place of "definite evangelistic, nurture, and witness responsibility . . . and a missional outreach responsibility," the rhetoric of contemporary church revitalization programs.

The juxtaposition—or collision—of these five ways of speaking about the local church, each reflecting a different era of development, demonstrates the varied expectations United Methodists have for their local churches.

Moreover, local churches themselves exhibit an enormous variety in their own understandings of the church's ministry and mission. The *Discipline's* description and rationale for organized units in the local church provides a measure of uniformity among churches. Considerable tension arises, however, from fundamentally ambiguous conceptions of what the local church really is, and how local autonomy and connectional uniformity should be balanced.

The Emergence of the Local Church

The discussion of the United Methodist Constitution (chapter 3 above) noted the significance of the term "local church." This name is relatively new in Methodist tradition. As recently as 1904 the MEC General Conference approved a new constitution with this provision:

> Members of the Church shall be divided into local societies, one or more of which shall constitute a Pastoral Charge.

In other words, MEC members were members of the whole connection first, then affiliated with local societies served by a pastor. The language of "society" was common in all branches of Metho-dism right up to the union of 1939. This is particularly striking in light of Methodism's movement into the American cultural establishment during the late nineteenth century, building magnificent Gothic structures in the cities and allowing its most famous "itinerant" preachers to take up long-term residence in prominent pulpits. Class meetings had long since ceased to be required, and the same 1904 *Discipline* did away with the rule of six months probation before one could become a member of a Methodist Episcopal Church.

Yet a "society" governed by a board of "stewards"—the leaders charged from earliest days with oversight of members and money—continued to be common lingo. It recalled Methodism's roots as an association for spiritual discipline within the established church. It resonated with times when the innumerable small societies scattered across the American rural landscape looked forward to "quarterly conferences" with the "presiding elder" of their region coming for worship, preaching, and sacrament, and encouragement of their growth in witness and mission.

"Local church" came into vogue by the 1920s. Retaining the sense of particular location—Methodist societies active in many "local" settlements—the term also maintained the connectionalism of the societies. "Local churches" were local mission outposts of the larger connectional church, expressions of the Methodist movement in local places. The first EUBC *Discipline* (1947) mixed old and new languages in a striking way by stating that "a local church shall be considered as a Class," and going on to describe the continuing role of class leaders and stewards (¶55-67).

Yet local churches were also now "churches," clearly responsible for Word and sacrament as well as discipline and mission. They were coming into their own as basic units of ministry to which the denomination would pay increasing attention. Thus the 1928 MEC episcopal address would determine the local church to be "the unit in our study of denominational progress, for it is there that we are to test the value of our organization and polity."[1]

The 1940 *Discipline* of the newly formed Methodist Church set up what would become an increasing tension in the connection.[2] While the Constitution for the united church (1939) stated that the annual conference was "the basic body in the Church," legislative paragraphs were pulled together from scattered headings such as membership and education to make a new section of eighty-one paragraphs titled "Local Church." The 1944 *Discipline* then brought that whole body of material to the front, immediately following the Constitution. This modification was made under the guidance of an influential consultant to denominations and local churches, Murray H. Leiffer, a professor of sociology at Garrett (now Garrett Evangelical) Theological Seminary and author of numerous research studies of the contemporary church.[3]

Among the significant effects of the new arrangement was the relocation of legislation regarding the quarterly conference from the conferences chapter to the local church chapter. The four annual meetings of quarterly conference had earlier been convened by the presiding elder who conducted worship and heard reports of the local work. By 1908 the *Discipline* granted permission for the second and third quarterly meetings to be dropped, and the presiding elder was retitled a "district superintendent"—a name more organizational than sacramental, as Russell Richey has pointed out, and more focused on a region than on a gathering.[4]

The 1944 revisions thus split the local conference off from the nexus of annual and general conference. The local church stood more on its own organizationally, its bridge to the annual conference being a district representative of the bishop. The name "board of stewards" was still permissible, but "official board" now became more common. After 1968, with the union of the MC and the EUBC, yet a new terminology was brought into use. The Administrative Board now carried responsibility for local church business, while the Council on Ministries—a term made over from the Program Council in recent EUB tradition—carried the program of the local church.[5]

These changes did not uniformly sit well in a connection as diverse as United Methodism. Nor did they reflect a consistent ecclesiology. The district superintendent now visited at least annually to conduct a "charge conference." This term related to the pastoral appointment from the annual conference, a "charge" being the local church or churches to which a particular pastor was appointed. Thus in situations where two or more local churches were on a "circuit" (a time-honored Methodist term) served by the same pastor, the charge conference still bore a strong resemblance to the old quarterly conference as a kind of small regional gathering for worship and appraisal of the work. Yet the new system obviously honored above all the ministries of *the* local church: the church with its own pastor—the "station" in older terminology—and the capacity to meet all the expanding requirements for local church organization in the *Discipline*. In these churches the charge conference was more like an annual congregational meeting.

This left an ambiguity that has been a persistent source of conflict in annual conferences. In what ways is the local church related to the connection? Are local churches who share a pastor and thus are joined in a charge conference related to the connection in the same way as are local churches which are charges in themselves?

The ambiguity has been compounded by the increasing use of the term "congregation" in the *Discipline*. It now appears frequently in legislative paragraphs, though not in the Constitution or in major headings or definitions—with the striking exception of the sixteenth-century Articles of Religion. The term is nowhere defined. In its ecclesiological use it suggests simply an emphasis on the gathering of the people of God in particular places, forming communities of witness, nurture, and service. No particular polity follows from the term.

Yet its use as an organizational term in the local church chapter continually suggests that somehow United Methodism has—or is moving toward—congregations in the political sense of self-constituted associations. To some extent the current Disciplinary usage originated with the EUBC. The annual meeting of a local EUB church was termed the "congregational meeting" and was called and convened by the minister for the purpose of hearing annual reports and informing the congregation of the work of the general church (EUBC *Discipline* 1967, ¶¶34-35). But the language of "local church," "charge," as well as the historic words "station" and "circuit" were also used (¶36). The body now called the Administrative Board was named the "local conference," another way of linking local EUB churches with the connection (¶52).

One way to sort out the confusion seems to be implied in EUBC usage. "Local church" referred to a church from the standpoint of its relationship to the connection—looking outward. "Congregation" referred to a church from the standpoint of its internal affairs—looking inward. But ambiguities persist. In the current *Discipline* some uses of the term "congregation" simply refer to congregation as assembly. Thus the pastor normally is to bring new members "before the congregation" to receive them (¶223). But other uses seem to have an organizational intent, such as the "Protection of Rights of Congregations" from having to alter their property titles in connection with the 1968 union (¶261), or the repeated use of the term in defining local church administration.

Thus while the Constitution still asserts that the annual conference is "the basic body in the Church," many current practices suggest that the local church is the basic body. An issue yet to be fully faced is that at present United Methodist connectional polity in no way is designed to support or interrelate congregations as independent units of ministry and mission. It is designed to support congregations as connectional outposts of a mission more widely shared "over these lands."

A Connection of Local Churches

That local churches are fundamentally connectional in nature (in current legislated polity) is apparent at many critical points. Paragraph 203 defines the local church as "a connectional society of persons who have professed their faith in Christ." Paragraph 205 places a definition of pastoral charge right in the forefront of the chapter, clarifying that in terms of the connection, local churches are defined by their status as a charge to which an itinerant pastor is appointed by the bishop. Paragraph 215 makes clear that a person joining a United Methodist church joins not just that church but the entire connection (an echo of the 1904 MEC Constitution—"members of the Church . . . divided into local societies").

Paragraph 245.1 establishes that "within the pastoral charge"—not the "local church"—the charge conference is "the basic unit in the connectional system of The United Methodist Church." Here the annual business of the local church is conducted under the presidency of an officer of the connection, the district superintendent. A charge conference may be convened as a church conference in which all members may attend and vote, but it is still presided over by the district superintendent (¶247). The charge conference elects a lay member of the annual conference as a "representative" of the charge, not the local church—one lay member per pastor under appointment (¶250.2). (Chapter 3 showed how this is not democratic representation in the sense of being proportional to membership.)

Some of the clearest evidence of the connectional nature of the local church is in the legislation governing the founding of a new one (¶259). Local churches may get started at the initiative of local persons, members of existing churches, a district superintendent, an office of congregational development in the annual conference, or under the guidance of the annual conference Board of Global

Ministries. But in terms of polity, the bishop and Cabinet must consent to the establishment of a new church. Then only the district superintendent of the district in which it will be located can serve as "the agent in charge of the project," recommend a site, and call together persons interested in forming a new local church.

When the interested persons come together to organize, the district superintendent (or a pastor whom he or she designates) presides. Persons are received by transfer of membership or by profession of faith, and thereby become members of a "constituting church conference." They in turn elect members of the church council. Once that is done, the "constituting" conference adjourns and reconvenes as a charge conference to elect officers. Thus at no point is a newly constituted local church a self-constituting congregation that begins meeting on its own, elects a president or moderator, or votes to accept its founding pastor. It is constituted as a local church within the connection.

Because they are not independent in polity but part of a connectional community of witness and service, local churches are critical to the vitality and effectiveness of the UMC. In the words of the episcopal initiative on *Vital Congregations—Faithful Disciples*, "the central, focal expression of ministry and mission in the name of Christ is found in the local church congregation." The connection depends on "particular assemblies of the faithful" discovering their unique mission in each place. At the same time, local churches are also held in communion with each other through a shared mission.

The *Discipline* encourages local churches to exhibit their own initiative in carrying out the mission and ministry of the UMC. Not only are local churches a primary "strategic base" with a "missional outreach responsibility"; they also share the classic definition of church as "a community of true believers" (¶¶201-4). In short, every local church is fully the church.

> The congregation is a place where life in Christ is visible, where the community of faith is made actual. *Everything is at stake in the life of the congregation.* The congregation is a place where the faith must be made real. In the congregation, ways to concretely live out the claims of God's kingdom must be discovered. The congregation must point to the reign of God if we expect that reign to be anticipated anywhere.

fractals

179

When the faithful gather for worship in a given place, there is no "real" church someplace else of which this gathering is just a subdivision or a branch office. Christ is wholly present in each place; Christ is not divided. The responsibility for witness and service in Christ's name lies not somewhere else in some more pure and holy setting, but in each place where Christians gather.[6]

Church Membership

The first major section of the local church chapter in the *Discipline* concerns church membership. Paragraphs similar to these have been placed near the front of the MEC, MECS, MC, and EUB *Disciplines* for generations. But in recent years the UMC has engaged in broad and serious debate about the church's traditions and contemporary understanding of what it means to be a member of the church.

The 1988 General Conference authorized a study of baptism which was eventually adopted by the 1996 General Conference. In brief, the study advocated a more "churchly" interpretation of baptism as an incorporation into the Body of Christ that initiates membership in the church. The study proposed creating two categories of membership in local churches. Baptized members would be listed on a local church roll but understood in the general sense as members of the church universal by virtue of baptism. Professing members would be those who took vows as adults and consciously joined the connectional and particularly the local church.

Adoption of the report immediately created confusion. The UMC Constitution defined the church as an inclusive body open to all persons "when they take the appropriate vows" of membership (¶4). The Judicial Council interpreted this paragraph to eliminate any possibility of a membership roll for persons who were baptized but had not taken conscious vows of joining the church. Moreover, many paragraphs about church members, including such items as eligibility for service as conference delegates or church officers, were not changed to define to which category of members the *Discipline* referred in each case.

Thus the 2000 General Conference had to address the issue again, and took the first step by adopting a constitutional amendment. As later adopted by annual conference members in aggregate, the new paragraph affirms that all persons shall "upon baptism be admitted as baptized members, and upon taking the vows declaring the Christian faith, become professing members in any local church in the connection." The 2004 General Conference will need to adopt legislation specifying the nature, rights and privileges of the two categories of membership in legislative paragraphs, particularly the local church chapter. Meanwhile, the 2000 *Discipline* contained the existing constitutional paragraph and the church membership paragraphs as authorized by the Judicial Council decision basically returning to pre-1996 wording.

The Baptism Study brought to focus the continuing tension between United Methodism as a church practicing baptism (including infants, as specified in the Articles of Religion XVII) and as an evangelical society inviting people to an experience of new birth in Christ. The study raised several issues unresolved in United Methodist polity. If baptism—even of infants—constitutes full reception into the Body of Christ, the Church, then what is the meaning of "membership" in the church? If the Holy Spirit is present in the sacrament of baptism to bestow the gifts necessary for following Christ in ministry, what is the purpose of the confirmation ritual (which clearly is not a sacrament)? After baptism, is there a further experience of the Holy Spirit sanctifying the believer? Should such an experience be expected of United Methodist church members? What should be the criteria of membership?

The *Discipline* affirms a middle way that synthesizes elements of the "churchly" and "evangelical" viewpoints. Baptism incorporates the baptized into the whole Body of Christ—yet it normally must be done in relationship to a particular church. United Methodism does not re-baptize persons coming into membership from another denominational tradition, but does expect them to transfer their membership—a distinction which pastors often have to explain to newcomers.

Membership is interpreted as a covenant entered into through formal vows and maintained through disciplines of full participation in the life of the church.[7] The covenant is a mutual bond in the community of the local church. "A member is bound in sacred covenant to shoulder the burdens, share the risks, and celebrate the joys of fellow members" (¶218).

Membership in a local church means participation in a community of faith, and the *Discipline* admonishes all members to welcome newcomers, to be involved in the ministries of the church, and to join in spiritual growth and small groups. One way in which the "care of members" is exercised is in efforts to bring inactive members back into the active fellowship of the Church. Such persons are to be contacted by pastor and laity, and encouraged to "reaffirm the baptismal vows," transfer to a church in which they want to be active, or withdraw.

This process is not taken lightly. The inactive member's name must be published in the charge conference minutes "for two consecutive years" and must be considered individually in a charge conference session. Only then can the charge conference vote to remove the person. Meanwhile the door is still open, since the church keeps a roll of persons removed. Thus the *Discipline* stresses the responsibility of members for each other, a quality that has roots deep in the class meeting structure of mutual care and accountability (¶227).

Nothing is more characteristic of United Methodist tradition than keeping exact records of how many members each local church has. The *Discipline* directs each church to have rolls for six different categories of membership (¶229), as well as a permanent register in which all members are recorded in chronological order (¶232.1). The register can make fascinating reading for people with historical or genealogical interests, particularly since members across the years have normally signed in their own handwriting.

Computer programs now make possible for many churches a continuously updated roll with much associated data from addresses to birth dates to skills and interests. At the other end of the spectrum, though, are local churches which—despite the many imperatives of the *Discipline*—have no reliable records of membership at all. Persons who long since moved away, or moved on to the Great Campmeeting, are still listed as members. Children who were baptized and grew up in the church but now live their adult lives elsewhere remain on the roll.

These anomalies are not necessarily oversights; they may reflect a different norm of church. For many people, the church of their childhood and/or family is the church for their lifetime—a continuing place of roots. In these situations "membership" is more organic and traditional in nature, such that to remove a person from the rolls is tantamount to expelling him or her from the family. This norm differs notably from an understanding of church as voluntary association, in which membership is a rational decision accompanied by information cards to be filled out for entry into the computer and pledge cards to indicate what one expects to give in the coming year.

Most local churches are a blend of these traditional and rational organizational forms. Whatever the mix, membership is primarily a matter of pastoral and congregational care, not a matter of formalities. All the paperwork involved in transfers of membership, for example, is worthwhile only in the service of making sure that a member continues to be under the care of a local church. There is no watertight bureaucratic system that tracks all United Methodist members—much less persons transferring in or out of other denominations. Many people who come seeking membership are never able to obtain a formal transfer from their old church (many denominations do not have or do not honor such a system). Many move away without ever requesting a transfer of membership.

The most pastors and laity can do is integrate people into the life of the local church, and when a person moves away, try to make sure that a pastor or layperson in the new community gets their name and address for contact. Then the former church can issue a certificate of transfer indicating the good standing of the member and lending a sense of continuity to their membership in the connection (or the wider church). The least desirable option, the *Discipline* makes clear, is to indicate that a person has withdrawn from membership, meaning either that they joined another church without requesting a transfer or simply that they no longer wish to be a member.

A growing edge for church membership issues in United Methodism is the inclusion and incorporation of persons of all racial, national, economic or social backgrounds. As a connection, United Methodism is remarkably diverse. Within its local churches, however, United Methodism continues to be sharply separated by race and class. In most towns, "First" UMC is higher on social status indicators (education, income, type of employment). "Epworth" or "Wesley" UMC is more likely to be comprised of people who make a living with physical labor. Everyone knows, moreover, what kind of people go to which church. Everyone knows which local church in town is "white" and which "black." In many towns and cities across the old "EUB/MEC belt" from Pennsylvania to Iowa, former EUB and former MC local churches continue to sit on opposite corners, preserving separate heritages. Hispanic, Asian, Native American, or other bilingual local churches are obvious from their signboards.

The UMC has tried to address these divisions with both constitutional and legislative language about inclusiveness. "All persons, without regard to race, color, national origin, status, or economic condition," the Constitution declares,

> shall be eligible to attend its worship services, participate in its programs, receive the sacraments, upon baptism be admitted as baptized members, and upon taking vows declaring the Christian faith, become professing members *in any local church in the connection* [¶4 as amended in 2000; emphasis mine].

This language is echoed—with the addition of including persons with disabilities—in the first church membership paragraph (¶214).

At this point connectionalism can be a real strength. All kinds of persons can and do participate in the connection. The issue is whether everyone can participate in any and every local church. If the UMC really consists of "local churches" *of* the connection then the answer has to be affirmative.

It is somewhat ironic that the *Discipline* falls back on human rights language at this point, stating that all persons are "eligible" for membership. Of course, that is a foundation point that must not be taken away. But the real question is whether all people in the connection are in fellowship with each other such that they would welcome persons of any background into their particular local church. Will it make any difference to this connectional community if local churches increasingly call themselves and think of themselves as "congregations"? Will "congregations" be more or less hospitable and open to diversity than "local churches" have been?

The *Discipline* asks a lot of local churches, perhaps too much. Churches are inevitably local and adopt local customs. Nothing the *Discipline* says can make any local church become inclusive. Here connectional polity becomes more a model of Christian community than a reality. It is up to local churches to put it into practice.

184

The Organization of the Local Church

Since United Methodist local churches are fundamentally connectional in nature, their primary governing body is a "unit in the connectional system"—the charge conference. That is, local churches cannot make major decisions about such items as facilities, elected officers, pastoral salary, removal of members from the rolls, or candidates for ordained ministry, without the sanction of the representative of the connection, the district superintendent. Normally the DS is present, though he or she may designate an elder to preside if necessary. In any case, the DS authorizes and sets the time of the meeting (¶245.1, .4, .5).

The charge conference has "general oversight of the church council(s)" (¶249.1)—or to put it the other way around, the council of the local church is "amenable to and function[s] as the administrative [also termed "executive" in ¶243.1] agency of the charge conference" (¶251.1). Through the charge conference, under the leadership of the DS, a local church is to "review and evaluate the total mission and ministry of the church, receive reports, and adopt objectives and goals recommended by the church council" which are then to be carried out under the governance of the council (¶246.3).

Thus in United Methodist polity neither the pastor nor a lay president or moderator of the congregation presides over most of the crucial decisions in the life of a local church. The "charge" is a "pastoral charge," which means both that the bishop appoints a pastor, charging him or her with ministry in that place, and that the pastor is "in charge" of many basic responsibilities of ministry there. But in the charge conference, the pastor is under the superintendency of a representative of the bishop.

Likewise, while every local church elects a lay leader and a chairperson of the church council, neither they nor any other lay officers are "in charge" at the charge conference. In fact, no certain number of local church officers or members is even required to be present. Neither the charge conference or any other local church body—with the exception of the Board of Trustees—must have a quorum in order to conduct business (¶¶245.6, 251.6).

Obviously, of course, the health of the church depends on people wanting to attend and be actively involved. If they do not, the pastoral and lay leadership must take notice and try to find out what the poor attendance indicates. Many district superintendents and pastors are seeking new ways to conduct charge conferences with a more vital format in which the local church can worship, celebrate its story of ministry, and accept new challenges for mission. After years of emphasizing the collection of data and annual report forms, charge conferences may be picking up once again some of the threads of fervency and vigor from the older quarterly conferences.

The *Discipline* puts forward in very brief form a dynamic systems model of the local church, parallel to the systemic description of "making disciples" described above. The "primary task and mission" of a local church "in the context of its own community" involves a continuous flow and process of growth and transformation as persons

- are invited, welcomed, and received into the fellowship;
- encouraged in their relationship with God through Jesus Christ;
- strengthened in their "spiritual formation"; and
- supported in their everyday lives in the community as faithful disciples (¶242).[8]

To structure and support the primary task, the *Discipline* mandates certain organizational units for every local church. This assures a measure of consistency through the connection, making both superintendency by DSs and itineracy of pastors from church to church more feasible. It also meets basic legal requirements in order for local churches to own property, hire staff, and raise money.

The 1996 General Conference greatly increased the flexibility for local churches to structure themselves in their own way (¶¶243.2, 246.2). Certain *administrative units* are mandated for every church: committees on pastor-parish relations, finance, and lay leadership care for the provision of leadership and funding for the local church's ministries. The board of trustees administers the property. But the governing body—the executive agency of the charge conference—may now be simply the "church council," or may continue previous structures, either the administrative council or the administrative board with council on ministries.

Even greater choice of structures is now offered in local church *program*. Churches may continue with the administrative board model, created in 1960 to incorporate elements of both Methodist and EUB local church polity. In this model a separate council on ministries was charged with carrying out the program and mission of the church. Like other units, the council on ministries was amenable to the administrative board but was able to initiate a program agenda without always being overwhelmed by the administrative agenda of buildings, personnel, and money. The program divisions reporting to the council on ministries focused around specialized areas including (in alphabetical order) age-level and family ministries, and the "work areas" of Christian unity and interreligious concerns, church and society, community volunteers, education, evangelism, higher education and campus ministry, missions, religion and race, status and role of women, stewardship, and worship (1992 *Discipline*, ¶¶260, 261).

Churches may also continue with the administrative council model, devised in 1980 as a simpler alternative. In this model administration and program were under one governing body with four programmatic divisions: nurture, outreach, witness, and age-level and family ministries. While this structure was originally intended to respond to the needs of smaller churches, it was adopted by churches of all sizes as a way of eliminating duplication of meetings and consolidating decision making.

The new "church council" virtually makes the administrative council model the norm for United Methodist churches (¶251). Program ministries are grouped under nurture, outreach, and witness, with the "work areas" previously authorized under the administrative board and council on ministries model divided among the three headings. However, the *Discipline* no longer refers to the three ministry areas as having "chairpersons," and terminology of "commissions" for program no longer appears. "Persons who represent the program ministries of the church" are to be members of the church council, but no office is specified (¶251.5). A charge conference "may elect annually a coordinator or ministry group chairperson for any or all" of what were known previously as work areas. These persons are to "work with the church council" but are not specifically authorized to be members of it (¶253).

Moreover, the *Discipline* no longer contains any legislation describing the functions of "coordinators" or "ministry groups." No paragraph explains or authorizes the specific content of local church work in worship, Christian unity, status and role of women, or any of the others. No conference unit or general agency is authorized to define it, either. The council on ministries itself lacks any Disciplinary description or authorization. Thus these items, mentioned in name only, are left solely to the discretion—and creative leadership—of the local church.

The terminology of "committees" or "boards" is still reserved for administrative units of the local church (¶258). Unlike the program units, administrative bodies have certain required membership. The committee on lay leadership may have up to nine members, plus the lay leader and the pastor, with rotating classes of membership to ensure both stability from year to year and some turnover with fresh voices and perspectives. Whatever its size, this committee is chaired by the pastor, who has thereby the opportunity to shape the whole leadership of the local church (¶258.1).

The committee on pastor-parish relations (termed staff-parish relations in churches with numbers of paid employees, but widely known as "PPR") may range in size from five to nine members, plus the lay leader and a lay member of annual conference. Members are to be divided into rotating classes. The pastor is not a member, but is normally present at meetings; no meeting may be held without the knowledge of "the pastor and/or the district superintendent." This committee is charged with meeting at least quarterly to confer with the pastor and staff about "effectiveness of ministry," their compensation, as well as annual evaluation of the pastor and staff, and consultation with the district superintendent regarding the pastoral appointment. The *Discipline* is at pains to provide for a variety of perspectives in the committee—at least one young adult and preferably also a youth—and excludes having more than one person from the same family or persons from pastoral or staff families (¶258.2).

The committee on finance has oversight of the budget and handles the church's money. Its membership is composed primarily of officers such as the treasurer, a trustee, chairpersons of church councils, the pastor and lay leader. This committee, like all others, is amenable to the church council. It "compiles" a complete budget for the year. It develops and implements "plans that will raise sufficient income to meet the budget adopted by the church council." It is not authorized to decide how the local church will spend its money (¶258.4).

A later chapter of the *Discipline* devoted to all types of church property contains the provisions for a local church board of trustees. Unlike other units, this board elects its own chairperson. But it is still amenable to the charge conference—and thereby to the executive agency of the charge conference, the church council—for its actions.

Local church administration revolves around several key offices, to which persons must be elected by the charge conference itself. All members of the lay leadership, pastor parish relations, and finance committees, as well as the board of trustees, are so elected. The charge conference also elects the chairpersons of PPR and finance and (usually) a church treasurer, and three key leaders: the church council chairperson, the lay leader, and the lay member of annual conference (¶248).

Church councils have extensive responsibilities; the choice of chairpersons for these bodies is critical to the local church's ministry. The council has oversight of all planning for mission, all membership rolls, lay leadership, budgets and salaries, and connectional relationships. The chairpersons thus have key roles in initiating, guiding, and supporting the church's primary task (¶250.3).

The lay leader is the least defined but potentially the most influential lay position in a church. As a kind of organizational gadfly or ombudsperson, the lay leader is an ex officio (by reason of office) member of several key units: charge conference, church council, finance committee, and lay leadership committee. The lay leader, who is an ex officio member of the PPR committee as well, consults regularly with the pastor regarding "the state of the church and the needs for ministry" (¶250.1). The lay leader is charged with building up the ministry of the laity more generally. But because this is somewhat nebulous, many lay leaders also chair the church council, or otherwise serve in responsible positions.

The *Discipline* also places the lay member of annual conference on key local church units, mainly to provide a strong communication link between the annual conference and the local church. These persons are ex officio members of the charge conference, the church council, the pastor-parish relations committee, and the finance committee. They must have been members of the United Methodist Church for at least two years, so that they have some understanding of the connectional system (¶250.2).

The pastor is ex officio a member of the charge conference, church council, the lay leadership committee, the finance committee, and the executive committees of the local units of both United Methodist Women and United Methodist Men. The term "ex officio" in itself does not express whether a person can vote in the assigned body or not, and the *Discipline* does not specify whether or not the pastor can vote, leaving this as a matter of administrative and pastoral style. Most pastors and laity would consider the pastor to be an ex officio member of any church committee, not just the ones specified, but this too is a matter of pastoral style.

The pastor is charged with oversight of "the total ministry of the local church in its nurturing ministries and in fulfilling its mission of witness and service in the world." In particular, the pastor is "to be the administrative officer of the local church" (¶331). This is softer language than declaring that the pastor is the "CEO" and head of staff to whom all officers and program units report. Though there are some pastors who administer by this latter model, many others view themselves more as supporting and providing resources for lay leadership, who really determine the direction and mission of the local church.

In any case, the *Discipline* does not attempt to govern the leadership styles of diverse pastors serving in these varied branches of the United Methodist vine called local churches. All the *Discipline* establishes is that the pastor is charged with leadership responsibilities. It is important to be clear about the source of this "charge." Certainly a local church has hopes and expectations of its pastor and continually makes those known. But the "charge" itself comes from the connection. The pastor remains an outsider—appointed by the bishop, holding her or his membership in the annual conference and being finally amenable to that body, not the local church. Neither the charge conference nor the church council has authority over the pastoral appointment. Only the pastor-parish relations committee has a say in it, and that only consultative.

The organizational plan for the local church cannot say everything that must be said, especially about the relationship of the charge conference and the various associations active in a local church. United Methodist Women and United Methodist Men, for example, are officially represented in governing bodies. Yet they generate their own activities, raise their own money, and elect their own officers. The church council can only seek cooperation and coordination with these groups. The *Discipline* perpetuates the quasi-independence of another long-time association as well, the Sunday school, whose superintendent was in days past almost on a par with the pastor in influence. Today this work, while referred to as a program agency, is coordinated through a ministry group on education, and the traditional superintendent role can be difficult to interpret (¶¶254, 255.1).

Balancing Local and Connectional Mission

The *Discipline* sets out a plan of organization so that all 36,000 churches in the U.S. will have certain basic structures in common. To some extent the plan simply reflects cultural assumptions about what is required to be a responsible voluntary association in this society. A board of trustees, for example, is necessary for the corporate ownership of financial assets and property (albeit held in trust for the connection). A finance committee keeps the income and expenditures under the control of lay members of the organization, separate from the administrative officer (pastor). Local churches in Central Conferences may be under a different plan of organization adapted to their own culture and local laws.

The extensive plan of organizing for program and mission which grew up over twenty-five years of United Methodism—now largely deleted by the 1996 General Conference—was another expression of connectionalism. Program units and work areas were not required, but by force of connectional relationships seemed necessary. Annual report forms distributed to charge conferences by the general church appeared to reinforce them as a norm. Guidelines for chairing them (and all local church positions) were published and distributed each quadrennium by the General Board of Discipleship.

Work areas in particular were intended to provide a link between local churches and denominational units that could offer resources and support. Parallel bodies in the annual conference and general church created a network of shared purpose. A local church work area chairperson on the status and role of women, for example, carried special responsibility for "the church's continuing commitment to the full and equal responsibility and participation of women in the total life and mission of the Church" (1992 *Discipline*, ¶262.9). On its own, her local church might not have authorized such a work area or known what direction to take it. The connection offered both authorization and resources. For ideas about how to develop this work, she could turn to a district chairperson, an annual conference unit, and the General Commission on Status and Role of Women.

United Methodists experienced and interpreted the dynamics of these parallel units in various ways, of course. For many local churches, the scheme for organizing program and mission into specialized areas was appropriate and useful. These churches found the general church resource materials immediately adaptable to their circumstances. They experienced the connectional dynamics as a helpful support of local initiatives in ministry.

Other local churches found the scheme overbearing and the materials from general agencies unnecessary for local work. Some churches might list the same lay volunteer for several different jobs just to get the annual report forms filled out. Few people seemed to take an interest in or could relate to the content of the guidelines. They experienced the connectional dynamics as burdensome and even disrespectful of local initiatives in ministry.

Connectional culture has always collided with local church culture, of course. Connectional bodies inevitably view local churches as critically important mission outposts for the emphases on which the church more generally has reached consensus. They define local church vitality in terms of active involvement in carrying out connectional mission.

Local church culture, however, remains immensely varied and resistant to "outside" influence. Each local church has its own locale, story, character, and symbol system which distills into particular ways of choosing directions and making decisions. No "one size fits all" structural plan can possibly overlay such particularities. Any plan requires adaptation to local culture.

But to what extent should the connection honor local church culture, and to what extent should the connection challenge local church culture with new ideas and directions? This question has been sharpest in recent years around issues of race and gender. The connection has mandated that each local church open its doors to all persons and accept as pastors either women or men and persons of any ethnicity. There is still widespread resistance to these initiatives after twenty years or more.

The organizational challenge is twofold. On the one hand, the connection must empower local churches to undertake ministry and mission as local persons understand it in their particular situation. A number of connectional initiatives have sprung from this local vitality as effective ideas spread from church to church. On the other hand, conferences must seek the most effective way for initiatives that enjoy a wide connectional consensus to be interpreted and supported in the local church.

Indeed, a connectional church faces fundamental ecclesiological questions. If the church is both local and universal at the same time—fully church in each place yet also part of a universally practiced faith—how will that be embodied structurally? How can the local church be local without becoming parochial? How can the connectional church be general without losing its root of vitality in local places?

This balance is a continuing challenge for United Methodism, as it is for other traditions. The 1996 *Discipline* has shifted the balance toward local initiative and autonomy by removing most of the description of connectional program units. Yet this shift raises a host of polity issues. The *Discipline* as it stands no longer authorizes or defines a great part of local church work. The connection thus has much less role in the basic denominational function of congregational discipline.

Local churches are left largely to their own devices for organizing program and mission. Some have the staff, lay expertise, and resources for this task; many do not. In any case, local churches have less possibility of turning to the book for means of making decisions or resolving conflicts of authority, particularly if the local church is following an older structure no longer described in the *Discipline*. Meanwhile, connectional officers such as DSs will have an even more demanding task of learning about diverse local church structures so as to be effective in their superintendency. This situation promises to perpetuate in new forms the tension of local and connectional.

CHAPTER 7

Called and Set Apart: Ordered Ministry in United Methodism

No aspect of United Methodist polity and practice is richer in history and lore, denser with traditions and expectations, or more difficult to interpret than the ministries of pastoral and diaconal leadership in the church. Nowhere is the complexity of United Methodism's synthetic ecclesiological heritage of organic and evangelical elements more apparent. When the 1996 General Conference adopted a plan of ministry radically departing from over two hundred years of Methodist tradition, it introduced only the latest in a long line of controversies that result from an ever-shifting synthesis of understandings. The new plan, like earlier ones, will have to be lived into over time by a tradition that prizes its pragmatism.

Yet for all the confusion and frustration that sometimes results, United Methodism has been remarkably effective in providing leadership for the churches. Few local churches are left without a pastor for more than a short time; virtually all are served by a person with at least some training and certification. United Methodist churches enjoy the leadership of educated and credentialed pastors, educators, musicians, administrators, and many others.

A Dual Framework of Preaching Ministry

From its beginnings as an evangelical renewal movement within the established church, Methodism put preaching first among leadership roles. The preacher who could sway an audience and bring persons more closely into life with Christ has always claimed a central place in Methodism. Whatever one's standing in terms of education or ordination, one could still—inspired by the Holy Spirit—preach the Word of God. The members of this preaching order considered most effective and useful, of course, were those who were free to travel or itinerate, to carry their preaching ministry wherever they were sent. These belonged to annual conference to which they were accountable for their performance of ministry and through which they received an appointment from the bishop.

Thus the earliest *Disciplines* of American Methodism put the questions that have remained at the core of annual conference ever since, though the vocabulary has changed:

> On the Method of holding a Conference, and the Business to be done therein . . .
> We enquire,
> 1. What preachers are admitted?
> 2. Who remain on Trial?
> 3. Who are admitted on Trial?
> 4. Who desist from traveling?
> 5. Are there any Objections to any of the Preachers? Who are named one by one.
> 6. How are the preachers stationed this year?[1]

John Wesley took upon himself the ordination of preachers only under the exigency of needing to provide the sacraments for Methodist people in places where they were not otherwise attainable—in particular, in the "very uncommon chain of providences" that led to Methodism's independence in America.[2] Ordination was from the beginning presbyteral in form, the bishop presiding but joined by other elders in laying on hands. The roots of this form lay not in the organic church tradition but in the practical initiatives of the "primitive church" through which Methodism strove to find an authentic ecclesiology. Even as ordination requirements gradually increased—especially from the late nineteenth century on—the sense persisted that ordination was a pragmatic setting-apart of persons under definite needs of the traveling ministry in certain situations and contexts.[3]

As a consequence of the privileging of preaching and the pragmatic roots of ordination, United Methodism continues to authorize the ministry of pastors in two separate, sometimes parallel, sometimes discordant, frameworks. The one with clear priority, as demonstrated often by the grammar of the *Discipline,* is annual conference relationship. The other is ordination, which derives its importance not so much from its intrinsic value as from its relationship with credentials for full conference membership.

The roots of this double framework lie in the origins of annual conference as the gathering of itinerant preachers. As Frederick Norwood put it,

> Historically speaking, admission to membership in the annual conference as a traveling preacher had nothing to do with ordination. None of the early preachers, before 1784, was ordained. . . . The introduction of ordination provided for the sacraments, but it made almost no difference in the nature of the ministry. From that day to this, the really important factor in definition of the Methodist minister has been membership in an annual conference, not ordination.[4]

At the same time, however, the status conferred by ordination gradually became the distinguishing mark of full conference members. After 1784 the Methodist Episcopal Church made subtle distinctions between "ministers" and "preachers." While both were first and foremost called to preach, the former were ordained full members of annual conference; the latter served in local churches but were neither ordained nor members of conference.[5]

These local preachers, now called local pastors, illustrate the reality and the difficulty of the dual framework. They have provided a preaching ministry for United Methodist local churches from the beginning. They organized societies and class meetings in settlements scattered all over the countryside, and carried on with worship and preaching between visits of the presiding elder. For many local pastors, preaching has been a way for them to serve the church in a particular locale while continuing to make a living in some other form of work as well. Thus while they have been appointed by the bishop to a particular church, most have not itinerated from place to place like full members of annual conferences.

Local pastors also have not been expected to undertake the prerequisites for pursuing full membership and ordination. They are committed only to a course of study approved by the General

Board of Higher Education and Ministry (GBHEM). The course of study itself has deep roots in Methodist tradition, since it was the standard form of ministerial preparation before the founding of seminaries in the late nineteenth and early twentieth centuries.

For all that, however, local pastors do not really fit the dual framework. They are neither ordained nor consecrated, holding only a license for pastoral ministry from their district. They are permitted to administer the sacraments, but only in the local church(es) to which they are appointed. They are appointed by the bishop, but not required to itinerate. Full-time and part-time local pastors under appointment are considered to be no longer local church members but clergy members of annual conference with rights of participation—except that they still cannot vote as full members do (¶341.6).

Provisions for local pastors, along with multiple other categories of service—diaconal ministers, associate members, deaconesses, and so on—make it obvious that United Methodism continues in ambiguity over set apart ministries. Such ambiguity is not without its uses, of course; the lack of clear definitions allows for flexibility in meeting the pastoral needs of local churches. United Methodism's vaunted pragmatism has permitted the movement to adapt ministry to many different kinds of situations. At the same time, ambiguity can be deeply confusing and hurtful as people who faithfully serve local churches experience themselves as "second-class citizens" among the clergy, shut out of significant annual conference decisions that affect them and their local churches.

The 1996 General Conference adopted new forms of ministry that have shaken the dual framework to its foundations. For the first time in Methodist history, there is an ordained order of persons who do not itinerate and who initiate their own place of employment. Deacons are ordained to "Word and Service," including "proclamation of the Word" (¶¶319, 320). But this preaching and service ministry does not participate in the historic understanding of the missionary order of Methodist preachers willing to go where sent. (Local pastors do not have to itinerate, either, but they do not initiate their employment.)

The new ministry plan also disengages the dual tracks by eliminating ordination for those "on trial" (the historic language) as elders and members in full connection in an annual conference.

Probationary members are "commissioned" for their work, a minimum of three years in which they are "commissioned ministers" but not ordained as deacons—the historic practice (¶316).

Thus United Methodism is going through fundamental changes in its understanding of set apart ministry. In true synthetic fashion, the UMC seeks to maintain itineracy and superintendency as its definitive practices, even while moving toward a model that could greatly increase the number of clergy who are hired by local churches and do not itinerate. How this will settle out, only time will tell.

Specialized Ministries

All setting apart of persons for specialized, credentialed ministry in the church begins in the local church. Anyone who wants to proceed into any form of certified service or relationship with an annual conference must first have the approval and affirmation of governing bodies in the local church in which he or she holds membership.

Persons in specialized ministries normally relate to a connectional body outside the local church for credentials. But they cannot get to that point without the support of their own congregation. This puts the onus on local churches to take with utmost seriousness the recruitment and initial examination, as well as continuing support, of persons who express a call to serve.

United Methodism understands all baptized persons to have a call to ministry through their baptism (¶¶127, 310). But a person who recognizes an additional call to leadership in the community of faith must submit that call to be tested and confirmed by the community. The first place in which that testing occurs is the local church. There among people who know the person best, the church begins to determine what the gifts and graces of a called person may be, and whether the person has the integrity, understanding, and discipline to lead the community effectively.

This can be a demanding challenge for a local church; it may mean saying no to a devoted church member. But local churches must exercise their discernment at this initial stage to ensure that the "inward call" to leadership which a person has heard can be matched by an "outward call" of the church that confirms the person's ministry.[6]

Once a person's call has been affirmed by her or his charge conference, the process of preparation, training, testing, placement, and evaluation generally moves into connectional bodies. The local church gives over to the connection further claims of judgment on the readiness of the person for ministry. In a real sense, then, the local church sends the person out in mission where his or her leadership will be guided by the connection.

This sense of being sent in mission is most strongly reinforced through the itineracy—traveling preachers committed to going where they are needed. But a mission orientation is woven as well into the whole fabric of connectional understandings of ministry. The local church, having identified and affirmed the call of one of its members, turns him or her over to the connection for service. This is one of the most significant ways the local church contributes to the mission of the wider church.

Lay Speakers

The first category of persons set apart for leadership is lay speakers. Because these persons are not in any way separated from their local church and therefore have no membership in the annual conference, the legislation governing their practices is at the end of the local church chapter of the *Discipline*. The very title of this category, of course, resonates with early Methodist language of "exhorters" and "local preachers" who conducted worship, preached, led prayer and scripture study, and did pastoral work in local Methodist societies.

Lay speakers complete courses for certification in order "to develop skills in witnessing to the Christian faith through spoken communication, church and community leadership, and caregiving ministries." They are expected to have foundational knowledge of scripture and of United Methodist "doctrine, heritage, organization, and life" (¶266.1).

Districts or annual conferences are authorized to sponsor the courses and grant the certification of lay speakers. Persons may be certified either for their local church only, or—with advanced courses—for service in other local churches as well. District superintendents use lay speakers in a variety of ways, sometimes even to fill a vacant pulpit temporarily. But lay speakers are not in any sense appointed and have no standing beyond their local church membership.

Diaconal Ministers

In 1976, at the same time it was reorganizing the Disciplinary understanding of ministry by inserting Part IV on "The Ministry of All Christians," the General Conference created a new category of specialized ministry with the ungainly (and redundant) title of "diaconal minister." Several dynamics worked together to produce this anomaly in the conference system. First, for years the UMC had been seeking a way to provide permanent status in the church for the many laypersons who were performing essential work on local church and church agency staffs. Some means of regularized certification and recognition of their calling, skills, and professional rights and responsibilities was long overdue.

Second, the UMC was struggling to reconceive the traditional notion of the diaconate in order to locate it in United Methodist ecclesiology. In keeping with its Anglican heritage, the Methodist Episcopal Church simply took over the two orders of deacon and elder and made them correspond with the two categories of annual conference membership—probationary and full. The diaconate was normally a transitional order in Anglicanism, a status of preparation for full priesthood, which fit well with the Methodist idea of a preacher being "on trial" for judgment of his (or now her) gifts before being accepted into "full connection." Partly because of this merely transitional basis of deacon's orders, the EUB tradition never adopted it, but retained a unitary ordination.[7]

In company with widespread ecumenical conversations about the diaconate, the UMC began in the 1960s to debate what place permanent deacons could have in the church. That debate was complex primarily because in United Methodist ecclesiology there was traditionally no place for an order that did not exist to sanction itinerant preaching. The persons serving in a new diaconate would not be preaching—at least not primarily. Nor would they necessarily want to itinerate under the appointment of a bishop—because their placements are directly related to a church or agency's need for their professional skills.

The situation was further complicated by the "office" of deaconess (the feminine form of the word "deacon") traditionally held by women devoted to full-time mission work. With roots in the nineteenth century—at a time when women did not have access to ordained leadership roles and were limited to gender-specific lay leadership roles as well—this office enables women to serve as "itinerant" missionaries amenable to the General Board of Global Ministries (GBGM). That is, deaconesses receive "appointments" approved by the GBGM in consultation with the bishop of the area in which the deaconess will serve. The bishop then "fixes" the appointment and it is listed in the conference journal. Deaconesses are seated in the annual conference with voice but not vote. Yet they are not members of the conference, either lay or clergy, unless they happen to be elected by a charge conference as a lay member from that charge. Deaconesses hold membership in a local church and charge conference within the annual conference of their service (¶1313).

Thus the 1976 General Conference attempted to create a completely new category that would stand outside the itinerant preaching system but still be related to the annual conference. While it would bear some resemblance to the polity of the office of deaconess and be a "representative ministry" held to a great extent by women, it would also stand outside the deaconess tradition. But this attempt was in reality a transitional strategy while the church moved toward a permanent diaconate.

Diaconal ministry attracted a great many able people with a variety of professional skills. While most have been Christian educators, others have served as church business administrators, musicians, ministers of youth or evangelism, or other positions. Over 1,300 diaconal ministers became active in the UMC, with over 80 percent of them in the Southeastern and South Central Jurisdictions. About three-fourths were women, and the vast majority white. Most have served in larger churches since full-time program staff positions are more likely to be available there.[8]

The patchwork character of this category, together with its continuing growth in many conferences and its association with larger local churches, created deep tensions. At first glance, the parallels with procedures for pastoral ministry made diaconal ministry look like a comfortable fit. The candidacy processes for the two categories were parallel at many points; thus the diaconal ministry process required the recommendation of the charge conference of the local church in which the candidate held membership, psychological testing, certain educational standards, and a probationary period of employment. Even the historic questions asked of preachers since Wesley's conferences were revised to suit this form of ministry (1992 *Discipline*, ¶¶303-6). The entire category was under the care and supervision of annual conference Boards of Diaconal Ministry, the tasks of which paralleled the Board of Ordained Ministry (which until diaconal ministry was created was simply called the Board of Ministry).

But there the parallels stopped and the ecclesiological tensions began. The 1992 *Discipline* stated that diaconal ministers "shall be amenable to the Annual Conference in the performance of their duties as diaconal ministers" (¶308). Indeed the annual conference voted on their completion of candidacy, and their consecration took place in the annual conference at the hands of a bishop.

Unlike clergy members of conference, however, diaconal ministers were employed by a local church or agency with whom they had a contract for salary and benefits. They had no guarantee of employment in an annual conference. They did not itinerate, but initiated their own employment. While they held a "service appointment" from the bishop, who had to review and approve it, this was not to be confused with an itinerant—and guaranteed— pastoral appointment by a bishop (1992 *Discipline*, ¶¶310, 315-17).

The chapter on diaconal ministry did not explicitly say so, but the 1992 *Discipline* made clear in legislation regarding the annual conference that diaconal ministers were lay members of the conference (¶702.3). Therefore they did not participate in the clergy session devoted to the "conference relations" of clergy. On the other hand, the "conference relationships" of diaconal ministers were voted on by all conference members—lay and clergy—upon recommendation from the Board of Ordained Ministry.

Moreover, as lay members of conference diaconal ministers served on conference units and were eligible for election as lay delegates to General or Jurisdictional Conference (1992 *Discipline*, ¶309). But as paid program staff of local churches and agencies, they often were not viewed by other laity as being lay in the same sense. They appeared to some laypeople to take the place of laity who do not work for the church and who could serve in conference units and delegations instead. And since many diaconal ministers were employed in larger churches, their occupying lay seats in the annual conference tended to exacerbate tensions between rural and urban, smaller and larger churches.

Deacons

United Methodism's new permanent diaconate marks an effort to raise still higher the standard and status of persons who perform service ministries for the church, while expanding the scope of possible forms of service. The diaconate is increasingly understood as a distinct ministry of bridging between the worship and sacraments of the congregation and its service in the community and world. Deacons "embody, articulate, and lead the whole people of God in its servant ministry" through their leadership in both liturgy and acts of service (¶319). Not to be appointed as pastors in charge, deacons find their place in connecting the gathered worship, education, and care of the congregation with the needs of the world.[9]

Most deacons will continue to be directly related to a local church as their primary appointment. But the *Discipline* anticipates a potential expansion of the ministries of deacons into all varieties of social or community settings, while requiring that they maintain a specific relationship with a local church as a secondary appointment. That local church most likely would not pay a salary to a deacon with ministries beyond the local church, yet the deacon would "take missional responsibility for leading other Christians into ministries of service" through that local church (¶322.4).

Deacons are ordained to a "lifetime ministry of Word and Service" (¶320.1). They are clergy members of annual conference, ordained deacon and admitted to full clergy membership after a rigorous program of preparation, education, and probationary service. They form a distinct order within the annual conference, a "covenant community" of mutual accountability and support (¶¶311, 312). They also share in the conference role of clergy, as full participants in the clergy session voting on the conference relations of clergy, and as electors and candidates for clergy delegates to General and Jurisdictional Conferences (¶320.2).

At the same time, the order of deacon marks a radical departure from historic Methodist practice. Some groundwork for this change was laid by diaconal ministry, of course. Most diaconal ministers have chosen to become ordained as deacons, bringing to nearly 1000 the number of permanent deacons ordained since 1996. Oddly, diaconal ministers who have chosen not to become deacons and to retain their lay status found almost all paragraphs defining their work deleted by the 1996 General Conference. They are left to assume that their status falls under the 1992 *Discipline,* a polity practice unknown to Methodism before the 1996 General Conference.

Like diaconal ministers before them, deacons must be appointed by the bishop presiding over their annual conference, but they do not itinerate. They may initiate their own employment, as may the bishop or a local church or agency; but this employment is not guaranteed (¶322). Thus while they are members of annual conference, they are employed by a local church or agency on a different basis from other clergy.

Several ambiguities arise from this status now that the diaconate is expressed in a permanent order. The *Discipline* requires "an annual meeting of this covenant body, in executive session of clergy members in full connection" to vote on the conference relations of clergy (¶365.5). But deacons are not part of the same covenant as elders; "this" covenant body is actually two bodies. The term "executive" historically meant the core group of annual conference, the itinerating preachers. Now deacons are included as well. Thus nonitinerating clergy will be voting on the conference relations of itinerating clergy—a potentially volatile mix of roles.

Deacon's orders also confound other Disciplinary efforts to generalize about clergy. The "employment status of clergy" is clarified to mean that "clergy appointed to local churches are not employees of the local church"—thus the "historical covenants that bind annual conferences, clergy, and congregations" are still in place (¶141). But deacons would seem, indeed, to be employed by local churches—an entirely different covenant. Thus the amenability of "all clergy" to the annual conference seems quite different between deacons and elders (¶365.1).

The two orders are drawn more closely into parallel in the standards of preparation. Both require education at the master's degree level; both assume the ability to articulate a theology of Christian faith and ministry. Both deacons and elders must serve a probationary period during which they are commissioned to ministry appropriate to their order. After ordination, both must receive at least the minimum level of compensation established for pastors, as well as the right to participate in pensions and benefits for clergy. For deacons this will bring a heightened standard to their ministries and greater recognition and status in the church.

But whether deacons and elders can really be peers in United Methodism remains to be seen. Deacons can initiate their place of employment, work part-time indefinitely, or work for no salary at all. If appointed to a local church, they may serve there without any requirement to move. Meanwhile elders must work full time (with limited exceptions) and are expected to itinerate. How will these two orders work together in a particular local church, given that the elder is appointed as pastor "in charge" (¶330)? This will require a mutual and deepening acceptance of gifts and roles in an ever-changing church.

Local Pastors

United Methodism and its predecessor bodies have depended on local preachers from the beginning.[10] These persons usually were not ordained, but were authorized and assigned by the bishop to preach in a local church (or "society"). Since there have always been far more local churches than ordained clergy, local preachers played a critical role in the vitality of the movement, especially in rural towns and settlements. The average size of United Methodist local churches in the U.S. remains below 250, and a majority have 200 members or less.[11] Many of these smaller churches continue to be served by what are today called "local pastors."

Yet local pastors have always been caught between the cogs of the two frameworks for pastoral ministry in United Methodism. They have generally not been ordained, yet at various periods in recent history they have been authorized to administer the sacraments in the charge to which they are appointed. When the UMC was first created in 1968, this possibility was specifically excluded. The anomalous title "lay pastor" was adopted for this category of ministry, emphasizing the lay order of these persons. They were authorized to perform all the duties of a pastor in a specific charge except the administration of the sacraments of baptism and the Lord's Supper (1968 *Discipline*, ¶¶349-50).

By 1976, however, the General Conference reversed this position and adopted the new title of local pastor. This name emphasized the location and more particularly the conference relation, not the order. Local pastors were authorized to administer the sacraments in the charge to which they were appointed.

As Dennis Campbell pointed out, this arrangement is specifically contrary to the Wesleyan heritage of ordination. That is, Wesley undertook his extraordinary ordinations "precisely to avoid administration without ordination." Preaching without ordination was acceptable for evangelical purposes, in Wesley's view; administration of the sacraments belonged to the presbyterate or priesthood. On the other hand, Wesleyan Methodism's pragmatic approach to ministry is clear here as well.[12] The scattered smaller gatherings of United Methodist people need to receive the sacraments, the practical reasoning goes. Many laity do not make a great distinction anyway between a pastor who is ordained and one who is not, so long as the person has been appointed to their church by the bishop. Therefore, the local pastor must be allowed to administer the sacraments for the sake of the fullness of church in each place.

The relationship of local preachers to the annual conference has been equally ambiguous. Before 1976 all candidacy for the ministry began with "a license to preach." This historic license, originally granted by a quarterly conference, was later issued and renewed annually by a district. It was the initial basis of authority for the ministry of everyone who was proceeding toward a conference relationship, but was particularly the authority for lay pastors (1968 *Discipline*, ¶¶318-21). After 1976, however, the new basis for candidacy for all candidates, including local pastors, was the certification process, which continued to be a district matter (¶¶305-9). The license reverted solely to the local pastor category. Under the 1996 plan, "all persons not ordained as elders"— including probationary members—must have "a license for pastoral ministry" in order to serve as a pastor under appointment (¶¶340-41).

Local pastors are now divided into three categories, all three of which assume completion of candidacy certification and the issuance of a license (¶343). Student local pastors are appointed to a pastoral charge while attending pre-theological or theological degree programs. Their church membership remains in their "home church" or they may transfer it to the church to which they are appointed.

Part-time local pastors are appointed to a charge on a less than full-time basis. That is, they do not devote their whole time to the charge and they are not paid as much as the base salary for full-time local pastors. Full-time local pastors are appointed to a charge on a full-time basis with at least the minimum salary established by the annual conference.

Both full- and part-time local pastors are clergy members of the annual conference, not members of the local church. They have the right to voice and vote and may serve on annual conference units. However, they do not have all the rights of ordained members of conference in full connection. They cannot vote on constitutional amendments, the conference relations of clergy, or delegates to General and Jurisdictional Conferences—nor may they serve as delegates (¶341.6). Thus while they are allowed the rights of the ordained in their own charge, they are not allowed the rights of the ordained in the conference. What United Methodist polity withholds with one hand (no ordination rights and thus no full ticket to participation in conference) it partially gives back with the other (ordination functions in the charge). This double message has been the source of much tension and frustration.

Local pastors are required to complete a five-year course of study, the standard method of preparation for all Methodist preachers before a seminary degree became the norm for ordination. This course, conducted under the auspices of the GBHEM mainly at United Methodist colleges and theological schools, usually lasts one month each summer and encompasses biblical and theological studies, as well as United Methodist doctrine, history, and polity. Historically based on a list of specific books selected and approved by the bishops, the course today follows general guidelines within which teachers have latitude for their own approaches. At the point of completing this course, a local pastor may "remain in a local relationship with the annual conference" indefinitely (¶344.4).

An issue on which the church continues to change its collective mind involves the possibility of local pastors proceeding to elder's orders. Beginning in 1980 the *Discipline* offered the category of associate member of the annual conference. Local pastors who chose this option had to be at least thirty-five years of age and a full-time local pastor for at least four years, as well as meeting other requirements. In so doing they were committing themselves fully to "itinerant ministry" under appointment of the bishop, and they gained "the same security of appointment as probationary members and members in full connection" (1992 *Discipline,* ¶419).

Associate members did not receive any conference voting rights in addition to those of the full-time local pastor. But they did become eligible to be ordained deacon. Oddly enough, they could remain deacons indefinitely—belying the idea that United Methodism had no permanent diaconate. An associate member who had already been ordained deacon could choose, if qualified and elected by the conference, to become a probationary member of the conference. Two additional years of advanced studies, along with other requirements, opened the door to consideration for full conference membership and ordination as elder.

Relatively few local pastors proceeded all the way through these steps, partly because they had to itinerate and partly because their candidacy came under "special conditions" in which they had to show "exceptional" ministry. They had to receive a three-fourths affirmative vote along the way from the Cabinet, the Board of Ordained Ministry, and the clergy session of the annual conference (1992 *Discipline,* ¶¶416.2, 424.3.d). Many annual conferences never considered or approved anyone under these special conditions.

The 1996 plan removes the category of associate member, and simply allows local pastors at least 40 years old who have completed the Course of Study and specified graduate theological education, to apply as probationary members proceeding to elders' orders (¶315.6). The majority will probably remain as local pastors, though. Their service is critical to the pastoral needs of hundreds of smaller congregations. Their role has roots deep in Methodism's origins as an evangelical movement of preachers and disciplined societies. Their status has changed gradually as they have gained the right to be listed as conference members and to vote at least on many issues that affect the charges they serve. But local pastors continue to be outside the bounds of the core clergy membership of annual conferences—elders in full connection.

Traveling Ministers in Full Connection

Methodism began in England and America as a missionary cadre of preachers bound in connection with each other to spread the gospel and scriptural holiness over the lands. From the beginning their evangelical intention was embodied in a covenant to which all preachers subjected themselves. Every preacher would be given a place to preach; every preacher would agree to go where sent.

In America with its far-flung settlements, the system was in perpetual motion. As Francis Asbury and Thomas Coke stated it succinctly in their annotated *Discipline* of 1798, "Every thing is kept moving as far as possible." Preachers traveled around their circuits preaching and overseeing the discipline of their societies. They were also transferred regularly from circuit to circuit within an annual conference. Thus, as Norwood put it,

> the itinerant system went round and round, like a little hoop (the circuit) always turning around on a larger hoop (the annual conference), which itself was always in motion.[13]

Preachers were on constant pilgrimage, charged with "a mission to fulfill."[14] Their discipline was soon adopted by Evangelical and United Brethren groups among German-speaking Americans, the Methodist Episcopal churches that organized among African Americans, and other cultures and ethnic groups as well.

At the core of the preachers' discipline was their covenant commitment to each other—their connection at first with John Wesley and then in America with each other and the bishops who appointed them to their places. They held each other accountable for their conduct and effectiveness in ministry. They set standards for admission to their company and created means of caring for those who became "worn out" from the work.[15]

Within a few years after Methodism organized as an independent church in America, the standard for admission to this covenant connection became ordination. The terminology of "traveling minister" or "traveling preacher" was used interchangeably to indicate that one was part of the itinerant connection under appointment, with the authority to administer the sacraments as an elder. No further or "higher" order exists in United Methodism; bishops remain elders.

210

The elders in full connection—the missionary preaching order—governed the polity of United Methodism's predecessor bodies completely until the 1870s, and it was sixty more years after that before laypersons shared fully in annual conferences. Thus when one hears contemporary complaints that the laity do not have sufficient voice or that clergy dominate church affairs, one is hearing echoes of sentiments endemic to the way Methodism has always been organized.

Differing perspectives on what qualifies a person to be a traveling minister in full connection also run deep through Methodist tradition. The beginning point has always been the "call to preach," an inward call that arises from one's own encounter with the God who called Moses, purified Isaiah, and converted Paul to a new vocation. A conviction flourishing from a spring of companionship with God through Jesus Christ has been considered essential for all candidates for traveling ministry. To this must be added the gifts and graces necessary for effective leadership of the people of God in their disciplined journey of faith.

Wesley's questions posed to prospective workers in the Methodist movement ring as true as ever in this regard:

> Do they know God as a pardoning God? Have they the love of God abiding in them? . . . Have they gifts, as well as evidence of God's grace, for the work? . . . Do they speak justly, readily, clearly? . . . Have they fruit? . . . are believers edified by their preaching?[16]

The current *Discipline* places these questions in the forefront, at the point of candidacy for ordained ministry. Therefore local churches—not just committees of ordained ministers—that recommend a person as a candidate are asked to make these questions the basis of their consideration.

Once a person's call and candidacy has been confirmed initially, she or he begins a lengthy and thorough process of preparation and further testing of call, gifts, and effectiveness. During the course of the twentieth century the standards of preparation have become increasingly rigorous and detailed. Both a bachelor's and a seminary degree have become standard requirements (other than the few people who follow the local pastor track to ordination). A candidate must commit to at least seven years of education beyond a high school diploma, with most people being at least twenty-five years old before commencing a full-time ordained ministry.

Stories of disputes over this rising standard are well known. Was not the most effective preaching that which would convict hearers of their sins and bring them into the presence of a pardoning God? How much education was necessary for people who "have nothing to do but to save souls," in Wesley's words?[17] In a famous passage from his *Autobiography*, Peter Cartwright, one of the exemplary circuit riders of the antebellum age, stated that "preachers trained in schools were as pale as 'lettuce growing under the shade of a peach tree,' and their preaching as awkward as 'a gosling that had got the straddles by wading in the dew.' "[18]

On the other hand, voices increasingly were being raised to recall Wesley's admonition that Methodist preachers should "read the most useful books, and that regularly and constantly."

> Steadily spend all the morning in this employ, or, at least, five hours in four-and-twenty. "But I read only the Bible" . . . This is rank enthusiasm. If you need no book but the Bible, you are got above St. Paul . . . "But I have no taste for reading." Contract a taste for it by use, or return to your trade.[19]

Thus as early as 1834, when Methodism was at the height of its growth across an expanding frontier, John P. Durbin published an article calling for "An Educated Ministry Among Us" so that the call to preach could be made more effective.[20]

The vast majority of nineteenth-century preachers qualified for ordination and traveling connection through a course of study approved by the bishops. Higher education was considered both too costly and too time-consuming; preachers were needed in the field. This basic sentiment persisted well into the twentieth century as the debate over standards continued. Bishop Roy Short remembered that in a Methodist Episcopal Church South General Conference early in the twentieth century, a delegate rose to protest rising standards, saying,

> "If you pass this proposed legislation, you will make the requirements so high that Abraham Lincoln couldn't be admitted into the Methodist ministry." Bishop Purcell immediately got the floor and captured the conference as he said quietly, "Yes, but Robert E. Lee could."[21]

Gradually a bachelor of arts degree and completion of the course of study became normative for traveling preachers. But only in 1956 did the General Conference make a seminary degree (then called a bachelor of divinity, though it assumed also a completed bachelor of arts degree) the standard for admission to full connection in an annual conference.

The trend toward higher educational standards mirrored developments in the wider culture. A bachelor's degree became normative for any kind of professional work in America after 1950. United Methodism already supported a number of liberal arts colleges. They now became even more strongly the "feeder" schools for seminaries, creating a linkage of educational requirements comparable to medicine and law.

As theological education came to be located within institutions founded for that purpose, tensions between conferences and seminaries inevitably increased. Until 1916 the MEC bishops had to approve both professors and curriculum, and the seminaries were owned and governed by the General Conference. Succeeding generations loosened those ties of governance as teaching fields became more and more specialized. General Conference assumed a role of authorization and support; the founding of two new seminaries was approved in 1956, and in 1968 the Ministerial Education Fund was created to direct continuing financial support from the churches to the seminaries.

Thoroughly grounded in Wesley's "catholic spirit" and Methodism's character as *ecclesiola in ecclesia*, the seminaries have welcomed faculty and students of other denominations. Today's student bodies and faculties are quite diverse. Moreover, many candidates for United Methodist ordained ministry attend seminaries not affiliated with United Methodism, usually seeking the school closest to home or least expensive. All such schools have to be approved by the United Methodist University Senate, but may be of many different traditions (¶¶315, 326).

Little wonder, then, that theological education has become a major focal point for debate over perennial issues in United Methodist theology and polity. What should candidates learn that will particularly equip them for United Methodist ministry? Is there a United Methodist way of approaching theological questions? The current resolution of these questions comes down most simply to the academic requirement of study in each of the fields of United Methodist history, doctrine, and polity. This requirement is expected of all candidates for any form of set apart ministry (¶315).

One could certainly ask, though, whether this is sufficient to give a candidate more than a taste of United Methodism. The *Discipline* says nothing about the broader biblical and theological methods of study and reflection that may be most appropriate for United Methodist students to learn. Nothing is said about preaching and worship, or ways of thinking about ethics. The University Senate applies only the most general criteria in judging schools, and then mainly regarding their institutional integrity.

As a result, candidates enter the ordained ministry from a wide variety of theological perspectives and practical experiences. The Boards of Ordained Ministry carry the major burden of examination, with the *Discipline* specifying questions—but not answers—that cover many critical elements of theology and ministry (¶326). Boards have also been affirmed by the Judicial Council in their right to add expectations to the Disciplinary lists, such as to require a course in preaching. But since members of the Boards are themselves graduates of many different schools of various traditions, expectations may also vary widely within the Boards themselves.

Ordained ministers in United Methodism tend to learn United Methodist traditions and practices more from living and working in an annual conference, then, than they do from formal education. They are introduced to the "culture" of United Methodism by meeting with Boards and Cabinets, moving through steps toward ordination, and working under the guidance of a mentor assigned by the Board (¶347). This is another way in which the characteristic United Methodist focus on practices of ministry and mission is most apparent.

When a candidate has completed educational and other requirements, he or she may apply for probationary membership in an annual conference. Here the old language of admission "on trial" reflects the sense that probationers are "on probation as to character, servant leadership, and effectiveness in ministry." Probationary members have approximately the same conference standing as local pastors, being excluded from voting on constitutional amendments, delegates, or conference relations of clergy (¶318.2). If they serve as pastors they must have a license for pastoral ministry. They may not administer the Lord's Supper without the presence of an elder unless, like local pastors, they are appointed to serve a charge—and then they may administer only within that charge.

Probationary members are "commissioned" for their ministry. As of 1996 they are no longer ordained deacons as a transitional order to elder. Both prospective (permanent) deacons and elders must serve as probationary members, so each is commissioned to the appropriate form of ministry. Those intending to be elders have no ordained status prior to elders' orders, even if they serve as pastors.

A probationary member must serve for three years under full-time appointment, in relationship with a covenant group of peers. Then the Board conducts a new examination of the probationer, again based on Disciplinary questions and other criteria. The Board submits the names of approved persons to the annual conference clergy session for election to full membership.

The *Discipline's* wording about elders in full connection resonates with generations of clergy relationships in the annual conferences of United Methodism.

> Elders in full connection with an annual conference by virtue of their election and ordination are bound in special covenant with all the ordained elders of the annual conference. In the keeping of this covenant they perform the ministerial duties and maintain the ministerial standards established by those in the covenant. They offer themselves without reserve to be appointed and to serve, after consultation, as the appointive authority may determine. They live with all other ordained ministers in mutual trust and concern and seek with them the sanctification of the fellowship [¶324].

Participation in a covenant community entails mutual accountability. Elders are responsible to each other for adhering to standards of conduct and for supporting each other in their ministries. Covenant accountability begins at the moment one is elected into the fellowship and continues until one withdraws from the traveling connection or dies.

Admission into the covenant of traveling ministers is not to be taken lightly. As the *Discipline* makes clear, the requirements [for ministerial qualifications] set forth herein are minimum requirements only. Each person voting is expected to vote prayerfully based on his/her personal judgment of the applicant's gifts, evidence of God's grace, and promise of future usefulness for the mission of the Church [¶304.5].

While a Board of Ordained Ministry bears major responsibility for examining candidates, the whole body of clergy participates in the decision. Debating the merits of a candidate may be awkward for many people, but if they have questions or misgivings the *Discipline* implicitly urges them to speak their piece.

Once elected, full members are responsible to the covenant community of clergy at every point thereafter. The *Discipline* mandates an "executive session" of the covenant body at each annual conference. This wording perpetuates the sense that the clergy comprise the primary or core function of annual conference. Conferences hold this meeting—otherwise called a "clergy session"—for the purpose of passing on the character of each member as well as considering the conference relations of anyone requesting a change of status. Admission to the conference, sabbatical leaves, leaves of absence, family leaves, maternity/paternity leaves, disability leaves, and retirement all must be reviewed and recommended by the BOM and voted by the clergy session. A decision to locate or discontinue service in the itinerant ministry must also be voted by conference, as must withdrawal from conference with surrender of ordination credentials (¶365.5).

Clergy are responsible to each other for their conduct. "Ordination and membership in an annual conference in The United Methodist Church is a sacred trust," the *Discipline* declares (¶359). This trust has three covenant dimensions. By calling and ordination, the trust is a covenant between God and the ordained minister. By election into the conference connection of clergy, the trust is a covenant among itinerant ministers or deacons. By appointment to a local church or charge (or other assignment), the trust is a covenant between minister and people.

While the discipline of "ministerial duties" and standards is under the stewardship of the annual conference clergy as a whole, a pastor of a charge in fact has great latitude in the style and manner of carrying out pastoral responsibilities. One of the *Discipline's* most audacious paragraphs attempts to outline what the church

216

expects of a pastor (¶331). It names traditional duties of preaching, conducting worship, teaching, preparing new persons for membership, performing marriages and conducting funerals, that one would expect of any pastor of any denomination.

The paragraph goes on, though, with distinctively connectional responsibilities. That is, the United Methodist pastor is clearly a missionary assigned to a local church or charge on behalf of a wider connectional church. Thus the pastor is charged with "evangelistic outreach" as well as leading a congregation in planning and goal-setting for mission. The pastor takes initiative in "the selection, training, and deployment of lay leadership" utilizing "denominational and conference programs and training opportunities." The pastor is "to administer the provisions of the *Discipline*," fill out appropriate reporting forms, and lead the congregation in "full and faithful payment of all apportioned . . . funds." A United Methodist pastor is, in short, an officer of the connection.

Tensions in the Itineracy

Throughout its history the covenant community of "traveling ministers in full connection"—the missionary order of preachers—has been subject to two major kinds of tensions. While the tensions have sometimes produced creative change, on occasion they have provoked painful and lasting schisms.

Tensions Between Laity and Clergy

One major source of enduring tension is the relationship between the itinerant clergy covenant and the laity. Many laypersons experience this tension primarily within their own local church at the point of receiving the pastor appointed to them by the bishop from among the ranks of the conference. The *Discipline* mandates that "the unique needs of a charge, the community context, and also the gifts and evidence of God's grace of a particular pastor" be taken into account in making appointments (¶432). At the same time, the *Discipline* mandates that "all elders in full connection who are in good standing in an annual conference shall be continued under appointment by the bishop" (¶328.1). Putting these two demands together among the particular charges and clergy available is, to say the least, a challenge.

Laity have a voice in appointments and in evaluation of their pastor through their pastor-parish relations committees (PPRC), and can, of course, approach the district superintendent or bishop at any time to express their desires. But the committee's role is "advisory" only (¶431). Since 1976 the *Discipline* has made room for greater participation of both laity and clergy in the appointment process. It requires "consultation" between the bishop and/or district superintendent, the pastor, and the congregation regarding every local church appointment. The DS in particular is to "confer" with the pastor to propose a change of appointment. The *Discipline* appears to mandate that the DS "confer" with the PPRC at least twice—once to indicate that a change is forthcoming and to hear the congregation's needs and desires, and again to present the name of the new pastor (¶433).

However, consultation processes vary widely among annual conferences and bishops, so much so that "the Council of Bishops shall inquire annually of their colleagues about the implementation of the process of consultation in appointment-making in their respective areas" (¶431.2). Ultimately, in her or his own way of approaching these matters, the bishop—an elder among elders—holds sole responsibility "to make and fix the appointments" (¶416.1). A local church in no sense calls its own pastor, nor does the *Discipline* provide for even so much as a discussion of the pastoral appointment in a charge conference or any other church meeting aside from the PPRC.

At periods in Methodist history the laity have managed to assert more control over this process. From at least the 1920s until the 1970s, many larger local churches virtually called their pastors by sending out "pulpit committees" to hear candidates from anywhere in the country and then telling the bishop whom they would accept for their pastorates. The 1950s generation of clergy viewed this practice as unfair, and the bishops elected from among them would not cater to large church autonomy in this way. As a result few local churches have "special privileges" any more, and few clergy change annual conferences as senior pastors except through a rare transfer initiated and arranged by the respective bishops.

The appointment-making process is also for many laity a window into the covenant community of clergy that constitutes the annual conference. The annual conference is "the basic body in the church" not as a covenant body of congregations, but as an order of preachers accountable to each other for their conduct and effectiveness. Laypersons have been full participants in conference only since the 1930s, and the Constitution first required equal numbers of lay and clergy members in annual conference only in 1976 (¶¶30, 31).

How do I feel about this?

While efforts to include laity in decisions have increased in recent years, the conference relations of clergy remain a matter for clergy only. That the clergy covenant is the raison d'être of annual conference is evident in many *Discipline* wordings. "The annual conference may admit into clergy membership only those who have met all the Disciplinary requirements..." here does not really mean the whole conference, but only the clergy (¶604.3). Likewise, the "annual conference" that makes "inquiry into the moral and official conduct of its ordained ministers" is not actually the conference as it exists today with lay and clergy members, but only its "clergy session" (¶605.6).

As stated above, the *Discipline* also refers to this as an "executive session," implying that the clergy hold "executive" power in conference decisions. Lay membership on the BOM is one effort to redress this exclusion of laity from the constitutive process of annual conference. These lay members of the BOM are now constitutionally eligible to vote in the clergy session (¶31). But clergy remain largely unwilling to allow themselves to be judged by persons outside the covenant connection.

Tensions Within the Clergy Covenant

The second range of tensions are those that arise from within this covenant body of traveling ministers. Persons elected to full membership travel through the years together, supporting each other especially in times of personal crisis or grief, and becoming friends and colleagues. At the same time the inevitable jealousies, hurts, and competitions arise as well. While there is a steady stream of new members coming in to replace retiring or withdrawing members, conferences tend to have relatively closed boundaries.

A number of conferences have merged in recent years, in part to expand their territory and increase the range both of pastors and of possible appointments a bishop can make. But despite their missionary intention, conferences retain many attributes of a closed union shop. Once an elder is in the fold, she or he naturally expects to move up gradually through the system from smaller to larger churches, from lesser to greater salaries.

With the advent of computers, the salary scale of an annual conference can be even more readily available to bishops, district superintendents, and pastors alike. Charges usually are arranged on a master list by salary, and the effect of each appointment on the salary scale is certainly one major factor in appointment-making. Clergy can find the limits imposed by salary on their steps from church to church extremely frustrating. The gap between the lowest and highest salaries continues to grow, even as the largest single cluster of salaries hovers within a range of perhaps $5,000 per year. At the same time the guarantee of appointment can too easily become an assurance of security based on minimum performance, especially as pension and insurance plans have been further elaborated in recent years.

Thus a professional contract runs in and through the vocational covenant of the clergy. The contract reflects and reinforces changing definitions of professional work in American society. It includes extensive benefits packages of health, disability, and life insurance, provisions for maternity or paternity leave, various kinds of sabbaticals or study leaves, and a pension plan. Mandatory retirement rules parallel similar patterns and expectations in the wider workforce.

One of the fine moments at annual conference is the retirement ceremony when retiring clergy have a last chance to speak to the whole conference. Many will build their remarks around the thought that ministry is a calling, not a career. They admonish their younger colleagues not to let the work become just a tenured, professional job with expected perquisites. But of course, those retiring are precisely the ones who now get the benefits promised by the system in exchange for their years of service. They are living reminders of the professional contract contained within the clergy covenant.

Many people talk of standardizing salaries to alleviate competition, remove the salary scale as a factor in appointments, and open the way to a rebirth of missionary spirit. But this would be immensely complex for the same reason that itineracy itself has become increasingly complex. Itineracy was originally designed for an order of preachers. From Francis Asbury to the present, it has been evident that the system works best with single pastors who are willing to "travel light" (as does, for example, Roman Catholic priesthood).

Later, of course, the ethos of the system did a complete turn-about. Marriage became so much the standard practice in Victorian America that the single preacher became suspect. Itineracy now was asking not only the preacher, but his (almost always his) wife and children—and perhaps other relatives—to join the itinerant life as well. Annual conferences expected local churches to provide a house adequate for an entire family. In northern regions parsonages were only partially furnished and the family moved with its own possessions, but in southern areas they were more completely furnished in order to facilitate mobility. The middle class family ideal called for the woman to serve as homemaker and mother. Many churches assumed that wives would share in their husband's vocation and be an active church volunteer. Thus was developed a rich history of often invisible and underappreciated contributions that wives made to the ministry.

As more and more clergy spouses—women or men—have working careers of their own, the missionary mode of itineracy has been strained almost to the breaking point. The making of appointments has become immensely complicated by the vocations and educational needs of spouses and children, or of clergy couples. Local church expectations of receiving a male pastor with willing wife and helpmeet have run headlong into new social assumptions about women's employment outside the home.

One result of the changes in personal and family circumstances of clergy has been the gradual lengthening of tenure in appointments. Through much of the nineteenth century, Methodist preachers were to stay in one appointment no more than two years. The MEC eventually expanded this limit to three and then to five years, and then did away with it altogether. The MECS moved to a four-year rule after the Civil War and retained it either formally or informally well into the twentieth century.[22]

● Today's *Discipline* contains no limit on pastoral tenure. Many church consultants, clergy and laity, have come to believe that local churches are better served by longer pastorates, especially in situations of rapid transition in the community. Yet appointments continuous for ten years or more do begin to give the appearance of exempting those particular clergy from itinerating. There have always been a few clergy in every annual conference who have managed to stay in one local church for twenty or more years, which is more typical of Presbyterian churches, for example. Other clergy generally write this off to the personality of the preacher or to the luck of the draw. But such a tenure can be extremely difficult to follow.

Appointments to extension ministries beyond the local church further muddy both salary and tenure issues. Some such appointments are closely tied to the annual conference, such as district superintendency and campus ministry. Others such as chaplaincies or professorships create a kind of double amenability, as the clergyperson becomes an employee of an institution independent of (though usually related to) the church.

Bishops, Cabinets, and Boards of Ordained Ministry have worked to tighten the accountability of extension ministries to annual conference, and the *Discipline* reflects this in a detailed paragraph added in 1976 (¶335). Clergy in extension ministries must report their salary for printing in the conference journal. They must relate to a charge conference where they live and work. They are expected to attend annual conference. They are available annually for appointment by the bishop just like any other clergy. But in reality, those not closely related to annual conference administration and ministry generally do not itinerate on the same basis. Other clergy members often do not regard their work as a true extension of the mission of the annual conference, at least not in the same sense as pastors of local churches extend it.

With all the stresses created by the complexity of ministry in changing social contexts, the deep questioning of itineracy across the church is hardly surprising. Some observers have noted "the erosion of a strong theological base (the covenant) and the absence of a missional outlook to direct it (connectionalism)."[23] Others have questioned who is being best served by the system with its tenure and seniority for clergy—the clergy themselves, or the churches that need effective leadership well matched to their circumstances?

Itineracy is best suited to making sure that clergy leadership is available to as many local churches as possible. So committed is the system to this broad coverage that a plan of subsidies is necessary in every annual conference. Smaller churches can obtain funds from the conference in order to bring their salary and benefits package up to the level of a full-time ordained pastor.

But as a result the system puts disproportionate energy and money into providing clergy for what is actually a definite minority of church members. Larger churches collectively comprise the largest percentage of United Methodist members. They pressure the itineracy to put more resources into making sure that they are well served—for example, by providing additional pastors for growing local churches.[24] As retirements of the '50s clergy generation increase and the total number of clergy continues to fall, the question will become sharper: how should United Methodism honor and support the ministries of smaller churches that in many ways are most loyal to the connectional traditions at the heart of the United Methodist way of being church?

Itineracy also was best suited to a uniform culture. Itinerant pastors needed to be able to assume that the people they were going to meet in a new charge would be much like the people of the old one. They had a lot invested in believing that all United Methodist congregations are basically alike. As Willimon and Wilson put it,

> The clergy have a stake in generalizing their congregations, in making every United Methodist congregation look much like every other, in suppressing differences and distinctive characteristics, in ousting maverick members, and in fostering as much uniformity as possible. Clergy do this because it is easier for our clergy to serve such congregations. Uniformity among congregations requires less adaptation among the clergy who serve them. Uniformity also requires less creativity among the clergy who appoint other clergy. It is easier for bishops and district superintendents to move clergy around among such churches.[25]

This mentality ignores the fact that every congregation is a unique culture in itself. A pastor must learn and appreciate that culture in order to be an effective leader within it. An itineracy that is too quick to move pastors does not reward their acquiring this deep knowledge of the people under their care.

But itineracy calls for traveling clergy to adapt to the diversity of racial and ethnic cultures as well. With the full union of African Americans from the MC, EUBs of German heritage, and predominantly white (northern European) Methodists in one United Methodist Church in 1968, and with the increasing ethnic diversity of local churches, itineracy faces even stronger challenges of diversity and inclusiveness.

In 1964 the MC General Conference first declared that appointments should be made "without regard to race or color" (1964 *Discipline*, ¶432.1). By 1980 the *Discipline* had become even more explicit about "open itineracy" (1980 *Discipline*, ¶527.1). According to the 2000 *Discipline* this "means appointments are made without regard to race, ethnic origin, gender, color, disability, marital status, or age . . . through appointment-making, the connectional nature of the United Methodist system is made visible" (¶430.1). Clergy must be willing to go where sent, and superintendents must be willing to send them where their gifts best match a congregation's needs. At the same time, responsibility for "open itineracy" falls not only on the clergy but the congregation as well. In the local church the PPRC is required "to communicate and interpret to the congregation the nature and function of ministry . . . regarding open itineracy" (¶258.2.f(4)).

The church is still finding its way into these declarations. Relatively few cross-racial appointments have been made, but in some cases they have marked significant breakthroughs into new understanding for the local church, the pastor, and the whole conference. Women now comprise about sixteen percent of the active United Methodist clergy, though unevenly distributed among conferences. Over 100 have been appointed as district superintendents, about a dozen serve as annual conference council directors at any given time, and fourteen have been elected bishops. But few have served as yet as senior pastors of larger, multiple-staff churches. Some raise the question of whether an unspoken "glass ceiling" exists in the local church as it does in many parts of the business and professional world.

The UMC is wrestling today with how to view all these tensions in the itineracy. While the elements of mission covenant remain, many people take the tensions to mean that the church must move toward some kind of modified call system. Others argue that times like these offer precisely the challenges that the itineracy was called into being to meet. If United Methodism really is a missionary order of spiritual discipline and renewal, then surely it must not turn away from the risk of becoming an ever more diverse connection drawing into its covenant people of both genders and many ethnicities. And some would argue that United Methodism with its connectional ministry has a better chance than many churches—and even a particular calling—to model an inclusive church for a society and world of many cultures.

Finally, tensions in the clergy covenant over issues of sexuality and personal conduct have become increasingly prominent over the last twenty years. One cannot help noticing that the footnote elaborating this matter has grown to occupy the better part of two pages in the *Discipline* (¶306, n.2). The footnote originated in 1968 as an effort to reassure United Methodist people that although clergy no longer had to pledge specifically not to drink alcoholic beverages or smoke tobacco, they were actually being held to a higher standard of "thoroughgoing moral commitment . . . [to the] highest ideals of the Christian life" (p. 188). This assurance glossed over the reality that many clergy and laity no longer interpreted "temperance"—with which Methodism was so strongly associated—to mean total abstinence from alcoholic drinks, but rather, responsible, temperate consumption. Many no longer viewed moderate drinking as inconsistent with "responsible self-control by personal habits conducive to bodily health, mental and emotional maturity" (¶306.4.f).

The defensive tone of this footnote, as if to shore up a shifting reality, only increased as more paragraphs were added to it in 1980 and 1984. Doing little more than repeating what was already in the *Discipline*, the footnote puts an exclamation point now not only on the alcohol and tobacco issue, but more on sexuality as well. It draws together all the paragraphs marking the examination of candidates for ministry, as if to point to all the gates through which one must pass to be admitted. It stresses the exclusionary aspect of the process, as if to assure members (or someone) that inappropriate persons will not be able to get into the fold.

The 1984 General Conference added to ministry qualifications a phrase of seven words that appears no less than six times in the *Discipline*. Candidates for all forms of set apart ministry in United

Methodism are to practice "fidelity in marriage and celibacy in singleness." This phrase appeared to be directed at three groups within the clergy covenant (or candidates for it). First, the standard was a response to the rising level of divorces and cases of adultery among married clergy. Some United Methodists apparently thought the situation so critical that a kind of restatement of the marriage vows needed to be printed as a regulation.

Second, the standard was directed toward single heterosexual clergy who, not being under the guidance of a marriage vow, now were implicitly and informally being asked to vow their celibacy outside of marriage (a striking recollection of the single clergy of early Methodism). This also applied to the increasing numbers of clergy now single following a divorce.

Third, the standard served to reinforce a rule also placed in the *Discipline* in 1984 that:

> Since the practice of homosexuality is incompatible with Christian teaching, self-avowed practicing homosexuals are not to be accepted as candidates, ordained as ministers, or appointed to serve in The United Methodist Church [¶304.3].

The exact impact of this statement is still subject to varying interpretations. The first phrase mirrors the Social Principles statement that homosexuality is "incompatible with Christian teaching" but does not address the Social Principles' further declaration that homosexuals are under "the ministry and guidance of the Church" (¶161.G)—presumably as members of local churches. The wording leaves unclear why a self-avowed practicing homosexual could serve, for example, as a lay leader of a local church, but not as its pastor.

The second phrase, lacking a comma, evidently means that a homosexual must be both self-avowed and practicing before he or she can be denied candidacy, admission, or appointment. In relation to the standard of "celibacy in singleness" the crucial factor here appears to be the "practice" of homosexuality. A celibate but self-avowed homosexual would seem to meet existing standards. A homosexual who is not "self-avowed" (and most are not in American culture) but who practices homosexuality (and the church has not defined what such "practice" means) would violate the "celibacy in singleness" standard.[26]

One could certainly question at this point whether the exclusionary strategy has proved to be the most helpful way to strengthen the clergy covenant. As instances of sexual misconduct among married male clergy proliferate across the church—greatly outnumbering instances of practicing homosexuals avowing their homosexuality—one might ask whether the need here is not far more pastoral and communal than legal.

The bonds of fellowship among the clergy apparently in many cases do not create friendships and mutual support through which clergy can care for their personal needs. No work can be lonelier than the pastorate. In an atmosphere of competition and defensiveness, clergy have not been adequately bonded together in shared ministry and care for each other. They often tend to see themselves less in a covenant to which they are accountable—and to which they hold other clergy accountable—and more as individual professionals in a culture of personal privacy. In this sense, the itinerant connection suffers from the same individualism, isolation, and anomie as much of the rest of Western culture.

Perhaps United Methodism could ask if there are not ways to support disciplined clergy conduct more rooted in Wesleyan tradition and more in the evangelical spirit than trying to erect new legal barriers to protect an already troubled covenant community. It is disheartening, to say the least, to begin a chapter on ordained ministry by reading of the profound blessings of the ministry of all Christians and the specialized ministry of those called of God and set apart by the church, only to follow with sentences excluding one ill-defined class of persons from consideration.

The footnote itself declares that the UMC "has moved away from prohibitions of specific acts, for such prohibitions can be endless" (p. 190). There is great wisdom in the church focusing its zeal rather on its understanding of ministry in fulfillment of its mission—a focus which the 1996 plan for ministerial orders demands if the church is to live its way into a new discipline.

CHAPTER 8

Superintendency in United Methodism

The superintendency as expressed through the bishops and district superintendents of the church is United Methodism's unique office. Other church traditions have bishops, to be sure, and most have "middle judicatory" officials to administer church discipline and program in geographic regions. But none combine the ecclesiologies of churchly episcopacy and mission administration in quite the way United Methodism does.

As the discussion of the Constitution indicated (chapter 3), United Methodist episcopacy is not monarchical in nature, with the bishop ordained to a distinct order through which the apostolic succession of ministries is sustained. The bishop is not understood to preside over a diocese, the parishes of which are extensions of the bishop's ministry. Nor does a bishop transmit sacramental authority through the ordination of priests (elders), again as an extension of the bishop's authority.

At the same time, United Methodist episcopacy is not simply an administrative office, either. Bishops are not executive officers of any church body. They do not direct any programs. They serve on the boards of many church agencies and institutions, and by tradition often preside over those bodies. But they are in no sense the "chair of the board" as that term is commonly used in business corporations.

United Methodist episcopacy uniquely combines elements of both a monarchical and an administrative ecclesiology. From the monarchical side, while the office of bishop remains in the same order with the other elders, the bishop is set apart for life and remains "a bishop of the Church in every respect" even in retirement (¶410). The *Discipline* assigns to bishops alone the

229

"presidential duty" of ordaining, consecrating, and commissioning others to their offices (¶415.6). Bishops hold constitutional responsibility for appointing clergy to their charges (or other assignments) (¶¶52, 416.1).

From the administrative side, bishops are charged with "general oversight and promotion of the temporal and spiritual interests of the entire Church" (¶45). They are asked "to provide general oversight for the fiscal and program operations of the annual conference(s)" (¶415.2). They are expected to organize missions (¶414.7), rearrange "circuit(s), station(s), or mission(s) as judged necessary for missional strategy" (¶416.2), and "ensure fair process for clergy and laity" by monitoring the bodies which conduct administrative and judicial proceedings (¶415.3).

If this "job description" is beginning to look exceedingly complex and demanding, so much the more remarkable is the brevity of description of superintendency in the *Discipline*. The entire chapter three requires only twenty-seven pages, expanding on the ten brief articles of Division Three of the Constitution. The 400-numbered paragraphs did not even constitute a separate section until 1976. Material on the superintendency was simply an extension of the chapter on ordained ministry.

One would think that such a multifaceted office would require more explanation. Particularly given the unique mix of ecclesiological elements, one might anticipate some degree of theological justification for the superintendency. But this, too, is practically nil, consisting of a single paragraph (¶403). Here the *Discipline* makes reference to "sharing a royal priesthood that has apostolic roots" and cites five biblical passages. Yet none of the passages offer a specific argument for either episcopacy or ordination as the church has practiced them. As J. Robert Nelson noted,

> The member of another episcopal-type church who reads the *Discipline* is no doubt disappointed in the total lack of any theological or historical warrant for episcopacy. . . . Nothing is said about the bishop's ministry as made familiar in recent ecumenical discussions of the office. Is the bishop *pastor pastorum* [pastor of the pastors]? Is the bishop guardian of the faith "once delivered to the saints" and henceforth a teacher? Is the bishop a sacramental figure, a eucharistic leader? Does the bishop symbolize the unity of the whole church on earth?[1]

The answer to these questions is by and large "yes"—but in a uniquely United Methodist way.

Rather than specify episcopal responsibilities in each dimension of the office, the church has chosen the opposite course. The *Discipline* grants the bishops enormous latitude in interpreting the office for their own times and circumstances. By the same token, the church has latitude in sharing the responsibilities of the episcopal office.

Thus the bishops are indeed charged with a teaching office—"to guard, transmit, teach, and proclaim, corporately and individually, the apostolic faith" (¶414.3). But no one understands this domain to be the bishops' exclusive right. Only the General Conference can effect any official change in church doctrine or teaching. Likewise, bishops ordain, but in company with other clergy; and they ordain only those candidates whom the whole body of clergy in an annual conference concurs are ready to be ordained.[2]

Bishops do symbolize the unity of the connection, and their presence—or that of the district superintendents as extensions of their office—legitimizes the formation of new congregations, dedication of facilities, and many other church actions. But the unity they represent is not embodied in their office so much as in the whole connection of conferences and local churches—the collective body of people called United Methodist.

General Superintendency

Three words are key to understanding the authority of the episcopal office. "Superintendency" is a term that Wesley created as a translation of the biblical *episkopos*—the office of oversight of the church. He appointed Francis Asbury and Thomas Coke as superintendents of the Methodist work in America. They then took the simpler term bishop for their office.

United Methodism has wavered back and forth about this terminology ever since. The *Discipline* refers to the whole function as superintendency, but clearly names the discrete offices within it as "bishop" and "district superintendent" (the latter an extension of the former). The older language of "general superintendency" to describe the episcopate has fallen into disuse, even though the

Discipline describes bishops as "general superintendents of the whole Church" (¶427.1) and they are understood to have oversight of the general church, i.e., the whole connection.[3] Meanwhile, in common parlance "the superintendency" has come to refer to the district superintendent, and many people do not grasp how the DS shares a larger superintendency with the bishop or "general" superintendent.

In any case, the term "superintendency" indicates the oversight of the connection. This is expressed through two offices and two collegial bodies comprised of those officers—bishops serving in a Council of Bishops, and district superintendents serving in a Cabinet.

Upon their election, bishops are consecrated, not ordained, to their office (¶44). They become members of the Council of Bishops first "before they are subsequently assigned to areas of service" (¶427.1). While this may be a legal fiction in the sense that assignments are made in the Jurisdictions or Central Conferences immediately upon completion of elections, it is true that upon election and consecration a bishop's sole membership in the church moves from the annual conference to the Council of Bishops.

Through much of Christian history the episcopacy has taken a conciliar form. As Bishop James Mathews (elected 1960) argued, "bishops acting in concert antedates all other agencies of the church." In United Methodism the effect is that the bishops in council comprise the "chief executive arm to carry out the mandates of the General Conference."[4]

> *Bishops*, not *a* bishop, are administrative and executive heads of the church . . . one office of general oversight is shared by a number of persons; collectively they are charged with the temporal and spiritual interests of the whole church; each and all of them are bishops of the entire church and pastors of all the parts; wherever one bishop is, the whole of episcopacy is there in his or her person.[5]

Meeting in Council twice a year by current custom—the Constitution mandates at least an annual meeting (¶45)—the bishops consider a range of issues encompassing the whole life of the church. At one six-day meeting, for example, among the items the Council discussed were:

- the Ministry Study which the 1992 General Conference asked the bishops to undertake;

- the role of deaconesses in an annual conference;

- the work of the Council task force on Ministry with the Poor;

- United Methodist work in Russia;

- a Council study of the Global Nature of the Church (contemplating the restructuring of United Methodism into a global body);

- world crises: the former Yugoslavia, Bulgaria, Sierra Leone, Cuba;

- an episcopal statement on "wisdom" in Christian theology;

- reports from committees on various aspects of the Council's internal work; and

- an impending visit of the active bishops to the Korean Methodist Church.

Suffice it to say that no one knows the entire connection in all its activities, celebrations, and agonies in quite the way bishops do. From that standpoint as a Council they address the church on major issues at General Conference and other occasions, and make statements to the world about current events. They also act corporately as United Methodism's ecumenical officer in relations with other communions and faiths; bishops have been key figures in bringing about the various unions in this century.

While all bishops share in the discussions and actions of the Council, no legislation states that they are individually amenable even to their own Council. As Bishop Short put it (somewhat in contradiction to Bishop Mathew's generalization quoted above), "no Methodist bishop is bound even by any action of the bishops meeting in council, except as he chooses so to be."[6] Bishops generally understand themselves to be set apart for an office that relies on their independence of thought and action. On occasion a few bishops have refused even to sign their name to the episcopal address to General Conference; and in the administration of their areas they must, of course, exercise their own conscience and judgment.

The Council has expanded greatly in recent years through the 1968 union, the addition of bishops within jurisdictions, the continued participation of retired bishops, and the full membership of Central Conference bishops. Retired bishops attend Council meetings with expenses paid and voice but not vote. Some proposals have suggested that retired bishops come at their own expense, or only once a year or less. But it remains true that the Council is the only locus of church membership for bishops—retired or not—and their only peer group in the church.

Central Conference bishops have attended in increasing numbers as the churches in their regions continue to grow. Only in 1960 were all Central Conference bishops considered fully part of the general superintendency and thus full participants in the Council. Only in 1970 were retired bishops from Central Conferences permitted to attend Council meetings.[7] The earlier restrictions hinged on two factors. Central Conference bishops generally were elected to four-year terms, not to life tenure. Moreover, historically their superintendency had been limited to the conferences over which they presided, and they were known as "missionary bishops." Only in 1939 did the MC Judicial Council rule such a limited "general superintendency" unconstitutional in light of the Third Restrictive Rule.[8]

Today Central Conference bishops are full members with vote, and retired Central Conference bishops are eligible to attend Council meetings and General Conference with expenses paid. A non-U.S. bishop recently served as President of the Council for a year, and several have presided in General Conference. In these small steps, United Methodism moves toward becoming a global church.

Episcopal superintendency is also expressed through Colleges of Bishops in each Jurisdiction or Central Conference. This term originated in the MECS, in which all the bishops together constituted the College of Bishops. (The MEC and EUBC both called the whole body of bishops the Board of Bishops.) The term evokes the collegial relationships through which bishops confer about their own work and the work of the church in their region.

Colleges of Bishops are constitutionally responsible for arranging "the plan of episcopal supervision of the annual conferences, missionary conferences, and missions within their respective territories" (¶46). In case of a vacancy in the office of bishop occurring other than in the regular course of retirements, the College nominates to the Council a bishop to fill the vacancy until a new bishop can be elected (¶408). In the case of a temporary vacancy due to illness, for example, the College assigns a bishop to preside over a Conference. A temporary assignment does not, however, include the right to make clergy appointments, tempting as this might be in some cases (¶410.1). The College can also call a special session of a Jurisdictional Conference for the purpose of electing a bishop to fill a vacancy, but given the expense involved this is a rare occurrence (¶¶408, 519.2).

Under normal circumstances, items for discussion in a College might include scheduling the renewal leaves for each bishop (three months in each quadrennium—¶411.2); issues in United Methodist institutions in the region; rulings that a particular bishop made in presiding over a conference; or planning for episcopal presence in forthcoming regional events.

Colleges meet more often than the Council and serve as the more immediate peer group to which bishops are accountable. In the case of a complaint against a bishop, for example, the current president of the College receives the written statement and "shall make a supervisory response" involving consultation with all parties, attempting reconciliation of the matter if possible (¶413.1-3). If the matter is not resolved, it proceeds to the Jurisdictional or Central Conference Committee on Investigation, though obviously the College retains a vital interest in the disposition of the complaint.[9]

The bishops' general superintendency is also practiced in the annual conferences over which they are assigned to preside. In this capacity they "make and fix the appointments" of all clergy members of annual conference and "announce the appointments" of deaconesses, diaconal ministers, and home missionaries (¶416). In other words, bishops are charged with knowing the work assignments of everyone employed in or a clergy member of an annual conference.

Here again, no one has an overview of the whole mission of the church in quite the way a bishop does. The clergy alone may comprise a "congregation" of several hundred—in some cases over a thousand—individuals about whom together with their families the bishop needs to know at least something. Likewise there are several hundred charges comprising even more local churches, about each of which the bishop needs at least some knowledge.

In the appointive task, of course, the *Discipline* provides for superintendency to be shared by a second office and conciliar body, the district superintendents meeting together in Cabinet. Usually a district has about fifty to seventy charges, making it possible for a DS to have deeper knowledge both of the clergy and of the local churches themselves. Bishops are dependent on DSs to bring that knowledge to the Cabinet meeting when appointments are being considered. But the bishop has the broadest view of the conference and its needs, must adjudicate between competing demands and desires of districts and the local churches within them, and ultimately must make and fix the appointments.

General superintendency is an enormously demanding task. Bishops must be able to balance varied pressures and demands, allotting time and energy wisely to their roles in the general church and in the annual conference(s) over which they preside. Annual conference members often complain that the bishop is not present enough in the conference, does not know the clergy or the local churches well enough, and is not sufficiently a pastor to the pastors.

But bishops also are needed for oversight of the astonishing variety of activities that comprise a global connection. These two dimensions need to be viewed not in competition, but in complementarity. As Gerald Moede put it, "Constant attention to local church problems helps bishops keep their national and global commitments in touch with reality."[10] The work in a region is not complete without the wider mission of the connection, and the connection is not complete without the vital work in each region.

Travel

Much of the bishops' knowledge and oversight of the whole connection hinges on a second key role: travel. Like their peripatetic forebears Wesley and Asbury, McKendree and Newcomer, bishops are continually on the move.[11] By their sheer presence in so many different places, they embody and enhance the unity of the church.

Bishops travel throughout the annual conferences over which they preside. Most Sundays of the year a bishop will be found preaching in a local church or dedicating a new building; often several such events will be arranged on the same day. Bishops are on the boards of any church-related institutions in the area; were they to attend all sessions of all such boards that task alone would occupy a month or two of every year.

The *Discipline* charges them also as a Council "to travel through the connection at large" (¶414.4). The Council sends each of its members in a rotation of "global visitations" to observe Methodist work in various parts of the world. Bishops serve as members of general agencies, which may lead to varying degrees of involvement in initiatives throughout the connection and meetings all over the world.

In this sense the bishops exemplify the itinerant ministry of United Methodism. They travel almost constantly. Moreover, they themselves are assigned to their episcopal residence by the Jurisdictional or Central Conference much as the "traveling ministers" are appointed by the bishops. Depending on the length of their service they may have several such assignments during their episcopal tenure. Little wonder then that the older term for retirement from the episcopacy was a bishop's request to "cease to travel."

Presidency

In all this continually itinerant superintendency, the bishops' unique role is captured as well in a third term, "preside." The bishops are the presiding officers of the connection and much of their authority derives from their presidential duties.

This role must not be confused, however, with executive power as it is practiced by the "Presidents" of other entities such as nations, universities, or commercial companies. In the most literal sense, the presidency of bishops means presiding and serving as chief parliamentary authority over the conferences of the church. The *Discipline* mandates that normally every session of every conference other than the local church or district—annual, jurisdictional, central, or general—will have a bishop in the chair presiding.

In a church comprised of as many diverse voices and unique personalities as United Methodism, presiding is no simple task. Not only must the bishop master the rules of procedure by which a conference is governed—usually Roberts' Rules of Order accompanied by other rules such as limits on debate. The bishop also must make an effort to ensure that all voices are heard as fairly and fully as possible.

Part of the lore of general and annual conferences especially preserves the memories of parliamentary bogs in which presiding bishops have found themselves mired. When someone moves to table a motion to which both an amendment and a substitute have been put before the house, and then a point of order is requested just as the "order of the day" such as a performance by a large visiting choir arrives, what is a presiding officer to do?

All bishops do not have the gift of presiding. Bishop Short (elected 1948) recalled that

> the greatly loved and genial Bishop Kavanaugh [elected 1854] of the Church South was never cut out for presiding, and often had matters in hopeless confusion . . . in his late years [he] was even known to nap while in the chair.

Other bishops have carried their presidential duties to the extreme, attempting to govern matters with an iron hand.

> Bishop Henderson [elected 1912] [was] intrigued by what was then called "church efficiency," giving the most minute attention to program planning and to timing, both in his own operations and in the life of the bodies over which he presided. His desire to see the Board of Bishops operate upon what he considered an efficient pattern met with strong reaction from some of his episcopal brethren, particularly Bishop Quayle [elected 1908] who inquired of him on one occasion, roughly and somewhat disrespectfully as he saw it, "When do we have time to spit?"[13]

A presiding officer competent in procedure who can keep the agenda moving in good humor and with respect for all voices can make all the difference in a conference, of course. Bishops take this responsibility with great seriousness.

The Constitution requires that in the course of presiding over annual conferences, bishops also make rulings on questions of church law. In some cases the matter is relatively simple, such as ruling out of order a motion that mandates something for the general church—only the General Conference can do that. Other matters can be exceedingly complex, such as rulings about whether annual conference procedures for fair process are in keeping with the *Discipline*. All decisions of law have to be reported in writing annually to the Judicial Council for review (¶¶49, 54.3).

Presiding also encompasses wider tasks. The Constitution charges the bishops in Council with "carrying into effect the rules, regulations, and responsibilities prescribed and enjoined by the General Conference" (¶45). That is, the bishops must ensure that legislation passed by General Conference is put into effect in the bodies over which they preside. This is no simple task, either, if it involves changes in the way local churches or conferences are structured or demands certain new kinds of record-keeping or reporting. Bishops are regularly in the position of advocating what General Conference has mandated, whether or not the bishops agree with it, and in any case without having had a voice in the new legislation.

Bishops have complained for many years that as the activist programs and missions of United Methodism proliferate, the bishops become little more than promoters and managers. Even in 1920 Bishop Quayle of the MEC wrote that

> We are at present in the church programmed to the point of nervous exhaustion, and if it is desired that a bishop add to the already overprogrammed preacher and church, a program of his, we shall go program mad. . . . The bishop who can make spirituality to be apparently the great design of the church and is not simply reduced to a maid of all work in financial matters . . . will render a superior service to the church.[14]

In a 1948 address Bishop James H. Straughn (elected 1939) complained that "the high office of bishop is used up in petty details" and "promotional responsibilities."[15] Four years later Bishop Paul B. Kern (elected 1930) noted in the episcopal address to General Conference the bishop's

> diminishing role as a thinker, a writer, or a preacher. . . . The dynamic activism of our Methodist way of doing things has much

to commend it, but . . . We must beware lest in the multiplicity of our endless emphases we lose our sense of direction.[16]

Bishops have often been in tension with general agencies on this account, since the latter are carrying out a mandate from General Conference that relies on the former to make it effective in annual conferences.

Over the past decade the bishops in council have been more deliberate about articulating and exercising their teaching and spiritual leadership roles on behalf of the church. Both their 1986 statement *In Defense of Creation* and their 1990 document on *Vital Congregations—Faithful Disciples* were efforts to address both church and society on critical issues. Both were publicized and studied widely. These were followed by a broad initiative on children and poverty. The bishops have also made collegial covenant among themselves, often inviting the whole church to join them, for prayer and fasting about such pressing concerns as the drug traffic. In 1991 they even asserted their Disciplinary option—never before used—of designating one of their own, Bishop Felton May (elected 1984), for a special assignment to take on the issue of the drastically poor quality of life in poverty neighborhoods of American cities—eventuating in the establishment of "shalom zones" throughout the U.S. (¶407.3).

Issues in the Episcopal Role

The complexity of the episcopal role in United Methodism has led to numerous controversies or even schisms over the years. James O'Kelly and his followers left in the 1790s in protest over Asbury's right to appoint preachers without appeal. Methodist Protestants organized in 1830 to free themselves of episcopal authority and give laity a voice in church governance. While the schism of the MEC in 1844 was provoked by the issue of a bishop owning slaves, the constitutional standing of the bishops as either amenable to or coordinate with the General Conference was also at stake. The pages of MECS newspapers in the late nineteenth century were full of articles protesting what was perceived to be the autocracy of the bishops. The southern bishops at that time were also the judiciary, ruling on the constitutionality of General Conference actions. While a Judicial Council distinct from both General Conference and episcopacy was created in 1934, the bishops remained fiercely independent in their actions, while northern bishops were viewed more as amenable to General Conference.[17]

Thus when The Methodist Church was created in 1939, and again when The United Methodist Church came into being in 1968, a simple statement from the pen of Bishop Nolan B. Harmon (elected 1956) was adopted to cover a multitude of sins.

> There shall be a continuance of an episcopacy in The United Methodist Church of like plan, powers, privileges, and duties as now exist in The Methodist Church and in The Evangelical United Brethren Church in all those matters in which they agree and may be considered identical; and the differences between these historic episcopates are deemed to be reconciled and harmonized by and in this Plan of Union and Constitution [¶43].

This was consensus by fiat, but by and large it worked.

In recent decades General Conference has attempted to channel disagreements about episcopacy into study commissions to propose judicious adjustments and reforms. In the early 1960s and again in the mid-1970s commissions examined the office and published studies. In the latter case, several paragraphs were adopted by the 1976 General Conference and placed in the *Discipline* to begin a new chapter on superintendency (¶¶401, 402).

But these paragraphs, laden with organizational management jargon of the period (with the 1996 addition of the "disciple-making" mission of the UMC), add little to an ecclesiological understanding of episcopacy. They do point to some of the immense challenges that confront this office in societies comprising many cultural practices. They call for alertness in reading consensus and "team-building." They note that bishops must pace themselves to allow time for reflection and friendship. They suggest strategic skills that bishops need in order to be effective in a diverse and ever-changing church.

Arguments for a limited term episcopacy have surfaced in all these studies and debates for over a hundred years. Some branches of what is now United Methodism have always had four-year episcopal terms. The Central Conferences can set any term they wish, and generally elect bishops for four-year terms (¶48). The EUBC

241

elected bishops for four-year terms, but usually a bishop was re-elected as a matter of course until retirement. A term episcopacy was said to protect against accumulation of power, enable the church gracefully to relieve an incompetent bishop from office, and allow greater flexibility and variety in filling the office.

Life tenure for bishops of United Methodism in the U.S., though, is set by the 1968 Constitution. Before that in The Methodist Church and prior bodies, life tenure was simply assumed in the same way that life tenure for all clergy was assumed—one served until retirement or removal from office. The constitutional standard of life tenure recognizes that while episcopacy is not an order, as a practical matter a former bishop would have great difficulty simply rejoining the itinerant ministry. Bishops must make decisions that affect other people's lives and careers. They must inevitably learn much not only about connectional bodies but about the people who serve in them. If they had also to keep an eye on their own future reelection as bishop or appointment as clergy, they would lose a good measure of their independence. Other officials in whose spheres they exercised their general superintendency would have greater tenure than they did. As the 1976 report stated the case,

> the connectional system of The United Methodist Church is best served by placing strong authority into the hands of the elected officials [bishops] rather than creating a vacuum into which bureaucrats could step.[18]

The enormous and broad-ranging demands on the office necessitate a long-term commitment and continuity in the work.

In fact, of course, many bishops are not elected until they are eligible for only one or two four-year terms before mandatory retirement. Moreover, bishops are limited to two terms in any one episcopal area unless the Jurisdictional Conference by a two-thirds vote determines a third term "to be in the best interest of the jurisdiction" (¶407.1). Thus in effect the *Discipline* does institute some features of a term episcopacy.

Election of Bishops

Bishops are elected by the lay and clergy delegates of Jurisdictional and Central Conferences meeting in the months immediately following each General Conference. Since 1976 the *Discipline* has made provision for Annual Conferences to designate a nominee(s) about whom information can then be distributed to all Jurisdictional Conference delegates. But voting is open and not restricted to persons so nominated (¶406.1). In fact, delegates may vote for any ordained elder in the connection, and a few bishops have been elected by Jurisdictions other than their own.[19]

Prior to 1939 in the MEC and MECS, and 1968 in the EUBC, bishops were elected by the respective General Conferences. Those elected tended to be well known across the connection, often as college or seminary presidents or general secretaries of church agencies. Under the Jurisdictional system, far more pastors and other regionally known persons have been elected. This has brought the episcopacy closer to the local church in a sense, but at the price of electing persons who are not known more generally.[20]

A great deal of personal and political lore has grown up around episcopal elections. American United Methodists expect certain "manners" of nominees or candidates for episcopacy. They must not be too aggressive or appear to be seeking the office, yet they must be willing publicly to acknowledge their sense of vocation for the office. Persons who are said to have maneuvered their election or exercised "power politics" may never recover their reputation in some quarters. Persons who withdraw from consideration to free up the election process after voting deadlocks are often considered to be frontrunners "next time" in return for their sacrifice. Other bishops have been completely surprised by their election, but few have ever turned it down.[21]

The impact of an episcopal election not only on the church but on the new bishop's career and family can hardly be underestimated. The new bishop begins an entirely new life in which she or he has no peers except within the Council of Bishops. The church must now find a place in which the new episcopal leader can serve effectively. The family must adjust to the sometimes cloying prestige of the office, and to the regular absence of their loved one. Bishop Eugene Hendrix's wife, Ann Eliza Scarritt Hendrix, put the trauma as poignantly as anyone ever has upon his election in 1886:

> The telegram bearing the sad tidings of your election to the office of a bishop reached me about an hour ago. How can I give you

up, my husband? I hope I appreciate the honor the church has bestowed upon you, but what a lonely life my future will be.

On the other hand, when William McKinley was elected President of the United States in 1896, his mother, Nancy Campbell Allison McKinley, publicly stated that she would have much preferred that her son be a Methodist bishop.[22]

Episcopal Assignments

The assignments of bishops to their residences are determined by Jurisdictional or Central Conferences upon the recommendation of the respective Jurisdictional or Central Conference Committees on Episcopacy. These committees are usually composed of the first elected lay and clergy delegates from each annual conference (¶¶48, 407).

The *Discipline* goes to great length to provide for one possibility that has never happened—the transfer of a bishop from one jurisdiction to another. This provision, placed in the Constitution in part to preserve the sense of a general—not jurisdictional—superintendency, allows for the transfer of bishops who have served at least one quadrennium in the jurisdiction that elected them, but only with the consent of the bishops involved (¶47). Legislation calls for the convening of an Interjurisdictional Committee on Episcopacy at the General Conference session to facilitate such transfers in advance of the Jurisdictional Conference sessions (¶511). The Jurisdictional Conferences must all meet on the same days, in part so that the Committees on Episcopacy will all be meeting at the same time and can vote on such transfers (¶¶24, 47). As a result of a 1992 constitutional amendment, no vote of the whole Jurisdictional Conference is required. But until recently few bishops have made it known that they would be amenable to transfers, and it remains to be seen whether various jurisdictions will accept them.[23]

One of the more puzzling lacunae in the *Discipline* is the complete absence of any definition of either term used to designate a bishop's assignment—"area" and "residence." In fact, there are far more Disciplinary references to the bishop's "residence"—meaning

244

the house owned by an episcopal area—than there are to "residence"—meaning place from which the bishop presides. Legislation standardizing the purchase and maintenance of a house for the bishop was added to the *Discipline* in 1984 (¶¶635, 825). But no paragraphs clarify what is meant by area or residence in the larger sense.

This absence reflects the long history of episcopal independence in Methodist polity. Throughout the nineteenth century and well into the twentieth, the bishops viewed their superintendency as a ministry of travel. They actually lived wherever they wanted; they divided among themselves the responsibility for presiding over particular annual conferences; and otherwise they continually traveled the connection.

Bishops did tend to gravitate toward those conferences that received them gladly. Well before the schism of 1844 MEC bishops elected from northern regions presided mainly in northern conferences, and likewise those from southern regions. Only Bishop McKendree insisted on traveling even where he was not much liked (the north).[24] But not until the turn of the twentieth century were either MEC or MECS bishops enjoined by General Conference to preside over certain annual conferences and actually to live in a place contiguous to them.

This requirement—or request—was only grudgingly accepted by many bishops, most of whom continued to feel that by virtue of their office they should make their own presidential assignments among themselves and live where they wanted to. But gradually the idea of an "episcopal area" began to emerge, designating certain annual conferences over which a bishop would preside from the residence assigned by General Conference. In the Evangelical Church this system was in place only in 1930, in the MECS only in 1934, in the MEC in 1912.[25]

The last MEC *Discipline* (1936) argued for an "Area System" in an appendix:

> [The system] relates the bishops to definite fields and thus assures a close and intensive supervision of the spiritual and temporal interests of the Church.

The bishop was to preside over annual conferences adjacent to the episcopal residence, but the legislation left it to the bishops to decide which annual conferences would be considered adjacent. (There were a great many more annual conferences at the time.) In the very next paragraph, though, the *Discipline* specified the conferences and the assignments of the bishops to them (MEC *Discipline* 1936, ¶¶1531, 1532).

When the jurisdictional system (both regional and racial) was instituted in 1939 the bishops were limited to presidency within the jurisdiction of their election. This served two implicit purposes: to inhibit northern bishops from exercising presidency in the south and vice versa, and to prevent African American bishops from presiding in predominantly white annual conferences.

At the 1939 Uniting Conference bishops were assigned to their areas on recommendation of the Judiciary Committee, with a request that the bishops accept their assignments despite the lack of any constitutional or legislative provision giving any conference the right to assign bishops. The Committee justified their action as instituting in the new church a system "which by custom, usage, and judicial decisions at least has had all the force and power of law."[26] Bishop Darlington (elected in the MECS in 1918) was well known for his refusal to abide by this request, as he administered the Louisville Area from his home in West Virginia.[27]

The 1968 Constitution of The United Methodist Church places assignment of bishops in the hands of the Jurisdictional or Central Conference, upon recommendation of the Committee on Episcopacy (¶48). But the Constitution perpetuates also the traditional prerogatives of the general superintendency:

> The bishops of each jurisdictional and central conference . . . shall arrange the plan of episcopal supervision of the annual conferences . . . within their respective territories [¶46].

According to the Judicial Council, even a 1992 constitutional amendment giving Jurisdictional and Central Conferences the power to "effect" changes in episcopal areas did not change the bishops' prerogative to "arrange" area boundaries (¶¶38, 46). The Conferences still only put into effect the changes upon which bishops decide.[28]

In practice this does not mean that bishops refuse their assignments. But it can mean, for example, that bishops decline to preside over more than two annual conferences. The College of Bishops in the Northeastern Jurisdiction so asserted in 1992, contributing to the formation of a New England Conference from the union of three annual conferences.

In recent years bishops have come to preside over fewer and fewer annual conferences. In fact, of the fifty bishops currently serving in the U.S., thirty-three preside over only one annual conference. This phenomenon is particularly evident in the Southeastern Jurisdiction, where only one of thirteen bishops has more than one annual conference. Particularly in these cases the average United Methodist has difficulty distinguishing between the episcopal area and the annual conference.

The "area" is in many ways a legal fiction. Only two committees administer its work: a Committee on Episcopacy and an Episcopal Residence Committee (and the former may be organized as a conference—not an area—committee) (¶¶634, 635). Few program committees are organized on an area basis (provision is made for this, for example, in the case of Higher Education and Campus Ministry, so that annual conferences with the same bishop can work together (¶631.4.a(10)).

However, the distinction is critical to United Methodist polity. Bishops are not the executives of the annual conferences over which they preside. They are not elected by particular annual conferences, nor is their superintendency limited to them. United Methodism does not have a diocesan episcopacy.

The term "area" maintains this distinction by clarifying that a bishop is assigned to a "residence" within the area. Twenty-three of the residences and areas associated with them carry the name of a city (e.g., Albany, Chicago, Richmond, Dallas, Portland), including all six in the Western Jurisdiction. This resonates with the metropolitan traditions of the ancient church. But the area name also serves to distinguish the area from the conference(s) over which a bishop presides (e.g., the bishop of the Ohio West Area presides over the West Ohio Conference). It prevents language that would imply that an area is constituted from certain annual conferences. In other words, episcopal areas are most adequately defined as regions of "residential and presidential supervision" (¶47) designated from within the whole general superintendency, rather than being geographic administrative units built up out of constituent annual conferences.

That the area and residence terms have not been further defined may be attributed to the way in which General Conference and the Council of Bishops have tried to respect each other's prerogatives. United Methodism has two bodies with general powers: the General Conference with "full legislative power over all matters distinctively connectional," and the Council of Bishops charged with "general oversight and promotion of the temporal and spiritual interests of the entire Church" (¶¶15, 45). For the General Conference to write legislation governing the bishops' superintendency would threaten this balance of powers and probably violate the Third Restrictive Rule; and the bishops do not directly write or propose legislation. Thus the *Discipline* maintains the freedom of the bishops to fulfill their unique office of oversight without being tied to any administrative or governing unit of the church.

District Superintendency

For many United Methodists the connection is most immediately embodied in the office of district superintendent. The DS is present at least once each year to conduct the charge conference. The DS consults with the pastor parish relations committee regarding the pastoral appointment. The DS is often in touch with lay officers of the local church regarding district, conference, and general church programs. The DS regularly reminds clergy and laity that their local church has a responsibility to pay its apportioned share of the annual conference budget.

In fact, the district superintendency is arguably the key office in making the connection work. Bishops depend on DSs for deeper knowledge of local churches and pastors; annual conference and general church agencies depend on DSs as their conduit for communicating with local churches; local churches depend on DSs to interpret their needs to the bishop and Cabinet.

For all that, however, the district superintendency has been little studied and its place ecclesiologically is neither well worked out nor widely understood.[29] The *Discipline* refers to it as an office, and it is established by the Constitution (¶51). But it is an office the holders of which are neither elected by the church nor consecrated to their work.

The district superintendency shares with the general superintendency a lack of ecclesiological definition. The role originated in the early nineteenth century as the office of "presiding elder." Often the only ordained Methodist, Evangelical, or United Brethren clergyperson in a region, the presiding elder traveled among the circuits assigned, holding quarterly conferences and administering the Lord's Supper. The arrival of the presiding elder was a high moment for the diverse elements of Wesleyan spirituality—worship, song, sacrament, and revival.

When the term "district superintendent" was adopted in the MEC in 1908—followed by the Evangelical Church in 1930, the MC in 1939, and the EUBC in 1946—it rang more administrative than sacramental. It indicated that the "elder" role was less important now than the "district" subunit of the larger connection.[30] District superintendency has become increasingly a managerial and promotional function.

District superintendency is an extension of the general superintendency. The office derives from the office of bishop. DSs are elders in full connection in the annual conference whom the bishop appoints to assist "in the administration of the Annual Conference" (¶¶51, 417). DSs share fully in the bishop's task of making clergy appointments.

The bishop chooses and appoints DSs, in consultation with the Cabinet and the receiving district's committee on district superintendency (¶417). But the *Discipline* insists on the legal fiction that upon being chosen, DSs become members "first of a Cabinet before they are subsequently appointed to service in districts" (¶429.1). Therefore, the DSs most immediate place of amenability in the church is the Cabinet, which is a conciliar body extending the superintendency in an annual conference. The *Discipline* draws a parallel between this conciliar superintendency and that of the Council of Bishops itself, which extends superintendency throughout the global connection.[31]

In another sense, though, the district superintendency is not much distinguished from the clergy membership of a conference. A DS may serve only up to eight years consecutively and no more than twelve years altogether (¶418). The DSs appointment is grouped with other extension ministries that are "within the connectional structures of United Methodism," such as general agency staff and United Methodist seminary faculty (¶335.1.a.1). Many if not most DSs return to a local church pastorate after their term or upon appointment by the bishop.

Thus DSs are also peers with other elders; they just happen to be asked by the bishop to fulfill a special task for awhile. This duality of the role—both peer with clergy and extension of episcopacy—creates inevitable tensions. The EUB tradition came down on the side of the clergy, with the annual conference electing what were then termed "conference superintendents" for four-year terms. The conference superintendent was a kind of representative of clergy working with the bishop (EUBC *Discipline* 1967, ¶100).

The Methodist Church gave bishops the power to appoint DSs. This power had been disputed to the point of schism in the 1820s, when it became a constitutional issue over whether the power to appoint "presiding elders" was part of the "plan of our itinerant general superintendency" protected by the Third Restrictive Rule. Later Methodists were disinclined to fight that battle again.

When United Methodism was formed in 1968, the bishop's power to appoint DSs was placed in a legislative paragraph, not the Constitution, making it easier to change to the EUB approach should the General Conference decide to do so. The 1976 study commission, though, reinforced the bishop's power to appoint by specifying that district superintendency is an extension of general superintendency.

Not only by nature of the office, but in most aspects of the role, a DS is always in between or standing in the middle of many competing pressures. The *Discipline* charges the office most generally with "maintaining the connectional order of the *Discipline*" (¶420.1). Thus the DS is a primary figure in mediating the connection of local churches, clergy, conferences, and agencies.

Five basic tasks occupy most of the DSs time. First is working with pastors—guiding them through candidacy and probationary membership, issuing licenses for pastoral ministry, consulting with all clergy on their appointments, holding them accountable for evaluation and continuing education, and supporting them and their families in times of need.

DSs are also key officers in handling complaints against the clergy of their district. Upon receiving a complaint ("a written and signed statement") the DS (or bishop) is charged with interpreting the complaint process for both "the person filing the complaint and the clergyperson." The DS (or bishop) undertakes a "supervisory response . . . directed toward a just resolution among all parties" (¶359.1). This has become an increasingly complex and demanding procedure as concerns for fair process increase in the church.

A second task is working with local church administration—conducting charge conferences at least annually in each charge, collecting statistics, reminding local churches of their financial commitments to the connection, and encouraging planning for mission. Third, DSs are the officers for handling all church property in the district—meeting with the committee on church location and building which must approve all property transactions, nominating members of that committee as well as the district board of trustees that holds property owned by the district, and keeping records of abandoned properties, church closings, and all local church or district assets.

Fourth, the DS is asked "to oversee the programs of the Church within the bounds of the district . . . working with and through the district council on ministries where it exists" (¶424.1). The district office is often the broker through which information about resources in annual conference or general church agencies passes to local churches and pastors.

A fifth task that has come into increasing prominence in the last decade is the DSs role in starting new local churches. Many annual conferences have undertaken "congregational development" programs, with major capital campaigns to help underwrite the costs of new churches. The bishop and Cabinet must give their consent to the founding of a new church and the bishop designates the district in which it will be located. The DS of that district then becomes "the agent in charge of the project," recommending a site and calling together the constituting church conference (¶259).

In these five areas of work among many others, the DS shares with the bishop the three key roles discussed above. The DS superintends by participating fully in appointment-making and by a thorough knowledge of the clergy and local churches in the district. The DS achieves much of this connectional work by traveling constantly through the district and conference, preaching and visiting regularly in local churches. And the DS continually presides in charge conferences as well as district conferences where they exist.

Over 525 clergy serve as district superintendents today. The office remains a highly visible leadership role in the church, and thus a focal point for expressing the inclusiveness of the connection. At the same time, the luster of the office has worn off for many clergy as it continues to bear many of the tensions in the connection without adequate rewards. While service as a DS is usually still considered a kind of "promotion," many clergy would prefer to remain in the local church.

Many annual conferences have reduced the number of districts partly in order to cut costs, since DS salaries and expenses are part of the conference budget. Just as bishops' salaries are set by General Conference, so DS salaries are set by annual conferences—but on widely varying bases. In some conferences the DS salary is based on an average of the top twenty or so local church clergy salaries. In others it is based on a certain percent more than the average salary in the conference. Expenses for district office space and staff support may be shared between the conference and the district. This may result in a district apportionment to help support office expense as well as district parsonage upkeep (¶¶612.1.a, 663.4.a).

Superintendency has become an increasingly demanding vocation. Bishops and DSs must balance many competing claims on their time. They are expected to be preachers and missionaries as well as administrators. They carry both the responsibility for placing the clergy in their appointments and the task of pastoral care and guidance of clergy and their families. They must devote much time and energy to teaching local church people the value of the connection—including the superintendency, their own office.

United Methodists continue to have high expectations of superintendency. In the 1994 annual conference survey conducted by the General Council on Ministries, every question regarding the role of bishops and district superintendents in the appointment system was ranked as needing higher levels of attention in the future. Respondents also wanted the superintendency to take leadership in generating new vision and direction for the church.[32]

Many voices today call for DSs to spend more time in local churches than in conference and district meetings, especially as those meetings preoccupy them with program promotion. DSs need to be free to give time and attention to the particular challenges and opportunities of local churches. In particular, DSs need to bring skills in conflict resolution, in long-range planning for mission, and in staff development. Complex as it is, superintendency obviously remains a constituting element of the connection and a key expression of discipline in the denomination.

CHAPTER 9

General, Jurisdictional, and Central Conferences and the General Agencies

The conference is the signature form of United Methodist polity and politics. To confer—to gather for song, prayer, preaching, teaching, discussing, debating, and acting—is to join in a Christian conversation that has spanned over two hundred years of Methodist history. Conferences have met regularly for generations and have developed their own distinct traditions. At the same time conferences are ephemeral; in a real sense they do not exist except when they are meeting. Methodist people have always resisted powerful continuing executive bodies. They prefer to govern themselves in conference, from the broadest connectional legislative body of General Conference to the regional judicatory of annual conference to the local charge conference overseeing ministry and mission in each place.

General Conference

The General Conference of United Methodism is the most improbable and vexing, eventful and stirring church body one could ever hope to see. Meeting for eleven days out of every four years "in the month of April or May" (¶13), the General Conference brings together a thousand United Methodists from over twenty nations to set policy, approve legislation, and issue pronouncements on behalf of the entire connection. That it works at all is amazing. That it holds central place in connectional polity is indisputable. That it will continue to change in composition and function to reflect a global church is certain.

General Conference began as the distinctive political form of American Methodism. All denominations of Wesleyan heritage—including African Methodist Episcopal, African Methodist Episcopal Zion, Christian Methodist Episcopal, Evangelical, Methodist Episcopal, and United Brethren—adopted this procedure of gathering in a large delegated body to confer on teachings and practices of the church, elect bishops, worship, enjoy fellowship, and make policy.

The name originated in the late eighteenth-century Methodist Episcopal Church as an adjective with a lower-case "g"—that is, the conference was an annual general meeting of all the Methodist preachers who could travel to it, usually to Baltimore. The Christmas Conference of 1784 was such a general gathering in Baltimore, but it was a special or irregular meeting for the purpose of constituting a new church and ordaining clergy to lead it. The regular conference met in the summer months of 1784 and 1785 as usual.

As Methodism grew, conferences were held annually in various regions and records of their proceedings were assembled into one collection titled "Minutes of the General Conference of the Methodist Episcopal Church in America." Each conference considered issues facing the new church and deliberated on changes to the emerging *Discipline*. But passing legislation sequentially through various regional conferences was burdensome, and the last conference to consider an item usually had the final word. Thus in 1792 all the preachers gathered in Baltimore, where they agreed to meet as a general body every four years thereafter.

The 1792 General Conference was the first such conference by that name meeting as an assembly separate from the regional conferences collectively. It met again in 1796, 1800, and 1804, with a gradually emerging authority over the connection distinct from the authority exercised by the collective annual conferences. For example, the General Conference of 1796 set the first geographic boundaries of annual conferences, confirming their regional nature. In 1800 with the body of preachers continuing to grow, the General Conference limited participation to preachers who had traveled for at least four years. In 1804 this was limited still further to traveling elders in full connection.

256

The 1808 General Conference gathered at a critical juncture in Methodist Episcopal history. While the movement was expanding rapidly, it lacked permanent structures of authority and continuity. Thomas Coke was no longer visiting America as a general superintendent. Richard Whatcoat, elected a bishop in 1800, had died in 1806 leaving the church with only Francis Asbury to serve as general superintendent. Asbury himself was now over sixty years of age and in failing health. Meanwhile the General Conference was continuing to meet without a constitution or any limits on its powers.

Led by a young Joshua Soule, master parliamentarian and later bishop, the 1808 General Conference of all the traveling elders created a new governance structure for the church which is essentially still in place. General Conference was now to be delegated, in two senses. First, the traveling elders were to elect delegates—at first one for every five traveling elders—to serve in the General Conference.

Second, General Conference was to have limited powers delegated to it by the whole collective body of elders. The powers to legislate for the connection were broad, yet on certain issues they were subject to confirmation by all the annual conferences collectively (the originating body of elders). These limitations to powers were set in the Restrictive Rules, which have continued in more or less their original form ever since (¶¶16-20).[1]

Beyond those restrictions, though, the General Conference has continued since those early days to exercise "full legislative power over all matters distinctly connectional." The Constitution names fifteen specific powers, concluding with a permissive statement: "to enact such other legislation as may be necessary, subject to the limitations and restrictions of the Constitution of the Church" (¶16).

In practice this means that the General Conference considers legislative proposals in virtually any and every area of church life, from doctrine to committee structures to major initiatives in mission. It can establish study commissions on any topic. It can pass resolutions on any issue facing church, society, or world.

However, the *Discipline* is specific that the General Conference "has no executive or administrative power" (¶501). In fact, then, it has no executive office or administrator. Bishops are charged with putting its legislative enactments into effect, but they are not executive officers of the General Conference. Bishops preside in the business sessions, but no one person is elected president or moderator of the conference. No single body is designated to maintain the work of General Conference between sessions. When it adjourns it is no more. When General Conference convenes again four years later it does so as a completely new conference and is free to undo everything the conference of four years ago has done.

The *Discipline* has surprisingly little to say about General Conference procedure. The Constitution mandates that bishops be the presiding officers (¶¶15.11, 503). The General Conference must elect a secretary upon nomination from the Council of Bishops—a hugely demanding position for which the rightly gifted and willing individual must be sought carefully (¶504). The Plan of Organization and Rules of Order from the previous General Conference are continued in the new one, so that they do not have to be completely rewritten but can be modified as needed (¶505). Immediate passage of the Plan, Rules, and agenda is critical, since without them any delegate could, upon being recognized, begin a speech on any subject and talk until his or her voice gave out—much like a filibuster in the U.S. Congress.[2]

The *Discipline* also establishes a quorum so that the General Conference can officially convene long enough to get its own Rules in place. The quorum rule (¶506) makes certain realistic exceptions in order to prevent the General Conference from being unable to approve its journal or adjourn, for lack of sufficient numbers (often a problem on the last day).

These meager provisions fortunately are not the only lines of continuity from one conference to the next. Normally about half the delegates have served in a previous General Conference, and a fifth in three or more.[3] While some traditions such as the bishops' hymn—all the bishops singing together from the platform—come and go ("elect more tenors" was the plea from a bishop one year), many others continue, such as opening communion, daily worship, an episcopal address and a lay address.[4]

Delegates

Part of the improbability of General Conference comes from its ungainly size. The Constitution allows for a range of 600 to 1,000 delegates, half of whom are clergy, half laity. Every annual, missionary, or provisional annual conference is entitled to at least one clergy and one lay delegate. Beyond that, the overall composition of General Conference membership is based on a complex formula factoring in the number of clergy members in an annual conference and the number of lay members of local churches in an annual conference. In 1996 the secretary was able to work this out to 998 delegates and in 2000 to 992, just under the maximum.

Both the Methodist and EUB General Conferences prior to 1968 were considerably smaller than this. They were able to have meaningful floor debate on agenda items and each delegate could see the importance of his or her voice. The larger body has brought less sense of ownership by individual delegates and unwieldy discussion of issues on the floor.[5]

The increasing size of General Conference over the years has allowed for a wider diversity of delegates to be full participants in United Methodism's highest legislative body. One notable change that began over a hundred years ago was lay representation. The scope of General Conference work expanded in the 1870s, incorporating enterprises in education and missions that had previously been under independent boards made up largely of laity. Since these lay leaders wanted to continue their activities, gradually the need for lay participation in decisions affecting the whole connection became obvious.[6]

The 1872 MEC General Conference included two lay delegates from each annual conference. The definition of "layman" at this time was "members of the Church who are not members of Annual Conferences," since annual conferences were still assemblies of the traveling preachers in those days. Thus lay delegates were elected by special Electoral Conferences held on the third day of each annual conference, with one layperson attending from each local church or charge (then called stations and circuits).

Sixteen years later, in 1888, five women who had been elected by their respective Electoral Conferences came to the MEC General Conference. The conference refused to seat them; opponents argued that "layman" meant male. Twelve more years and three General Conferences went by before the new MEC Constitution of 1900 changed "layman" to "lay member" opening the door to women, and at the same time equalizing the numbers of laity and clergy in the General Conference. (These provisions went into effect in 1904.)[7]

The MECS voted lay representation in both General Conference and annual conferences in 1870. Lay rights for women were not established until 1922, however. The Evangelical Association voted for lay participation in 1903, and the United Brethren Church some years earlier with much debate over the ratio of lay membership to clergy. Methodist Episcopal clergy and laity who had demanded full lay representation in the MEC in 1830 had left to form the Methodist Protestant Church, of course. Women first served as MPC delegates in 1896. Thus when the church unions of 1939 and 1968 bringing all these traditions together were completed, equal lay representation inclusive of women was firmly established in all the uniting bodies.[8]

The qualifications for serving as a delegate are stated in the Constitution, not in legislation. Ministerial delegates must be members of the annual conference that elects them. There are no nominations; every clergy member in full connection is eligible (¶33).

Lay delegates must have been "active participants in The United Methodist Church for at least four years" and members of a UMC for at least two years. They do not have to be members of the annual conference itself, but must belong to a UMC within its bounds. Again, there are no nominations although some conferences distribute information about any persons who wish their interest in being a delegate to be known (¶34).

About a third of the 2000 General Conference delegates were women, including 23 percent of the clergy delegates. This contrasts sharply with the 1972 General Conference, in which only a little over 13 percent of the delegates were women.[9] Over 13 percent of the 2000 General Conference delegates were African American, reflecting a proportion similar to the U.S. population (though much higher than the proportion of African Americans in United Methodist membership). The proportion of Asian American and Hispanic American delegates continues to rise as well (3 percent and 2 percent, respectively).

General Conference is also rapidly becoming a truly international body. In 1992 116 delegates were from Central Conferences or autonomous non-U.S. Methodist churches, and by 2000 that number grew to 162, over sixteen percent of the total. While the

260

language of conference business remains English (or American), the conference provides for the simultaneous translation of its proceedings into Chinese, Spanish, Portuguese, German, and French.[10]

Delegates come from many walks of life, standing for the diversity of United Methodist adherents. Clergy delegates include pastors, district superintendents, annual conference Council on Ministries directors, camp directors, seminary professors, deans, and retreat center directors. Lay delegates include job titles like violinist, auto dealer, attorney, dental assistant, social worker, banker, freelancer, office manager, industrial distributor, homemaker/volunteer, archivist, travel agent, farmer, fisherman, and retired. In short, General Conference itself could be the basis of a good small town.

Petitions and Procedures

One of the remarkable practices of General Conference is its reception of petitions from "any organization, ordained minister, or lay member of The United Methodist Church." Formerly termed "memorials," petitions can address any topic, but only one topic— in particular, one paragraph of the *Discipline*—in each petition (¶507). The secretary for petitions has latitude for combining peti-·tions that have essentially the same purpose. In 2000, 1,967 legislative items—consolidated from about 14,000 petitions—were presented to the General Conference for consideration.[11]

For purposes of handling this mass of material the General Conference Plan of Organization divides all delegates into eleven legislative committees. While still large with as many as a hundred members, these committees provide at least a more manageable forum within which to consider petitions. Each committee is convened by a bishop for the purpose of electing officers, who then assume their presiding duties. Bishops, of course, are neither members nor officers of any committee or of General Conference itself. The committees often divide into subcommittees, which in turn may divide to produce working groups of half a dozen people. This makes real hands-on work possible, especially if new material or revisions must be drafted.

Each legislative committee covers a certain area of church work, such as church and society, global ministries, the local church, or financial administration. Petitions are distributed according to those topic areas. After debating or revising them, the committees then vote concurrence or non-concurrence with each petition that comes before them.

Obviously the plenary sessions of all delegates cannot consider the legislative committees' actions on each petition individually. Most, as many as 80 percent, are simply printed as part of a "consent calendar" on which General Conference votes en masse. Occasionally a significant item will slip into the *Discipline* this way, without any floor debate at all. But petitions are at least discussed in legislative committees.

The concurrence or nonconcurrence procedure is probably as efficient as any process in such a large body could be. But it still creates tangles that can tax the most logical mind. For example, if a committee has voted nonconcurrence on a petition, a delegate's vote of "yes" in plenary—that is, agreement with the committee—actually means "no" in the sense of agreeing with the nonconcurrence and thereby voting against the petition.

If a substantial minority of a committee disagrees with the majority committee action, they can prepare a minority report that the plenary must vote on as well. A minority report cannot be simply the opposite of the majority position, though, since in that case the conference would simply have to reverse the committee's action. Rather, a minority report must make some substantive change to the original petition. Voting on a minority report may require the opposite valences, then, with a "yes" actually meaning "yes" to the petition as modified in the minority report, and "no" meaning agreement with the majority of the committee.

A number of petitions originate from larger bodies of the church, including annual and jurisdictional conferences and general agencies. These are printed in an advance edition of the *Daily Christian Advocate (DCA)*, along with reports of any study commissions created by the preceding General Conference, since lengthy explanatory material may accompany them. Studies on such topics as baptism, ministry, homosexuality, mission, and theology must be available to delegates for careful reading ahead of time. Petitions from individuals or local churches are printed in a *DCA* advance edition available on the first day of the conference if not before.

Legislation proposed by general agencies is usually the product of much research and debate among members of those boards during the quadrennium preceding General Conference. Since agency membership is largely comprised of people who were members of the previous General Conference, many of whom are members of the current one at which the legislation is being presented, there is a good deal of continuity in the process of considering these ideas.

The privileging of material from general church bodies does create a kind of "populist" backlash, however. Many delegates and observers of the church have expressed a wish that more petitions from individuals and from local churches would be considered seriously. The problem is that General Conference realistically can handle only petitions that are clearly written and well worked out in advance, and that express some emerging consensus in the church. This tends to favor proposals that come from conferences or agencies, where a process of full consideration, refinement and consensus-building has already occurred.[12]

Nevertheless "populists" have attempted various ways of intervening in the established process, such as petitions with large numbers of individual or local church signatories from around the church. Similar voices have pushed through procedures which mandate that the staff of general boards and agencies in attendance at General Conference be listed in the *DCA*. Some delegates have felt that staff have too much influence on the legislative process, and want staff presence (and the financial cost of that presence) to be public knowledge. On the other hand, the expertise of staff is almost invariably called upon when legislative committees are weighing the sense and impact of petitions.

The compulsive record-keeping of United Methodists is evident at General Conference. The *DCA* is printed each day with a complete transcript of plenary sessions of the previous day, plus reports of all actions by legislative committees. In 2000 the Advance Edition with petitions from all over the church was over 1,400 pages long; the daily edition added up to over 600 pages during the course of the conference. The *DCA* then becomes the Journal of the conference, the permanent record of its actions.

Following the conference, a group comprised of the conference Secretary, a small Committee on Correlation and Editorial Revision, and the Book Editor and Publisher for the United Methodist Publishing House, goes through all General Conference actions. They consider all legislation that must be printed in the

Discipline, making minor language changes as necessary for consistency and figuring out the exact numbering of paragraphs. This can be an exceedingly complex task, given the errors and questions of intent that can creep into the process between legislative committee decisions, plenary action, and printing of reports.[13]

Resolutions

The *Discipline* makes clear that the General Conference is the only body of United Methodism that "has the authority to speak officially for The United Methodist Church" (¶509). Thus the conference considers various resolutions addressing contemporary issues. Many of these receive publicity in the press after the conference passes them; many others are passed on without any fanfare. All are published in *The Book of Resolutions* as a reference volume available to all United Methodists.

Resolutions are organized into the same headings as the sections of the Social Principles. An editorial team decides their placement, and removes those which "have been rescinded or superseded."[14] The resolutions currently present policy statements on about two hundred different subjects, ranging from the law of the sea to gambling to HIV/AIDS.

While these are official positions of the UMC, they are not binding in a legislative sense. The General Conference asks all United Methodists to consider these positions and accept them as the collective wisdom of the church, but it does not expect all United Methodists to agree with all such statements. Whether any resolution is really acted upon or fulfilled is up to United Methodist people. The policy can be stated, but is meaningful only in practice.

The published resolutions can be helpful to the church in two primary ways. First, they can be the basis for pastoral care and congregational discussion of major issues facing world societies. Second, they provide grounds on which church leaders can approach civil governments and elected officials by presenting carefully worded and well thought out official positions of the church.

A Diverse Public

As General Conference has grown in size, it has become not only a more diverse public in itself, but also the focal point of varied interests represented in the diverse public of the church. Particularly since the 1960s, interest groups and caucuses have been highly visible at the conference site. In 2000 a delegate entering the convention center was likely to be handed a daily news sheet from any of several different groups, ranging from the Good News caucus and the Institute on Religion and Democracy to the Methodist Federation for Social Action and the National Women's Caucus.

The UMC (unlike the Presbyterian Church USA, for example) has never created a mechanism for certifying caucuses or incorporating them more formally into decision-making processes. Yet established caucus groups are present and active at every General Conference. Each represents a constituency of United Methodists that because of its minority status at General Conference would have trouble making its voice heard with a corporate presence.

Caucuses have been organized under various historical circumstances and for various purposes. Ethnic caucuses originated in the 1950s and 1960s as African American and Asian conferences merged with the majority white annual conferences from which they had previously been separated. By the time United Methodism was formed in 1968, the only nonwhite ethnic conferences allowed to remain were the missionary conferences for Oklahoma (Native American Indians) and the Rio Grande (Hispanics).

These mergers had many advantages. New rules for inclusiveness brought ethnic minority persons into decision-making bodies for the whole church. Ethnic minority pastors had at least the promise of open itineracy and full place in the salary ladder of annual conference.

However, nonwhite ethnic groups became increasingly concerned by the failure of the UMC to attract new leadership and start new congregations among growing ethnic minority populations. Many leaders felt that the promises of "integration" had produced a church built on the assumptions of the white majority, and that nonwhite ethnic groups had lost control over the mission among their own people. Caucuses formed to provide a collective voice in moving denominational resources toward congregational and leadership development as well as missional needs of ethnic minority communities. These now include Black Methodists for Church Renewal (BMCR), Methodists Associated Representing the Cause of Hispanic Americans (MARCHA), the Native American

International Caucus (NAIC), and the National Federation of Asian American United Methodists (NFAAUM). Among other programs that grew from their efforts were the churchwide emphasis on the Ethnic Minority Local Church from 1976–1984 (with continuation of aspects of it to 1988) and the Hispanic and Native American ministries plans approved by the 1992 General Conference.[15]

Some voices in the church have complained that ethnic caucuses are divisive. While they may receive some operating funds from church bodies, they have no official standing in United Methodist polity or in the General Conference. Their program proposals sometimes appear to force delegates to choose between ethnic groups in allocating resources. They imply that general church programs are not adequately inclusive. They tend to heighten the differences among United Methodists, so this argument goes.

On the other hand, when the overwhelming majority of United Methodists and General Conference delegates are white persons of northern European heritage, it is hard to see how the voices of persons of other ethnic and cultural heritages could be heard without some kind of deliberate action. The 1994 survey of annual conference members conducted by the General Council on Ministries confirmed that ethnic groups who have been excluded in the past still want much greater attention to inclusiveness than does the ethnic majority.[16]

Moreover, any comparison of ethnic minority and ethnic majority segments of the church shows huge disparities in the value of church property, the number of seminary-trained pastors, salaries and housing for pastors and staff of local churches, and monies available for mission. The caucuses have been a voice for economic justice, calling for the church to redistribute its resources. The majority is unlikely to think of redressing economic differences without some focused pressure from minority groups.

Other caucuses have organized as advocates for certain kinds of issues and concerns in the church. The oldest of these is the Methodist Federation for Social Action, founded in 1907 to address major issues of social justice. This "fellowship" has chapters in many annual conferences, lobbies for social justice legislation at General Conference, and for many years has published a *Social Questions Bulletin* on current concerns and actions with the slogan, "seeking global justice through The United Methodist Church."

The Good News "renewal movement" began publishing a bimonthly magazine called *Good News* in 1967. The masthead refers to the mission of the caucus as "an evangelical voice within The United Methodist Church, urging the Church to be faithful to the biblically based principles of its historic Wesleyan heritage."[17] The caucus has particularly worked to prevent changes to the church's position on homosexuality, and has led organized protest against the use of general church funds for events in which speakers or leaders advocate theological or social positions opposed by Good News.

The National Women's Caucus organized in 1971 to support General Conference legislation creating a General Commission on the Status and Role of Women (GCSRW). After the Commission was established, the caucus continued to work for such causes as the election of female bishops. While the GCSRW is now officially part of general church structure, the caucus carries on its own advocacy role for the full participation of women.

The Affirmation caucus emerged in the 1980s to work for full participation of gay and lesbian persons in the UMC. The caucus has consistently urged General Conference to remove language placed in the *Discipline* in 1984 that excludes "self-avowed practicing homosexuals" from the ordained ministry and that calls the practice of homosexuality "incompatible with Christian teaching" (¶161.G). The caucus also helped bring into being a network of "Reconciling Congregations" who welcome gay and lesbian participation. A newsletter called *Open Hands*, in publication since 1985, is the voice of this network in United Methodism and several other denominations.

The continuing vitality of caucuses demonstrates as clearly as any feature of contemporary United Methodism that an older cultural consensus has passed from the scene. The taken for granted world that gave General Conference a certain unity and consistency has given way to a diversity of voices seeking a full hearing. One has only to compare photographs or minutes from twenty, fifty, or a hundred years ago to see that assumed roles of men and women, whites, blacks, and other ethnic groups have changed dramatically.

General Conference has become an enormous experiment in Christian community. How can a conference of a thousand people from over twenty nations create unity out of their diverse needs, interests, and perspectives? Is "Christian conversation"—Wesley's ideal of mutual accountability in the Christian life—possible on this scale? How can divergent opinions be heard and acknowledged even as the conference votes on issues? Is there a way to avoid creating "winners" and "losers"? Can General Conference still reflect the consensus or "mind of the church" on important matters? To what degree is it possible for any international church body to reach a common voice? The General Conference lives through these and like questions every time it gathers.

Jurisdictional Conferences

Since the 1939 MC Constitution, certain powers of the General Conference have been delegated or "conferred" to Jurisdictional Conferences (¶25). These conferences meet simultaneously at five different sites around the U.S., normally in July following the General Conference. All General Conference delegates are also delegates to this body. An equal number of additional lay and clergy delegates are elected by annual conferences solely to participate in Jurisdictional Conference, thus exactly doubling the size of the General Conference delegation (¶¶24, 32, 513).

Each Jurisdictional Conference adopts its own rules of order, but the *Discipline* establishes a simple majority of delegates to constitute a quorum (¶517). Bishops of the Jurisdiction rotate in presiding over sessions (¶520).

All powers of Jurisdictional Conferences formerly belonged to General Conference, and are undertaken on behalf of the general church. Only the power to create jurisdictional boards and agencies is uniquely a jurisdictional power, but only the Southeastern Jurisdiction (the primary territory of the former MECS) has exercised this power to any notable degree (¶25).

Foremost among Jurisdictional Conference powers is the election of bishops. Balloting usually begins almost immediately after opening worship, and reports of ballots often interrupt whatever other business is on the floor at the moment. Often a recess is called after each ballot report in order to allow time for delegations to consult with each other and with other delegations about their votes. The *Discipline* recommends but does not require that at least sixty percent of ballots cast be necessary for an episcopal election (¶406.2.b).

Many church folk express the wish that episcopal elections were conducted more in keeping with their ecclesial purpose, and Jurisdictional Conferences have adopted various procedures to try to open the way for spiritual discernment. These might include silence and prayer before each ballot, or singing hymns and reading scripture. Some conferences have tried to discipline the exuberance accompanying an election by replacing applause with the singing of the "Doxology" or the like.

Yet it would be naive to insist that elections could occur without politics. Indeed, without an open political process in place, many people would not have an opportunity to make their voices heard. Critical decisions like the choice of episcopal leaders require full participation on everyone's part so that the conference can make the most informed and fully discerned decision possible. Everyone brings certain perspectives and interests to the process and inevitably joins groups or coalitions of persons who share similar interests. Only from the expressing and balancing of these can a good decision emerge. In this sense politics are absolutely necessary to the episcopal election process, and the means through which the Holy Spirit can move in the church.

Since most annual conferences now designate a nominee for the episcopacy a year in advance of Jurisdictional Conference, delegations from other annual conferences have a chance to meet the nominee in the months before they vote. At times a strong consensus about nominees may develop through these meetings, so that when delegations assemble in the Jurisdictional Conference session the elections move very quickly. In the 1992 South Central Jurisdiction, for example, three bishops were elected on a single ballot, indicating a clear consensus formed largely ahead of time.

On the other hand, the church's need to acknowledge the many critical needs and interests represented by nominees may create a long struggle for discernment. The 1992 Western Jurisdiction conducted thirty-one ballots, with African American, Native American Indian, Asian American, Hispanic American, and European American nominees—both men and women—all receiving support. Finally several candidates withdrew,

leaving many supporters in tears, and offered their support for
the election of Ms. Swenson [The Reverend Mary Ann Swenson,
a European American female pastor]. Then—with only a couple
of hours left before the consecration service was slated to begin—
the standing, cheering delegates elected her by acclamation.
Swamped with hugs and surrounded by applause, the newly
elected bishop was escorted to the bishops' platform.[18]

Such a spontaneous celebration that acknowledges also the pain
and grace of those who were not elected is a political process at its
best. The entire Jurisdictional Conference then gathers for worship
in which the new bishops are consecrated for their work.

Because of this primary task of Jurisdictional Conference, its primary committee mandated by the Constitution is the Episcopacy
Committee (¶¶48, 522). The Committee usually is made up of the
first elected lay and clergy delegates of each annual conference in
the jurisdiction. They begin their service at the conclusion of
Jurisdictional Conference, thus serving on through the next
Conference four years later. In this way the Committee is better
experienced and prepared for its main charge, which is recommending the boundaries of episcopal areas (upon recommendation
of the College of Bishops) and the assignments of the bishops to
their areas. The Committee also consults with bishops regarding
their retirement plans and other matters, and must "review the
work of the bishops, pass on their character and official administration, and report to the Jurisdictional Conference its findings"
(¶522.3.a). The Conference as a whole then votes on the standing
and assignments of the bishops in the jurisdiction.

The second major power of Jurisdictional Conference is the election of members or directors of the general boards and agencies of
the church. Through this complex process the *Discipline* attempts to
provide for as wide a representation of gender, age, ethnicity,
region, handicapping condition, and lay or clergy status as possible.

The first step in the nominating process is for each annual conference in a jurisdiction to elect persons to a "jurisdictional pool."
This normally occurs after an annual conference has elected all its
delegates to General and Jurisdictional Conferences. The newly
elected delegates meet with the bishop and propose names for the
pool. This report is then presented to the annual conference, with
the floor open for other nominations. The *Discipline* mandates that

all General Conference delegates are to be nominated for the pool, and often the Jurisdictional Conference delegates are included as well.

The Jurisdictional Nominating Committee (curiously absent from jurisdictional legislation but named in ¶705 on the nominating process) then takes all the names elected from annual conferences in the jurisdiction—the jurisdictional pool—and develops a slate of nominees for each general board and agency. The number of nominees permitted each jurisdiction has to be worked out based on the membership formula for each board or agency. The Jurisdictional Conference then votes on that slate of nominees.

A third Jurisdictional Conference power is support of mission agencies within the bounds of the jurisdiction. This may take the form of adopting a budgeted amount of financial support which is then divided among annual conferences (and thence local churches) in the jurisdiction as either a goal for giving or an apportionment.

A fourth power is the setting of the boundaries of annual conferences within the jurisdiction. A number of annual conference mergers have occurred in the last forty years. These affect clergy conference membership, local church relationships with conferences, and episcopal assignments. The *Discipline* charges Jurisdictional Conferences with weighing such mergers carefully. The power of altering jurisdictional boundaries belongs to General Conference, of course, meaning that a jurisdiction cannot move annual conference boundaries outside the lines of jurisdictional boundaries.

Finally, the Constitution locates in the Jurisdictional Conference the appeal process from the trial of a traveling preacher in an annual conference (¶25.6). The College of Bishops nominates and the Jurisdictional Conference elects a Committee on Appeals, which "shall have full power to hear and determine appeals of bishops, clergy members . . . local pastors, and diaconal ministers" (¶2716.1). Fortunately, few matters reach the trial stage in the church, and this Committee is rarely called upon to meet.

The *Discipline* provides for jurisdictional agencies to be created, such as an Administrative Council to oversee program initiatives undertaken by the jurisdiction. Only the Southeastern Jurisdiction has developed jurisdictional entities to any extent, however. The original (1939) vision that some of the work of general boards and agencies would be assumed by regional conferences has never materialized. The cost of maintaining both general and regional structures is simply too great and has been viewed—even within the Southeast—as a duplication of effort.

Some United Methodists feel that the rationale for Jurisdictional Conferences, created to make a particular church union possible, has dissipated. Region alone does not justify locating these tasks and the expense of carrying them out on a regional basis. At the same time, the size and brevity of General Conference makes it unlikely that elections of bishops and general agency members could practically be accomplished in its sessions as in decades past. Moreover United Methodists from regions of smaller membership would want some guarantee that their nominees would have a chance of being elected. Those who want to change the jurisdictional system will probably seek a new regionalism that looks toward a connection organized globally. New regional conferences might assume more powers from General Conference, with the latter meeting less often as a global body. Such a plan could build on similarities between Jurisdictional and Central Conferences.

Central Conferences

All the predecessor bodies now part of United Methodism began mission work outside of the U.S. in the nineteenth century. At first through mission associations and then increasingly through denominational units, American churches supported the building of churches, schools, hospitals, agricultural stations, and many other institutions. This was a pragmatic evangelism that put the gospel into action in the everyday social and economic problems of many nations.

As increasing numbers of indigenous people became active in mission churches, they wanted training as lay and clergy leaders. They sought some measure of participation and control in church matters in their own countries. The 1884 MEC *Discipline* passed legislation authorizing delegated bodies called Central Conferences, perhaps borrowing the terminology from "central committees" then common in mission and ecumenical work. The first of these organized in India, and over the next fifty years several more came into being along with numerous annual conferences.

Many conferences that originated as missions from the U.S. sought autonomy under indigenous leaders. Some autonomous conferences have retained an affiliation with United Methodism; some remain separate. Thus contemporary world Methodism is comprised partly of The United Methodist Church, partly of British Methodism, partly of autonomous churches begun as missions from either the U.S. or Britain (e.g., Korea, Kenya), partly of united churches which Methodist groups joined (e.g., Church of South India), and partly of continuing missions from the U.S. or other countries.

Affiliated Autonomous Methodist Churches and Affiliated United Churches are those which enter a covenant agreement with United Methodism for mutual recognition of members and ministers. They have delegate representation at General Conference, with expenses paid and voice but not vote (¶¶546, 547). Nonaffiliated autonomous and united churches may retain a relationship with United Methodism, particularly through the Board of Global Ministries.

The longtime relationship of predominantly white U.S. United Methodism as sender of missionaries and resources and conferences of other countries as receivers endures in many provisions of the *Discipline*. The Council of Bishops, for example, is still charged with undertaking episcopal visitations to Methodist work in non-U.S. countries but not within the U.S. The Board of Global Ministries remains the most significant American contact point and conduit of resources for non-U.S. churches. The *Discipline* (¶¶554-563) retains legislation for Provisional Annual Conferences (lacking sufficient members to constitute an annual conference), Missionary Conferences (organized to meet the unique needs of a region or ethnic group), and Missions—all entities put into practice mainly in non-U.S. countries and/or with nonwhite populations in the U.S. (Red Bird Missionary Conference, deriving from EUB mission work in Appalachia, is one exception).

Over the last fifty years the assumed relationship of mission sender and mission receiver has changed dramatically. Central Conferences have had a growing place in United Methodism. They have enjoyed remarkable membership growth and consequently

273

greater representation in General Conference. Indigenous leadership is strong enough now that U.S. bishops no longer are assigned to preside over non-U.S. conferences, as they were even into the 1960s.[19]

In 1940 the MC established a General Conference Commission on Central Conference Affairs in order to coordinate the relationship of the widespread Central Conferences with the predominantly American General Conference. In current UMC polity the Council of Bishops has close oversight of this Commission. A bishop chairs it; its members are named by the Council of Bishops; a bishop from each Jurisdiction and Central Conference serves on it, along with a clergy and a lay member of each as well. The Commission meets simultaneously with General Conference (¶2201).

The powers of Central Conferences are broad in some decisions and specifically dependent on General Conference in others. The Commission mainly handles the latter, such as authorization for creating new annual conferences or episcopal areas within Central Conferences. The Commission's recommendations then must be approved by the General Conference. Current conferences are listed legislatively in the *Discipline* (¶535.3).

Central Conferences have wide latitude to adapt United Methodist polity to indigenous cultures and practices. They may govern themselves with their own *Discipline*, which must incorporate the Constitution and general church legislation, but then may add a Central Conference's unique legislation for local churches, annual conferences, and other matters. They are free to manage church property according to local laws, and of course, to interpret Article XXIII of the Articles of Religion (loyalty to the U.S. government) in relation to their own civil governments. They may adopt their own forms of rituals, ministerial preparation, or lay membership qualifications.

As part of United Methodism, though, Central Conferences may not enact legislation contrary to the Constitution, including the Restrictive Rules. This results in constant tests of what is appropriate for cultural adaptation and what is necessary to remain part of one internationally constituted ecclesiastical body (¶537).

Central Conference sessions are held within one year after the General Conference, with an equal number of lay and clergy delegates from all annual conferences and provisional annual conferences within its bounds. A bishop presides and decides questions of church law, which may subsequently be reviewed either by the Judicial Council or by the Central Conference's own Judicial Court (¶536). The Conference elects bishops as necessary, sets their terms, and assigns them to areas and residences.

Central Conferences also elect clergy and laypersons to a nomination pool for general agency membership. Each agency has its own designated number of Central Conference members, whom they elect from the pool. Most agencies also provide for a Central Conference bishop to be a member.

Jurisdictional and Central Conferences are somewhat similar, then, as regional conferences mediating between annual conferences and the General Conference. They have certain powers of election and assignment of bishops and election of general agency members. Their roles differ most markedly in that Central Conferences must adapt the *Discipline* to the laws and cultures of various nations, while all the Jurisdictions are within the U.S.

Obviously the current place of Central Conference participants in the general church is inadequate. While all bishops from Central Conferences may attend Council of Bishops meetings, they are thrown together in one "college" there even though they represent entirely distinct cultures from various parts of the world. They remain in outsider status in this regard. Similarly, U.S. participants tend to lump together all Central Conference delegates to General Conference and members of general agencies. Yet the only thing they have in common is being United Methodists—and not being from the U.S. Any plans for a global church will need to embody a fresh understanding of all United Methodists as full and equal members of the church.

General Agencies

From a constitutional standpoint, the general agencies of the church are an expression of General Conference powers. General program boards derive from the General Conference power "to initiate and direct all connectional enterprises of the Church and to provide boards for their promotion and administration" (¶15.8). Administration and finance agencies carry out the General

Conference responsibility "to determine and provide for raising and distributing funds necessary to carry on the work of the Church" (¶15.9). General Conference creates commissions through its power "to establish such commissions for the general work of the Church as may be deemed advisable" (¶15.13).

Therefore general agencies are a creature of General Conference and amenable to it. "Amenability" is generally understood to mean that they are expected to carry out the programs and mandates adopted by General Conference. Their basic powers, membership, and structure must be passed by General Conference and printed in the *Discipline*. This creates an "Administrative Order" chapter of over 200 pages.[20]

General agencies must report to the General Conference each quadrennium, and *ad interim* they are accountable to the two General Councils created by the General Conference. The General Council on Ministries has oversight of the program responsibilities of general agencies. The General Council on Finance and Administration has oversight of their financial affairs. This accountability is not, however, the same as amenability. That is, general agencies must report to GCOM and GCFA, but only General Conference can give general agencies certain mandates or responsibilities. Neither GCOM nor GCFA is a continuing executive body of General Conference between its sessions; they are councils of "review and oversight" (¶703.1).

The members or directors of the general agencies are elected from Jurisdictional and Central Conference nomination pools. Many of these persons were delegates to the General Conference initiating the quadrennium in which they serve as members. Many return as delegates to the next General Conference, thus providing a continuous link of accountability and communication.

The Council of Bishops shares constitutionally in the oversight of general agencies as part of the episcopal power of "general oversight and promotion of the temporal and spiritual interests of the entire Church" (¶45). Bishops serve as members of each general agency. By tradition bishops are elected president of each as well.[21] While bishops do not report the activities of general agencies to General Conference or in any other way act as executives of the general agencies, they are critical links in communicating and promoting agency work.

Constitutionally, then, general agencies are the creature of General Conference. They are amenable to it. They are presided over by and subject to the oversight of bishops.

Historically, though, general agencies originated from many different lines of development and their purposes have evolved in response to a variety of needs and circumstances. They comprise a number of enterprises, some of which have enjoyed wide autonomy over the years and expressed the interests of distinct constituencies. Some activities have continued for generations, with their own histories, leaders, meeting places, and cultures of language and symbol.

Even the program boards have parallel functions only in the most general terms; their actual activities vary enormously. In this way they express something of the scope of United Methodist people and their vocations and interests.

The 1968 union of the Methodist and EUB Churches was the occasion for reconsidering how best to manage general church activities. Both uniting denominations had their own agencies which needed to be merged in some way. The General Conference created a Structure Study Commission which reported in 1972, and its proposal was largely accepted.

The Commission sought mainly to reduce "the number of boards and agencies which would have as an end result a more efficient and effective organization." The plan was intended to eliminate "overlapping and multiple approaches to the annual conferences and the local churches," and to create more accountability, flexibility, and inclusiveness.[22]

The 1972 plan forced the merger of previously separate Boards for Education, Evangelism, and Laity into a single General Board of Discipleship (GBOD). In a very few years the staffs in education, evangelism, youth ministry, campus ministry, and other departments were vastly reduced. This eliminated many programs and resources on which local churches and annual conferences had depended.

Separate Boards for Missions and Health and Welfare Ministries were joined in a new General Board of Global Ministries (GBGM). The new Board was in turn divided into three Divisions—World, National, and Women's—pushing together many different mission institutions and initiatives with their own organizational cultures.

One need read only ¶1305.3 to see the names of seventeen historically separate mission enterprises the new Board was expected to
coordinate and manage. The Commission on Ecumenical Affairs
was also lumped into this Board, even though it had a distinct purpose; this was later recognized and remedied by creating a separate
General Commission on Christian Unity and Interreligious
Concerns (GCCUIC).

Ministry, higher education, and theological education offices
were brought together into a single General Board of Higher
Education and Ministry (GBHEM). The old Board of Christian
Social Concerns was renamed the General Board of Church and
Society (GBCS).

In addition to the four general program boards, the new structure continued four administrative units. The General Board of
Pensions needed to be independent for legal reasons and was managing vastly expanded pension monies for individuals and annual
conferences. The General Board of Publication continued to oversee the United Methodist Publishing House. The Commission on
Archives and History was authorized to manage historical records.
United Methodist Communications (UMCom) was originally a
Joint Committee on Communications, but in 1976 became a separate general agency.

Given the continuing mergers of former Central Jurisdiction
annual conferences with majority white annual conferences, and
the racial integration of lay and clergy leadership in all parts of the
church, the 1968 General Conference also created a General
Commission on Religion and Race (GCRR). Its purpose is to advocate full and equal participation of all persons in the life of the
church, and to monitor the progress of local churches, conferences,
agencies and institutions toward that goal.

Similarly, as women began to move into lay and clergy leadership roles in the church, the 1972 General Conference created what
became the General Commission on the Status and Role of Women
(GCSRW). This commission advocates full and equal participation
of women, monitors the church's progress on gender issues, and
acts as a catalyst for new structures that ensure inclusiveness.

A Commission on United Methodist Men was created by the
1996 General Conference, for "the coordination and resourcing of
men's ministry." This commission does not share the formative his-

tory of the other advocacy commissions (GCRR and GCSRW). Rather it came about through the splitting off of existing programs for UM Men from the much larger GBOD, where this office had been located since 1972. It focuses on programs that are "geared to men's needs" and seeks to "assist men in their ever-changing relationships, roles, and responsibilities in their family setting, workplace, and society" (¶2302).

The genius of the 1972 structure was its design for units in each annual conference and local church parallel to the General agencies, creating a continuous chain of communication between local, regional, and national and international units sharing a similar purpose. The 1972 plan thus also forced mergers and reorganization in every annual conference and local church.

In particular the General Council on Ministries (GCOM) and parallel annual conference and local church units was centrally placed to initiate and coordinate program and mission. The idea for the GCOM came partly from the EUB unit called the Program Council, and partly from a Methodist unit called the Co-ordinating Council. The former existed to initiate and carry out programs of ministry and mission. The latter existed to encourage joint planning by program boards and eliminate duplication of effort. The GCOM idea brought the two purposes together into one planning and coordinating effort.

Coordination also means control, however, and the COM structure in annual conferences and the general church has often been criticized for trying to do too much. The GCOM, for example, is charged with evaluating the program work of all the general agencies (¶906.14). This alone is an enormous undertaking and overwhelms the relatively small GCOM staff and resources. As a result the GCOM may tug and slow the program process to fit its management limits, rather than freeing up agencies to do what they are charged to do. Similarly the annual conference COMs have often tended to act as a funnel through which all initiatives must pass. This may dampen fresh ideas and prevent creative persons from attempting new programs.

The General Council on Finance and Administration (GCFA) acts similarly as a body for coordination and control. It receives recommendations from the GCOM about the program needs of the general agencies. It then devises a budget for all general agencies and refers it back to GCOM. From this process emerges a sum for the World Service Fund, by which all general agency budgets are supported. Over seventeen other funds also come under the management of GCFA. Many of these funds are then apportioned by a balanced formula to the various annual conferences to become part of the annual conference budget. That budget is in turn apportioned to the local churches by the annual conference CFA.

The GCFA has to try to anticipate what people will give in the coming quadrennium and budget accordingly. Since annual conferences generally pay less than 100% of their apportionments, GCFA has to negotiate between what money is likely to come in and what money the general agencies need in order to operate. Here again the agencies may be limited by such a process. While it does produce a definite income by which they can plan their work, the process may also prevent them from raising funds to support new activities.

The GCFA also monitors and coordinates the personnel and employment policies of all the general agencies through a committee made up of representatives from each (¶¶805.4.d, 807.11). It conducts regular audits and financial reviews of all agency treasuries through another committee (¶805.4.b).

Numerous additional controls have been legislated besides the "review and oversight" functions of the GCOM and GCFA. The heads of general agencies, titled general secretaries, cannot serve more than twelve years in their posts without special action. They must be reelected annually by the GCOM.

Several controls over general agency response to public political issues are in place. Each general agency must "keep a continuous record of its advocacy roles, coalitions, and other organizations supported by membership or funds" with particular attention to the "federal or state legislation" such coalitions may be advocating or opposing (¶717). Any general agency issuing a "written public policy statement" must make clear that it is a statement of the agency only, and not of the UMC (¶509.1). A general agency advocating a boycott must follow certain guidelines and cannot announce a boycott in the name of the UMC (¶702.5).

Other controls govern politics internal to the church. A general agency cannot initiate a program or expend funds in any region without consulting with the presiding bishop and annual conference bodies (¶718). No funds may be expended that "promote the acceptance of homosexuality" (¶806.9). All general agency meetings must be open to the public and the press, and all documents handed out in open meetings are considered public. Only certain considerations that must be confidential, such as property sales, personnel matters, or litigation, can be conducted in closed meetings (¶721).

All these controls reflect a long history of tension between general agencies and other units of the church, including bishops, conferences, and local churches. To understand the tension requires first a careful look at what general agencies are asked to do. They carry enormous responsibilities on behalf of the whole connection. They oversee and evaluate institutions supported by the whole church. They train and certify many kinds of personnel for ministry. They are charged with carrying out what General Conference puts in place as the mission of the whole church. In short, the general agencies perform the basic functions of denominations as discussed in chapter 2 above. They are not the only units by any means, but they are the only general church units to perform these functions.

In order to carry out these duties well, the general agencies recruit and employ the best persons possible. This brings into service talented, creative, and assertive individuals who want to get things done. They take their responsibilities seriously. They come to meetings—and especially to General Conference—well prepared to advocate a point of view that they have studied and discussed in depth. Their preparation and enthusiasm can sweep ordinary delegates and even bishops off their feet.

Thus tensions are inevitable. Tensions can be creative and productive; an organization without tension is not doing anything constructive. On the other hand, general agencies unquestionably do get wrapped up in their responsibilities at times without adequate communication to the wider church. In the 1960s, for example, mission and social concerns staff wanted their agencies to be a catalyst for civil rights. They did not want to wait on agreement from annual conferences in areas resisting civil rights. They thought themselves to be acting on behalf of the whole church, even if it rankled some parts of the church. Similarly some general agencies have undertaken protests and boycotts against major corporations, not taking into account the lag between their action and church members becoming better informed about the issues provoking the boycotts.

Bishops have oversight of general agencies and serve as members or directors as well as presidents. But they usually do not serve as long a term as the agency staff or even general secretary does. Moreover, bishops have complained for a long time that the jurisdictional system limits their presidential responsibilities to a region, while general secretaries and staff must relate to the whole connection. How can bishops have oversight equal to that of the people whose work they are charged with overseeing?[23]

Members or directors of the general agencies are unquestionably the strongest connection between agencies, conferences, and local churches. Every member or director was originally nominated by an annual, jurisdictional, and/or central conference. Every one is a member of a local church, and must be "persons of genuine Christian character who love the Church, are morally disciplined and loyal to the ethical standards" of the UMC (¶710.2). The agency membership sets policy, oversees and evaluates the staff, and authorizes new initiatives.

Yet members also serve limited terms—a maximum of eight consecutive years on any one agency and sixteen altogether (¶710.3). They meet as a plenary body only twice a year at most. While they divide themselves up to oversee particular divisions within an agency, they are not as equipped as full-time employed staff to see the work of the agency in depth. Since two-thirds of the members are laity, they must carry out their oversight task as volunteers adding this work to their regular employment usually outside the church.

Thus the ministry and mission of general agencies relies on a high level of trust within the connection. The 1972 restructuring attempted to increase that trust by creating the COM as a body for accountability, and by moving the church toward greater inclusiveness in agency membership. The current *Discipline* calls for a ratio of one third clergy, one third lay men, and one third lay women, in most church bodies. The *Discipline* recommends that at least 30 percent of each jurisdiction's membership on a general agency be "racial and ethnic persons" (a euphemism for nonwhite)—thus far greater than the nonwhite proportion in the total membership (¶705.5.b). This helps create a critical mass of various ethnic groups so that all voices can be heard.

Many United Methodists question these measures of trust today. There are calls for greater accountability, for more immediate resourcing of annual conference and local church needs, for smaller agency memberships to reduce costs of meetings, for better communications. How all this can be accomplished in a global connection is always the challenge for reformers.

CHAPTER 10

Annual Conference

Anyone who has ever been a guest speaker or preacher at a United Methodist annual conference learns a fundamental truth about them: no one is in charge of annual conference. The invitation to speak may come from the bishop or any of a number of program groups. The letter explaining where the speech falls on the conference agenda will arrive from a planning or worship committee. Someone else may or may not contact the guest regarding housing and meals. A check for honorarium and expenses will come from yet another office. A guest cannot help but conclude that no one office or person is in charge of coordinating all these functions.

The *Discipline* mandates that a bishop (or an elder in the absence of a bishop) preside over conference sessions and guide the agenda. Certain powers and duties are spelled out; definite items must be covered and questions answered. Various conference units bring issues for discussion. Local churches may even present legislative petitions. But no single office or body has executive management of the enterprise as a whole.

Like the other conferences of United Methodism, then, annual conference is elusive. It exists only when it is meeting; when it adjourns it is no more, and no conference session can obligate the next session a year later. Yet General Conference gives to annual conference numerous powers and responsibilities which it must develop some permanent organization in order to carry out.

Thus annual conference functions because its participants need and want it to. Given its makeup as a disjointed set of members, offices, and interests, that annual conference works as well as it does is something of a marvel, a gift of the Spirit.

Annual conferences have grown by circumstance and necessity to a complex state that is part revival meeting, part educational forum, part promotional rally, part business meeting, part community of worship. As Russell Richey has noted, annual conferences originally developed around three common traits. They addressed polity, to be sure. They discussed and voted on arrangements of governance, authority, and decision making that embodied the connection. But they also became communities of "fraternity," a fellowship of the men in itinerant ministry. They were poignant moments of reunion for far-flung Methodist preachers. Conferences were times of revival as well, characterized by dynamic preaching, lusty singing, and magnetic gathering that brought Methodist people from across the surrounding countryside.[1]

The form and style in which those purposes have been carried out has been uniquely shaped in each conference's culture. The place of meeting, such as a denominational college or conference center, the personalities of major leaders, stories of past events, regional culture, and social interaction of people from all parts of the conference have combined to make each one a distinct organizational culture.

The traits of polity, fraternity, and revival have been vastly modified over the years, yet endure in many ways. Polity remains foremost. In fact, as annual conferences have grown more bureaucratized with large budgets and full-time staff, accompanied by printed agenda books and rules of procedure, they have become increasingly preoccupied with business matters.

Yet the quality of fellowship in conference is vitally important to many participants. No longer a "fraternity," the clergy gather once a year as a whole covenant community of both genders and many ethnicities to "see each other's face" and be reconnected with those to whom each clergyperson is accountable and from whom each draws some measure of friendship and collegiality.[2]

Of course, new communications technology and highway systems mean that conference members see or communicate with one another a great deal more than in days past. But conference is still the only collective gathering, and includes lay members who also become connected through friendship and shared interests. Conference is the only place through which members of all charges in the region have a chance to meet, express mutual concerns, and adopt common commitments.

Revival has given way to more formally planned worship, often set in the less than worshipful contexts of convention centers or gymnasia. Conference events do not draw large crowds from surrounding communities. Yet revival still breaks out. Preaching and Bible study are highlights of conference sessions. Spontaneous outpourings of the Holy Spirit are widely claimed and celebrated as clergy and laity together seek direction for the church in challenging times.[3]

The *Discipline* names the central purpose of annual conference as "mak[ing] disciples for Jesus Christ by equipping its local churches for ministry and by providing a connection for ministry beyond the local church" (¶601). Historically this purpose has focused on supporting a covenant community of clergy itinerating among the churches of the conference. From the beginning annual conference has been the gathering place of preachers, the community within the church to which the clergy belong, and the covenant of itineracy from which they receive annual appointments to places of ministry.

Laypersons were associated with conferences at first only as electors of lay delegates to General Conference beginning in the 1870s. In the MEC after 1900 a lay conference met alongside the clergy conference in order to discuss lay activities, vote on constitutional amendments, and elect delegates. In the MECS lay membership in conference was based on a numerical formula, with members elected at District Conferences.

In 1939 the MC adopted the Methodist Protestant practice of one layperson attending from each pastoral charge. Lay membership was dependent on the pastoral appointment, then, since one layperson could attend per pastor appointed to the charge. The UMC adopted the same method in 1968. In 1976 the *Discipline* mandated that a number of laity equal to the clergy membership of annual conference, including retirees, should be members. In most conferences the Districts elect at-large lay members to bring the number up to equality with clergy numbers.[4]

Lay members thus do not "represent" local churches in the usual sense of the term. Most attend as the lay member allotted per pastor of a charge, and many come from districts. Moreover, since charges range widely in size, lay members in no way represent certain numbers of members and their interests. Diaconal ministers, who attend as part of their amenability to annual conference, also count as lay members of conference.

Lay membership and clergy membership in annual conference are not equivalent, and the two continue to run on separate tracks when they are gathered. Laity are members for this conference only; they may or may not come back to the next one. They are constitutionally excluded from voting "on matters of ordination, character, and conference relations of ministers" (except for lay members of the BOM) (¶31). They play a critical role in interpreting to the "folks back home" what annual conference decides. But they may or may not take an active role in conference units, such as boards or committees, membership of which is not limited to lay members of annual conference.

Clergy membership, on the other hand, provides the vocational locus for clergypersons. Clergy church membership resides solely in the annual conference. Elders in full connection are in mutual covenant with the conference, committing themselves to accept an appointment (with consultation) and being assured of receiving an appointment each year. Clergy look to the conference to establish basic elements of their professional security, such as health insurance and pensions. In this sense, clergy members have much more at stake personally in annual conference than lay members do, and have their first loyalty there. Most clergy serve on some annual conference unit. Lay members have their first loyalty to the local church and have more stake than clergy do in protecting local church interests.

Annual conference is disjointed, then, in the way it is constituted. Moreover, it assembles the diverse interests of many different conference units, associations and agencies in the region. These may include program emphases (such as Vision 2000 or Ethnic Minority Local Church), organizations for men, women, and youth, institutions with strong constituencies (such as children's homes or colleges), or mission relationships with conferences in other parts of the world. How all these energies can be coordinated and to whom various bodies are amenable—given the absence of a single, central executive agency—are constant questions for annual conferences.

Annual Conferences and the Connection

Annual conferences are creatures of the General Conference and as such have certain limitations on their powers (¶604). Annual conferences cannot change their own boundaries, for example; this power belongs to Jurisdictional Conferences (delegated from

General Conference). Annual conferences are obligated to carry out whatever mandates and budgets General Conference adopts for the whole connection. They must report accurately on the forms provided by general church agencies. They cannot issue any statement on behalf of the whole connection, or financially obligate any unit of the UMC except the annual conference itself.

On the other hand, annual conferences enjoy remarkable autonomy. They alone can admit, maintain, or remove persons from clergy or diaconal relationship with the conference. They can undertake mission initiatives, capital funds drives, or special ministries without the approval of any other unit of the connection. Many conferences are reorganizing extensively within the limits the *Discipline* provides, in order to put more energy and resources into evangelism, missions, and leadership development.

In fact, both the *Discipline* and the practices of annual conferences across the connection indicate a tendency to make them permanent regional units of the church. This marks a shift in orientation from time (annual) to space (geography). A number of factors have contributed to this trend over the last forty years. Annual conferences are merging, with many corresponding to the state lines of the civil states of which they are a part. This creates a strong loyalty and autonomy of governance reinforced by the ethos of the civil state. Many clergy never transfer among conferences, serving their entire careers in the clergy system of their geographic conference. The majority of bishops now preside over only one conference, creating pressure on them to become executive administrators of conference program and ministry.

The 1972 structural plan for the connection created a strong Council on Ministries at the center of every annual conference, in most places the first bureaucracy ever established there. Instead of small, informal conferences lacking any major conference staff positions and focused almost entirely on the primary function of certifying and placing clergy, annual conferences have become large administrative units with full-time staff handling millions of dollars in pension and insurance plans as well as conference-wide programs. They are incorporated in order to own property, such as conference office buildings or the episcopal residence. Many of them have United Methodist Foundations that manage sizeable sums of permanent funds on behalf of the conference and its local churches.

These trends put the annual conferences in constant tension with the larger connection. Increasingly they resist relating to general church agencies, wanting to reserve more initiative and resources for their regions. They protest the amount of time bishops have to devote to the general church, repeatedly petitioning General Conference to mandate a certain amount of a bishop's time to be spent within the conference. They do not look to General Conference for guidance in program and structure, and more broadly do not view themselves as subdivisions of a single, unified national and global connection. They are more and more free-standing units who think of themselves as sending delegates or representatives to General Conference, much as the civil states have representatives in the U.S. Congress.[5]

The annual conference functions as a mediating unit between the local church and the general church. As United Methodists give increasing attention to the possibilities and prerogatives of local churches, they tug annual conferences toward the local as well, asking them to become the primary resourcing agency for local church ministry and mission. This trend puts General Conference and its general agencies in an adversarial position, defending their usefulness to regional and local units. Instead of annual conferences viewing themselves as regional units of one whole connection, they scrutinize, resist, protest, or warily accept General Conference actions as if "they" were a body of persons from some other organization, and not made up of delegates of each annual conference.

These tensions are inevitable and have persisted throughout Methodist history. The current atmosphere of conference autonomy may, however, bring a marked change to fundamental understandings of United Methodist polity. United Methodism may move toward becoming a coalition of regional churches rather than a unitary connection. What role the *Discipline* will then play in providing a common polity remains to be seen.

Conference Structures and Functions

The movement toward conference autonomy was greatly accelerated by the 1996 General Conference. New legislation moved the polity of annual conferences sharply away from mandated structures and toward a more functional approach. A constitutional amendment affirmed annual conference latitude in creating "structures unique to their mission, other mandated structures notwithstanding" (¶15.15). The only conference units mandated specifically by name are those governing ordained ministry (Board of Ordained Ministry, Board of Pensions, Committee on Episcopacy, Administrative Review Committee, and Committee on Investigation) and conference property (Board of Trustees).

Other annual conference units for administration and program are named and their functions described, but in each case with the phrase "or other structure to provide for the functions of this ministry and maintain the connectional relationships" (e.g., ¶609). Thus while Disciplinary paragraphs still specify the membership, powers, and amenability of conference units, only their functions are truly mandated. The conference is free to design and relate units as it sees fit.

This marks a dramatic shift in the understanding of authority and decision making in the conferences, and perhaps in the connection as a whole. Many conferences are moving toward functionalism and flexibility, using names drawn from current systems management lingo such as vision team or ministry team. The advantage of this style is its fluidity as persons work together to accomplish specific goals and then move to other tasks. The disadvantage lies in the loss of Disciplinary structures for accountability, amenability, and authorization for action. Each conference must now invent these for itself.

From 1972 to 1996 the *Discipline* mandated two Councils in each annual conference with primary responsibility for coordination and administration. The Council on Ministries (ACCOM) was "to be responsible for the development, administration, and evaluation of the program of the Annual Conference and to encourage, coordinate, and support the conference agencies, districts, and local churches in their ministry and various programs." In effect this made the ACCOM the central body through which all proposals for programs to be carried out by other conference units had to be funneled for review and authorization (1992 *Discipline*, ¶726).

Membership of the ACCOM was designed to represent all major conference units and all districts. The ACCOM Director and staff held crucial positions of communication and coordination, and served as chief liaison between various conference units and between the conference and the general agencies.

The entire legislation authorizing and describing this body was removed by the 1996 General Conference. A new permissive paragraph has been put in its place, allowing each annual conference to organize in its own way "in order to accomplish its purpose . . . [and] provide for the connectional relationship[s]" (¶608). A conference could continue an ACCOM structure, of course, but without the Disciplinary description and authorization to define it.

The *Discipline* mandates that each annual conference develop program units that correspond with or relate to parallel units in the connection as a whole. These include the areas of Church and Society, Discipleship, Global Ministries, and Higher Education and Campus Ministry; the specialized focus of Archives and History, and Christian Unity and Interreligious Concerns; and the advocacy work of Religion and Race, and Status and Role of Women. The functions of these areas are described, but those functions can be assigned to whatever unit an annual conference invents. No unit specifically for the coordination of these functions is mandated or described, either.

The second Council, for Finance and Administration (CFA), continues to be fully described in the *Discipline*, but with the qualifying phrase that an equivalent structure may be designed as long as it carries forward the functions. Since this body or its functions involve numerous financial and legal matters, a crucial issue will be whether equivalent structures also carry the amenability and authorization specified in the *Discipline*. The 2000 General Conference added a mandate for "clear checks and balances" in program and finance (¶608.1).

This Council (or equivalent) develops and manages a budget for the annual conference. Made up of no more than twenty-one persons, including at least one more layperson than clergy in total, the council is amenable to and reports directly to the Annual Conference. It normally has no designated director, but the conference treasurer in effect serves as its chief administrator (¶¶609, 617).

Among many responsibilities, the CFA must collate the budget requests of all conference units together with the amount apportioned to the conference by the GCFA as part of the general church budget. The CFA then has to make an educated estimate of how much the local churches are willing to contribute, along with other sources of income.

The CFA presents a proposed budget to annual conference along with a proposed "decimal" or formula by which to apportion the budget among the churches. The decimal is usually a combination of a local church's proportion of all funds raised in the conference (excluding capital improvements and other items) as well as its proportion of the total local church membership of the conference. Once a conference member knows the decimal, she or he can simply take the proposed budget, multiply by the decimal, and see exactly what amount his or her local church will have to contribute toward the budget (¶613).

The major item in every U.S. annual conference budget today is clergy pensions and health insurance. This figure comes to the CFA from the conference Board of Pensions, one of three additional administrative units. The Board in turn works with both the General Board of Pension and Health Benefits and with the insurance plan in which the conference participates to determine how much money must be raised to fund the chosen pensions and insurance program (¶636).

Support of retired or—in the old lingo—"worn out" or "superannuated" clergy has always been a central concern of the connection. One of the 1808 Restrictive Rules permanently designated all net income of the church's publishing enterprises to the support of retired or disabled clergy and their families (¶20). The United Methodist Publishing House continues to deliver a check to each annual conference every year representing a proportional share of that income. But contemporary economics require a great deal more than that for adequate pensions.

In 1982 the UMC undertook an enormous shift in the way pensions are funded, moving away from a general pension fund on which retirees could draw simply based on years of service, and into a plan that is based specifically on contributions made by the individual clergy and the annual conference toward the individual's retirement account. Some annual conferences have moved even further toward billing local churches (or charges) directly for pension contributions. This prevents any local church from enjoying the services of clergy under appointment without making the appropriate contribution to the pension plan.

A second administrative unit that makes a significant impact on the CFA's budgeting work is the Commission on Equitable Compensation (or equivalent structure). The *Discipline* charges this unit with setting "a schedule of minimum base compensation" for pastors. The Commission also must consider those local churches or charges which cannot meet this standard, and estimate an amount called the Equitable Compensation Fund to be raised by the annual conference to subsidize this minimum support schedule.

Many people have questioned this Fund as a form of "welfare" for churches that cannot support a clergyperson.[6] Yet most conferences have continued to provide such support either to enable small churches to continue an effective ministry or to sustain a United Methodist witness in certain communities. The *Discipline* mentions Native American ministries specifically as warranting special attention in this regard (¶623).

A third administrative unit, the Board of Trustees, handles all matters relating to property owned by the annual conference, either real estate or permanent funds. The latter may be managed by a Foundation in order to provide specialized attention to investments and distributions of funds (¶¶2512, 2513).

Thus the CFA assembles an annual conference budget in three divisions. Far and away the largest part of the budget is comprised of funds designated for clergy support: pensions, insurance, equitable compensation, support for district superintendents, and an amount for the support of bishops that comes as the Episcopal Fund apportionment from the GCFA.

The second budget division is administration of the conference itself. Though there is no executive office per se, there are various administrative and coordinating functions such as the conference treasurer and the program staff. All these require salary and benefits support, as well as office expense.

The third budget division is funding to support the ministry and mission of the connectional church. Much of this amount is apportioned to the conference from the World Service Fund approved by General Conference. Another major portion of it is the budget to support annual conference programs. These two amounts together are called "World Service and Conference Benevolences."

The budget may, of course, include other special causes that the annual conference adopts, such as a capital funds drive for an institution related to the conference. In any case, no institution or organization related to United Methodism is allowed to approach local churches in an annual conference without approval from the annual conference upon recommendation of the CFA (¶612).

Ministry

Two boards and one committee oversee matters relating to particular categories of ministry. They serve to enable annual conferences to achieve their central task of equipping, credentialing, and placing persons for ministry. The Board of Laity (or equivalent structure) exists "to foster an awareness of the role of the laity" both within and outside the church. The *Discipline* charges it with developing training opportunities for laity, especially for lay speaking (¶629). The conference lay leader, elected by the whole conference, chairs the Board. This position is granted wide scope for "enabling and supporting lay participation" in the activities of the conference and its various units. The lay leader serves ex officio on major conference bodies (¶603.9). Other conference units also work to enhance lay ministry, including United Methodist Women, United Methodist Men, and the council on youth ministry.

The Board of Ordained Ministry (BOM) carries on the primary historic function of annual conference, handling all matters concerning the conference relations of clergy. The BOM is comprised mainly of clergy nominated by the presiding bishop, with between one-fifth and one-third lay members elected by the annual conference.

The BOM must prepare a report each year, based on the historic Disciplinary question and answer format, that includes all requests for changes of conference relations (retirement, leave of absence, etc.), admissions of probationary or full members, and reports of satisfactory progress in studies for those preparing for clergy membership. The BOM also develops policies regarding such matters as grievance procedures, continuing education, and clergy evaluation.

While the BOM must carry out its duties in full cooperation with the bishop, Cabinet, Board of Pensions, and other conference units, it is "directly amenable to the annual conference" (¶632.1.b). This language mainly refers, of course, to the conference in its historic sense, that is, the clergy session which alone has power over conference relations of clergy.

Third, the Committee on Episcopacy acts as a kind of "pastor-parish relations committee" for the bishop presiding over an annual conference. The *Discipline* charges the committee with representing to the bishop the needs of the area as well as conditions that "affect relationships between the bishop and the people." One of its most important functions is to carry to the Jurisdictional Committee on Episcopacy a recommendation regarding "needs for episcopal leadership," that is, a request to return the current bishop or to seek the appropriate new bishop (¶634).

Districts

Districts hold a peculiar place in United Methodist polity. They have no mandated constitutional standing and thus no formal role in constituting the connection. Yet they serve a critical function as a link of communication and fellowship for both laity and clergy.

The Constitution states only that district conferences "may be organized in an annual conference," but gives them no constitutional powers (¶40). Legislative paragraphs make clear that the organization and responsibilities of such conferences are a matter for annual conferences to determine. Thus the actual practices of district organization vary widely around the connection (¶¶653, 654).

The Constitution does mandate that "there shall be one or more district superintendents who shall assist the bishop in the administration of the annual conference" (¶51). This makes districts most explicitly an expression of superintendency, with particular reference to the appointing of clergy to their charges.

Thus from a constitutional standpoint districts appear to be essentially a subdivision of the superintendency created to make episcopal oversight of the church more effective. They appear to be secondarily a geographic subdivision of the annual conference intensifying and making more local certain annual conference functions.

In fact, however, several critical powers do belong legislatively to districts. The *Discipline* mandates a district committee on ordained ministry, charged with supervising all candidacy for ordained ministry and issuing certificates of completed and approved candidacy—the first step toward ordination (¶660). The *Discipline* locates the organization and administration of new church starts with the district superintendent, and mandates a district board of church location and building (¶¶259, 2518). The latter must approve all church sites, building plans, property purchases, and renovations that exceed 10 percent of a building's value. Many districts also have a District Union or participate in a Church Extension Society to raise and manage funds for building or expanding local churches (¶654.4).

The *Discipline* mandates a committee on district superintendency to provide support and feedback for the DS, manage the district parsonage, and consult with the bishop regarding appointment of the DS (¶663). The *Discipline* requires that two lay organizations, United Methodist Women and United Methodist Men, also organize in each district as well as in each annual conference and local church (¶¶664, 665). A lay leader is elected in each district—usually by a district conference—and is a member of annual conference as well as key administrative and program bodies of the district (¶¶655, 30).

Moreover, in many annual conferences the districts are fully developed along the permissive lines suggested in the *Discipline*. Though the structure is no longer described in the *Discipline*, many have councils on ministries to act as liaison with the annual conference and to coordinate and initiate program and mission among the churches of a district. Many have district program officers parallel to the annual conference structure in areas such as church and society or religion and race. Many support youth ministry programs, lay speaking, and lay activities.

Districts may also play a crucial role in financing the annual conference budget. In some conferences the historic practice has been to apportion the budget to the districts. A district Board of Stewards then distributes to each local church or charge the proportional amount needed to meet the district apportionment

(¶613.3). In all conferences the DS is expected to notify each local church or charge of its apportionment (¶246.13).

The United Methodist Church in the U.S. currently has over 500 districts. They vary greatly in geographic area, membership size, and number of local churches. Some districts in the Midwest and West cover so many miles that any kind of district work is a major effort and expense. Other districts in urban regions are compact and highly organized, becoming an essential expression of connectional mission.

All districts have some role to play as the "glue" for connecting the actions of annual conference with the local churches. Like annual conferences, districts hold a mediating place and are caught in the inevitable tension between local autonomy and connectional authority. Many people advocate making district superintendency more local, more related to churches and their clergy and missional needs, and less a function of conference administration. Many districts would like to keep more resources available for sponsoring new churches and mission work in which local churches can fully participate.

On the other hand, local churches will be reluctant to support the expense of much organizational structure in districts. Most districts have minimal staff and office space, with administration done directly by the district superintendent. Districts depend heavily on clergy and lay volunteer time to carry out their functions. These commitments can build high morale among the churches of a district, which in turn builds enthusiasm for full participation in the initiatives of annual conference.

But district structures themselves are likely to remain lean and oriented to specific tasks. The development of districts will continue to depend heavily on the leadership of district superintendents and of interested clergy and laity.

CHAPTER 11

Church Property

The legal and ecclesiological status of church property in United Methodism exemplifies the character of Methodist tradition as a synthesis of polities. Neither entirely organic nor entirely congregational in its handling of property, United Methodism combines elements of each in a third mode. Largely unchanged over two hundred years, the model has been fiercely defended and consistently upheld in the civil courts of the U.S. Property laws vary, of course, in other nations in which United Methodism is active.

In organic polities with a monarchical episcopacy (such as Roman Catholicism), church property—including local churches or parish buildings—is owned in the name of the bishop of a diocese, who for legal purposes is considered to be a corporation holding title. All decisions about the disposition of property must pass through the bishop's office.

In congregational polities, each local church congregation owns its own property outright. Associations, conferences, and synods may have varying degrees of influence over how local churches dispose of property, but the title is in the name of a local church corporation with designated trustees.

In United Methodism, as well as the Presbyterian Church USA and other connectional churches, local church property is held "in trust" for the denomination.[1] This key phrase means, on the one hand, that the property deed is in the local church's name (preferably as incorporated under the laws of the particular state). Management, upkeep, and initiatives for renovation or expansion of property are in the hands of local church trustees and charge conferences. On the other hand, local church trustees can undertake no major transactions regarding the property under their stewardship without approval from the connection, specifically, the district superintendent and district committee on church location and building. While the bishop does not hold title, local church property and assets revert to the annual conference (if the local church is abandoned or discontinued) and thus are reserved for the exclusive use of The United Methodist Church.[2]

Model Deeds

The trust clause has its roots in eighteenth century English Methodism. While property laws were different there, similar legal issues arose. As a society or association, English Methodism had a peculiar status on the boundaries of the Church of England. Methodist chapels or preaching houses clearly were not Church of England property, since no Methodist activities were officially authorized or approved by the Church. On the other hand, John Wesley and other Methodist leaders were concerned that chapels and preaching houses not be held solely by local trustees. They wanted them used for services in accord with Methodist teaching under duly appointed preachers. In particular Wesley did not want local trustees to bring in Dissenting preachers who would advocate separation from the Church (even though the buildings themselves were obviously separate).

Therefore the English conference began as early as 1746 to require a "model deed" assuring that only those preachers appointed by Wesley or the conference and teaching Methodist doctrine would have use of the pulpits. Local trustees could neither bring in unapproved preachers or exclude preachers duly appointed. When issues of a succession of authority began to cluster around an aging Wesley, the exact meaning of the Conference had to be more closely defined. Thus the Deed of Settlement of 1784 specified one hundred names of preachers who would legally constitute the Conference. The Model Deed of that year included the wording to

> permit such persons and no others as shall be appointed at the yearly Conference of the people called Methodists . . . to have and to enjoy the said premises for the purposes aforesaid: provided always, that the persons preach no other doctrine than is contained in Mr. Wesley's *Notes on the New Testament*, and four volumes of sermons.[3]

The 1784 Deeds made even clearer Methodism's legal independence of the Church of England, which combined with the Church's refusal to approve Methodism under canon law to bring about the constitution of Methodism as a separate church in England in 1836.

Under the emerging laws of the U.S., the early Methodist Episcopal Church could have set up a property system more organic in nature. There was, after all, no established church from which to assert independence as a society. Of course, there was no established church to which Methodists could—in true Wesley form—pledge their enduring allegiance either. American Methodists ended by handling their property along the same lines as the English Methodists, only now in the context of a voluntary society. This gave them a system both more organic than many independent-minded Americans desired, and incorporating more congregational autonomy than organic polities would allow. It was, in short, a connectional property system.

The first Deed recorded in the Methodist Episcopal Church in America was contained in the 1796 *Discipline*. Here the Deed reserved church property

> *for the use of members of the Methodist Episcopal Church in the United States of America, according to the Rules and Discipline which from time to time may be agreed upon and adopted by the ministers and preachers of the said Church, at their General Conferences in the United States of America;* and in further trust and confidence that [the trustees] shall at all times, forever hereafter, permit such ministers and preachers, belonging to the said Church, as shall from time to time be duly authorized by the *General Conferences* of the ministers and preachers of the said Methodist Episcopal Church, or by the yearly Conferences *authorized by the said General Conference, and none others,* to preach and expound God's Holy Word therein.[4]

From the first, then, the General Conference and the annual conferences constituted by the General Conference had sole determination of how Methodist property would be used. On the other hand, at no time did the General Conference—or annual conferences—actually own or hold title to local church property. As Asbury and Coke interpreted the system in their explanatory notes on the 1798 *Discipline*, the property of the preaching houses will not be invested in the general conference. But the preservation of our union and the progress of the work of God indispensably require, that the free and full use of the pulpits should be in the hands of the general conference, and the yearly conferences authorized by them. Of course, the travelling preachers, who are in full connection, assembled in their conferences, are the patrons of the pulpits of our churches.

They quickly explained further, though, that this did not exclude from Methodist pulpits the local preachers who were not members in full connection.[5]

The Trust Clause and the Local Church

The legal character of General Conference (or its annual conferences) as the party controlling ministry in local churches but not as owner of local church property has continued unchanged. As we have seen, the current *Discipline* makes clear that "The United Methodist Church" does not exist as an entity (¶139). Therefore, no title can show either "The United Methodist Church" or "The General Conference of The United Methodist Church" as owner (¶2501). Many entities within the denomination are incorporated and thus can hold title to property—including local churches, annual conferences, agencies, and institutions. All such deeds must indicate that the property is held in trust for The United Methodist Church. But this does not mean that the denomination as a whole owns the property. As the trust clause states it,

> In trust, that said premises shall be used, kept, and maintained as a place of divine worship of the United Methodist ministry and members of The United Methodist Church; subject to the Discipline, usage, and ministerial appointments of said church as from time to time authorized and declared by the General Conference and by the Annual Conference within whose bounds the said premises are located [¶2503].

The *Discipline* further clarifies the same issue that troubled the English societies in the eighteenth century. A local church board of trustees

302

shall not prevent or interfere with the pastor in the use of any of the said property for religious services or other proper meetings or purposes recognized by the law, usages, and customs of The United Methodist Church, or permit the use of said property for religious or other meetings without the consent of the pastor, or in the pastor's absence, the consent of the district superintendent [¶2532.1].

Thus the connection retains its interest in the ministry that occurs in and through a local church, while not itself owning and operating the property.

What exactly the trust clause means in referring to uses of property being "subject to the Discipline" remains undefined. Presumably it must mean among other things that the doctrines expounded through the pulpit and program of ministry must accord with the standards protected by the Restrictive Rules.[6] But the local board of trustees is not the judge of such accord. A local church's very acceptance of a pastor under appointment indicates its willingness to be subject to the trust clause (even if the trust clause is not specifically written into a particular property deed). This in effect places the prerogative to determine local church ministries and to exercise discipline over local churches in the hands of the respective annual conferences (¶2503.6).

A denomination as expansive as United Methodism has been in the U.S. cannot expect to have consistency in all its property relationships, of course. The *Discipline* attempts to protect the name "Methodist" or "United Methodist" from use by organizations not authorized by the conferences (¶2502). It establishes control of the "official insignia" of the church, such as the cross and flame (¶807.8). But use of symbols is difficult to control in a large, international voluntary association in which United Methodist people are continually creating new parachurch organizations. Conversely, hundreds of local churches or chapels bear the name—especially in rural areas—but have only a tenuous relation with an annual conference. Many exist primarily as a cemetery association. Many are not incorporated, or not duly organized according to the *Discipline*.

The Disciplinary provisions for local boards of trustees attempt to allow some latitude for local traditions while also reining in some of the independence of these widely scattered local churches. The board may have as few as three or as many as nine members, but only two-thirds must be members of the UMC (thus allowing for churches, for example, that serve as chapels for a whole rural community). Trustees are in three equal, rotating classes of three-year terms to prevent domination by certain individuals (though nothing prevents a person's being reelected). The *Discipline* recommends that at least a third be men and at least a third women to ensure gender balance (¶¶2524, 2525). Unlike other church bodies, the trustees elect their own chairperson or president and other officers (¶2529.1). For legal reasons they also must have a quorum of a majority of their members (¶2531).

The *Discipline* makes clear that boards of trustees are amenable to the direction of the charge conference in such matters as sales, mortgages, gifts or bequests. This keeps property decisions open to the wider congregation as well as the district superintendent who presides (¶2528). Both the DS and the pastor must give written consent to any sale, transfer, leave, or mortgage of property (¶¶2539, 2540).

Any purchase, sale, mortgage, building plan or renovation of property amounting to 10 percent or more of its value must be approved not simply by the board of trustees but by the district board of church location and building and by the charge conference. Both of the latter are under the presidency of the district superintendent, thus reinforcing ties to the connection. Building and renovation plans must be studied first by a building committee established for that purpose. The whole congregation is invited to participate in any proposed decision through a church conference, the only occasion for which such a conference is mandated (¶2543).

Property and Prosperity

As United Methodist people have prospered economically, many local churches have acquired valuable investment property and endowments. While any such assets also are held in trust for The United Methodist Church and revert legally to the annual conference to be used for its purposes, in truth the connection has made little effort to influence the use of these holdings.

The *Discipline* provides for a permanent endowment fund committee or even a local church foundation to be established, which would give special attention to what is otherwise a trustees function (¶¶2533, 2534). Local churches are encouraged to invest their money in accord with the Social Principles, and to place their endowment funds with an annual conference or area United Methodist Foundation for management (¶2532.5).[7] The *Discipline* charges district superintendents with the almost impossible task of keeping "accurate and complete records" of "all known endowments, annuities, trust funds, investments, and unpaid legacies belonging to any pastoral charge or organization connected therewith in the district" (¶423.7.c).

The connection has not established much regulation of assets, though, or found any way to distribute income from local churches with plenty to local churches in need of resources. The *Discipline* does state that a local church cannot mortgage its property to pay current expenses, nor can it sell property to pay its current bills (¶2542). But these limitations do not speak to the growing issues of what a generously endowed local church should do when its current members either cannot or will not financially support the church's program, or what action a local church should take when it receives a bequest that dwarfs the gifts of even its major donors.

Should a local church of vastly diminished membership spend its endowment to artificially prop up the pastoral salary, hire professional musicians, or maintain an enormous building? Should a local church that receives a bequest worth millions of dollars simply retain that money as an investment? Is it appropriate for a local church to own land or buildings not used directly for church purposes (aside from the tax liability that may be incurred)? Does the stewardship of current members suffer under conditions of endowed wealth? What should the church teach about material possessions through its financial policies? The General Conference so far has not addressed these questions legislatively. Within the breadth of the trust clause, local churches retain autonomy to manage their own monies as long as they continue their ministries.

The point at which the trust clause really kicks in, of course, is when local church property is abandoned or the ministries of a congregation are discontinued. In such a case, with the approval of the district superintendent, property reverts to the administration of the annual conference Board of Trustees. That Board then must seek approval of the annual conference to sell such properties. The proceeds then must be used for other purposes within the connection (¶2548).

Despite the strong sense of connection that arises from a conference's being able to use for another need such money faithfully given to the church, no moment of annual conference business is more painful than the decision to sell a local United Methodist church property. United Methodists do not like to acknowledge that their ministries may be less than viable or at an end in a given locale. It may be some consolation that all documents, memorabilia, and any other assets of the church are kept in perpetuity by the annual conference.

When a congregation is relocating—continuing its ministries as a local church in a new place—it must first offer its property to another United Methodist church at fair market value. This is another effort to keep properties in the connection, and to avoid tensions that arise, for example, when a predominantly white congregation decides to move out of a predominantly black neighborhood (¶2540.3).

Other Church-Owned Property

United Methodist entities other than local churches also own a great deal of property. Such entities are incorporated with trustees of their property holdings. Thus jurisdictional or annual conferences often own office buildings, retreat centers, camps, or episcopal residences. Districts own parsonages and offices. General agencies own office buildings and other properties. All such trusteeship is amenable to the respective conference for whose purposes the property is owned. In the case of general agencies, the *Discipline* authorizes the General Council on Finance and Administration to receive reports on all property owned by general agencies and to approve any sale or purchase of real estate. In such actions GCFA and the general agencies are finally amenable to the General Conference (¶807.1, .4).

Institutions such as colleges, hospitals, and homes are related to The United Methodist Church in various ways. Those which are "owned or controlled" by any conference or agency are required to structure their trustees with at least 60 percent United Methodist membership (¶2552). Many institutions are now autonomous with self-perpetuating boards of trustees. However, even they often retain by charter a certain level of United Methodist board membership.

Over the last twenty years an important new literature has grown up around trusteeship and the stewardship of institutions.[8] United Methodism, with its heritage of over two hundred years of institution-building, certainly must train and prepare members to be faithful stewards of the church's assets. The 36,000 local churches in the U.S. now own over $37 billion worth of property, increasing in value at the rate of over $1 billion per year.[9] Conference properties along with church related institutions add several billions more to this total.

The stewardship of this mass of property entails a variety of legal issues. For example, church property normally is exempt from government taxation and is assessed only for special purposes such as "street lights or sidewalk repairs." Church organizations need only file an exemption form.[10] However, many voices in the U.S. advocate taxation of church property as the only fair way to equitably distribute costs of municipal government, schools, and public services. Churches may have to decide if they agree with such an appeal to equity, or if it is more important to continue to insist on the strict separation of church and state.

Another example is the increasing concern with preventative measures and adequate insurance, especially in areas of liability for everything from personal injury on church property to sexual abuse to misuse of endowed funds. In a litigious society like the U.S., churches must take more care with legal procedures and protections.

Stewardship

More broadly than legal issues, stewardship of church property must be centrally focused on the use of property for the mission of the church. This concern takes a variety of forms. For example, the *Discipline* charges the local church board of trustees with conducting "an annual accessibility audit of their buildings, grounds, and facilities" to see what barriers prevent the full participation of "people with disabilities" (¶2532.6). Churches and institutions generally exhibited little awareness of accessibility problems before the 1960s. This has left to current generations an enormous bill for modifying existing buildings. Yet accessibility is a critical witness to inclusive community.[11]

In its general mandates for local churches, the *Discipline* insists that "each local church shall have . . . a missional outreach responsibility to the local and global community" (¶204). The church council is responsible for carrying out its "primary task and mission in the context of its own community" (¶242). Many local churches have responded to changes in middle class family life by organizing or hosting "parents day out" or day care centers. Many host meetings of community organizations or rallies on community issues. Many use their buildings for soup kitchens, shelters, or health clinics. Yet many other churches have resisted allowing their facilities to be used for community programs.

The *Discipline* makes no specific demands for missional uses of property, and says surprisingly little about the stewardship of church assets. Yet as United Methodists in the U.S. and other nations know, churches have a critical role to play in fostering a sense of common good and justice in the communities of which they are a vital part. Through effective use of their assets they have an opportunity particularly to minister with the poor—a central concern for those who follow in Wesley's way.[12] This mandate of discipleship is not explicit in United Methodist polity, however, leaving it to local churches to realize how essential their buildings and assets are for witness and service in Christ's name.

CHAPTER 12

Judicial Administration

One of the most obvious ways in which American United Methodism has adapted to contemporary social trends is in its elaboration of judicial procedures. American society has become increasingly litigious, with a vastly expanded regulatory role for government on behalf of the public, and with a growing body of legal precedent shaping individual rights. Similarly, the church has become increasingly focused on the consistency of church laws and their conformity with the church's Constitution. The church has given increasing attention as well to rules regulating full participation in the church and fair process in church personnel and complaint procedures.

The creation of a Judicial Council for The Methodist Episcopal Church South in 1934 marked the beginning of a new era in church law. The uniting conferences that formed The Methodist Church in 1939 and The United Methodist Church in 1968 both made the Judicial Council a constitutional body.

Prior to 1934 in the MECS, decisions regarding the constitutionality of General Conference legislation, as well as decisions or interpretations of church law, were made by the College of Bishops. The episcopacy's power to interpret law was long considered to be a crucial balance to the powers of General Conference to make legislation. If it disagreed with episcopal interpretations, General Conference would have to amend the *Discipline*. At the same time, voices in the MECS increasingly were raised against the power of bishops to block the will of the General Conference. The EUBC similarly gave the bishops judicial power over the constitutionality of legislation, subject to amendments by the General Conference.

In the MEC before 1939, decisions of law were referred to a Judiciary Committee of the General Conference. The MEC had always had a "higher" view of General Conference as the final

309

authority in the church, to which even bishops were ultimately amenable. Yet again, gradually voices were raised against the power of General Conference to rule on its own actions.

The Judicial Council plan resolved both of these objections by setting up a third body, neither legislative nor episcopal, to which various entities in the church could appeal. Viewed in the context of broad social change, the perceived need for a distinct ecclesiastical court had at least two sources. First, the increasing diversity of both American culture and the church made traditionally ascribed authority of officials (civil or ecclesiastical) increasingly questionable. The time had long passed when the church could simply operate something like a family; roles were becoming more specialized and bureaucratized. Members wanted and needed a locus of legal appeal not directly involved in either legislative or administrative interests.

Second, legal issues were becoming increasingly technical and complex, much too involved for a legislative assembly to adjudicate. It is striking in retrospect that laity who were leading judges and attorneys in their communities were most active in working for changes in the denomination's judicial administration. As a result of their efforts as specialists, the General and Uniting Conferences decided to create a separate body that could concentrate all its energies on legal issues. The *Discipline* says nothing about the qualifications of Judicial Council members, but General Conference has often elected attorneys to the lay positions.[1]

Over the past sixty years, the successive Judicial Councils have made more than nine hundred decisions on church law. These are now on record and form an expanding body of legal precedent to which the Council refers in its deliberations. Moreover, all Judicial Council decisions are final, meaning that appeal from them lies only in amending the church's Constitution or *Discipline*. To date, however, despite the growing influence of this legal material, no one has published a critical assessment of the impact of a distinct judiciary on the ecclesiology or practices of the church.

Judicial Council Decisions

As presently constituted, the Council has nine members, with five laity and four clergy in one quadrennium, four laity and five

310

clergy in the next. The Council of Bishops nominates three times the number of persons needed to fill vacancies and the General Conference then votes among those nominees. This provision allows the bishops to consider fully who is best qualified for the work, while still leaving the actual choice to the conference. Members serve eight-year terms, though they may be reelected (¶2602).

The Council has latitude to organize in its own way and develop rules of procedure. The *Discipline* mandates only certain procedures. It insists that no Judicial Council member discuss any pending case outside of the Council. It requires a quorum of seven, and sets an affirmative vote of six as the minimum required to rule a General Conference action unconstitutional (¶¶2607, 2608).

Beyond that, the Judicial Council has created its own structure, electing a President, Vice-President, and Secretary. It has established rules for preparation of briefs and for oral arguments. It meets at the call of the President, usually at least twice a year, with a mandated meeting during every General Conference session.

Matters coming before the Council fall into four main categories. First are declaratory decisions regarding the constitutionality or legality of actions taken by General, Jurisidictional, Central, or annual conferences, or by bodies created by General, Jurisdictional, or Central Conferences. These decisions must be requested by a certain majority of members, or by the Council of Bishops or Colleges of Bishops (¶¶2609, 2610).

Declaratory decisions enable conferences to write or revise legislation in conformity with the church's constitutional law. This procedure is especially helpful at General Conference sessions. With the Judicial Council meeting simultaneously at the same site, the conference can refer even proposed legislation for a ruling on constitutionality or legality, correct it, and pass it confident that the new legislation will stand further legal tests. Legislation ruled unconstitutional can, of course, be resubmitted as a constitutional amendment for approval by the General Conference and subsequently by the whole body of members of annual conferences.

A second category arises from the bishops' power of presiding over conferences. The Constitution mandates that bishops "shall decide all questions of law" that arise "in the regular business of a session." Such questions must be presented in writing, and the ruling duly recorded. The Constitution then mandates that the Judicial Council review all such decisions of law made by bishops presiding over Jurisdictional, Central, annual, or even district conferences. Bishops report annually to the Judicial Council all their rulings, which the Council may either affirm, partially affirm, or reject (¶¶49, 54.3, 2613).

The bishop in this sense acts as the judiciary in presiding over annual conferences. But though the annual conference does not have the Judicial Council present at its sessions, it can rest assured that decisions of law will be reviewed. To make this more explicit, the *Discipline* also authorizes a third category of procedure through which an annual conference itself may appeal a decision of law to which at least a fifth of its members object. This allows the parties who disagree with the bishop's interpretation to prepare a brief for full consideration by the Judicial Council (¶¶54.2, 2609).

The fourth category, and that least used, is an appeal "on a question of Church law" that may arise in the conduct of a church trial. Few trials reach the stage of appeal from the Committee on Appeals of a Jurisdictional or Central Conference. But should one do so, the Judicial Council rules only on matters of a conflict of decisions or other questions of church law, not "upon the facts" of a case. The determination of guilt or innocence remains in the church trial procedures (¶2609.8).[2]

Historically the church has looked upon church trials as a protection of the accused more than as a useful measure of ecclesiastical discipline. The right of clergy and laity to a trial is a constitutional provision protected by a Restrictive Rule (¶18). No United Methodist clergy or lay member may be expelled without a trial if the accused person so requests it.

At the same time, the church's exercise of discipline has evolved more toward pastoral and moral persuasion than legal confrontation. Few clergy or laity would welcome formal challenges to their laxity of faith or practice. Few United Methodists have had the taste for extended legal proceedings over doctrinal issues, though "dissemination of doctrines contrary to the established standards of doctrine" of the UMC is a chargeable offense (¶2702.1). The *Discipline* devotes over twenty pages to the legal process of church trials, at the same time pleading that "church trials are to be regarded as an expedient of last resort" (¶2707).

Current Legal Issues

The apostle Paul urged the early Christians to be obedient to civil authorities, to pay taxes, and to respect criminal laws (Rom. 13:1-7). He also decried the practice of church members taking their disputes with one another to civil court (1 Cor. 6:1-11). These basic attitudes have informed church practices in various ways ever since.

The judicial procedures of the UMC derive from the church's understanding of itself as a community of faith to which all members are bound in mutual accountability. Disciplinary provisions are written in the church's language of pastoral and covenantal responsibility, not the legal terminology of civil law. Of course, because of the UMC's heritage as a covenant connection of clergy, the *Discipline* addresses accountability procedures and protections for the clergy far more than the laity.

This is especially clear in complaint procedures as spelled out in the ordained ministry section of the *Discipline*. While a complaint may concern any matter listed as a chargeable offense in the later chapter on trials, initial procedures attempt to head off the need for a trial. Chargeable offenses include immorality, crime, sexual abuse or harassment, and several other matters (¶2702).

The *Discipline* provides for complaints to be handled first by a "supervisory response" (¶359). This allows the district superintendent or bishop, upon receiving a complaint in writing, to confer pastorally with the clergyperson and the complainant. The bishop and cabinet are also charged with attending to "healing within the congregation," including "support for victims" and forms of mediation and reconciliation as needed. Resolution of complaints begins, then, as close to the situation as possible, and with a pastoral and covenantal method appropriate to the church.

If the matter "does not achieve a resolution" through the supervisory response, the bishop may refer the complaint to one of two bodies (¶359.1.d). A complaint concerning a chargeable offense may be referred to the committee on investigation of the annual conference. The bishop appoints a counsel for the church to "represent the interests of the Church in pressing the claims of the person making the complaint" (¶2708.7). This commences a procedure of inquiry into the complaint that may include written and oral responses from the parties involved. If a satisfactory solution is still not possible, a trial may be necessary.

A complaint regarding "incompetence, ineffectiveness, or unwillingness or inability to perform ministerial duties" may be referred to the Board of Ordained Ministry (¶359.1.d(2)). The clergy-person against whom the complaint is lodged has the right to a hearing. If the BOM decides upon administrative location or involuntary leave or retirement for the clergyperson, its decision is subject to review by the Administrative Review Committee to be certain that procedures were appropriately followed (¶¶359.3, 633).

The relative informality and flexibility of these procedures has allowed church authorities to handle complaints with sensitivity to the circumstances of particular clergy, complainants, and churches. The same response is not appropriate in every case. Since grievances may include anything from doctrinal differences to sexual misconduct, the authority receiving the grievance must exercise judgment about the appropriate response—mediation, immediate action, a form of redress, or other options. On the other hand, the flexibility of multiple options may lead to inconsistencies that the clergy of an annual conference, laity, and complainants have difficulty understanding. Moreover, it is essentially a peer review process to which laity, especially lay complainants, have less access (though a clergy committee on investigation must have two lay observers).

Indeed the church increasingly finds itself faced with pressures to develop more precise legal procedures—for reasons different from what earlier generations might have anticipated. Clergy and laity are, of course, still subject to civil and criminal laws, and to the ethical standards of the church. But in many cases people expect redress from the church, and when it is not forthcoming, a lawsuit may ensue.

Three major areas of law are forcing this increased attention from church bodies.[3] First, a devastating increase in cases of sexual misconduct, particularly by male clergy, has put tremendous strain on existing procedures. The United Methodist heritage of clergy accountability is well expressed in the *Discipline's* claim that "ordination and membership in an annual conference . . . is a sacred trust" (¶359.1). Yet some annual conferences have had a number of sexual misconduct complaints being processed at the same time, and most annual conferences have had at least one.

Existing procedures are vulnerable at the point of conveying to persons who bring complaints of sexual misconduct that the matter will not be "swept under the rug." Every effort must be made to assure the complainant that he or she will be fully heard and her or his hurt addressed both in fair process and in pastoral care. Moreover, the church sometimes shows too little care for a clergyperson against whom a complaint is filed. Especially those from whom the church removes ordination credentials are too often left without means of healing and reconciliation in a time of unemployment and transition to a new life. Ironically, while these are pastoral matters in which the church should excel, the church's failure to show sufficient care may be the springboard for offended persons to bring lawsuits. Certainly part of the reason for the church's shortcomings in responding to the complainant and the one complained against is a fear that open procedures will expose the church to even greater liability, public scrutiny, and embarrassment. But a hint of "scandal" not dealt with forthrightly may be far worse.

Second, in sexual misconduct, employment policy, and other areas the church is being forced to consider legal processes that will stand up to civil as well as ecclesiastical review. For example, every state has laws governing "hiring and firing" policies and the rights of employees to review, benefits, leaves, and other matters. General agencies particularly have had to make sure that their personnel policies are in accord with the state in which they are incorporated. A GCFA Committee on Personnel Policies and Practices coordinates and reviews these policies (¶805.4.d).

Personnel policies are especially relevant for lay employees of church agencies. The *Discipline* offers very little distinctly ecclesial procedure for handling employment of laity in local church or general church agencies, leaving this largely as a matter of civil law.[4] But personnel issues also affect clergy. By United Methodist tradition clergy work in a covenant body under the superintending authority of bishops and district superintendents. Yet clergy who feel they have been treated unfairly might turn to civil employment laws for legal redress.

The Judicial Council has ruled in several cases that church law must be brought into closer accord with civil law, especially in providing more explicit "due process" in terms familiar to civil courts.

315

The church continues to insist upon "fair process," however, in order to distinguish the practices appropriate to a covenant community of faith from those of civil procedure (¶2701). In an investigation, for example, the parties involved may have representation by counsel but not by an attorney (counsel may be a clergyperson or lay member of the church). The committee must attempt to bring the parties "face to face" in an effort to resolve the matter. No oaths are to be taken; the committee's executive deliberations do not have to be transcribed. In all these ways, church procedure is grounded on the integrity and trust of persons who share a common faith and practice (¶2706).[5]

In order best to advance justice and to protect itself from lawsuits, the church must develop the fairest procedures possible and it must follow them consistently. These procedures should be well-publicized so that all persons know what the chargeable offenses are, how to bring a complaint, and how their complaint will be handled. The church must also improve its screening of both volunteers and employees and its keeping of records. Local churches and conference agencies should take special care to screen all workers with children and youth, including background checks for criminal convictions. Bishops and conferences are developing policies for keeping more careful records on clergy, particularly complaints against clergy even after they have been resolved. These records should be shared among bishops and BOMs to the extent necessary to prevent a clergyperson from moving from conference to conference leaving a trail of misconduct complaints.

Of course, none of these legal measures touches the fact that the church should not seek as its standard a legal minimum of rights, but an ecclesial maximum of mutual responsibilities in a caring community of faith. The church as a fellowship of love and justice ought to educate its members about appropriate behavior and teach ways to express care even in situations of broken trust. Clergy in covenant and laity in congregations ought to practice calling each other to account for actions. But this has proved increasingly difficult in the American culture of individual rights and personal privacy.

A third legal issue for the UMC is its status as a connectional religious organization. The courts generally have held that no religious denomination can be considered a jural entity as a whole, but only the units incorporated within it. Since the UMC is not incorporated as a single organization, it would seem not to be suable (¶139). Yet the well-known Pacific Homes lawsuit of the 1970s opened the door for a future court to rule that "The United Methodist Church" is indeed a single, hierarchical structure. An appeals court in that case viewed the UMC as an organization governed by the Council of Bishops as its continuing executive body. The court read the many mandates of the *Discipline* as evidence that local churches and agencies are units under the authority of a continuous pyramidal structure from local to national. While this was a gross misreading of the church's heritage of discipline and order, legal experts have had to examine the *Discipline* carefully to remove wordings that might reinforce such a perception.[6]

In fact, United Methodism does appear sometimes to be trying to "have it both ways." The church wants clergy to be accountable to each other and to serve under the authority of superintendents. On the other hand, if a clergyperson is sued for some form of misconduct, the church does not want to assume corporate responsibility for the clergyperson's actions. Similarly, annual conferences rely on local churches maintaining their place in the conference salary scale for the purpose of making clergy appointments. The denomination has even had to concede that civil government may require clergy to be classified as employees for tax purposes. Yet the church insists that "such classifications are not to be construed as affecting or defining United Methodist polity, including the historic covenants that bind annual conferences, clergy, and congregations" (¶141).[7]

Much as one might want to insist that civil courts are barred by the separation of church and state from any effort to define the church as a corporate entity, the fact is that courts will inevitably try to do so. Meanwhile the church too often is not well prepared to articulate its connectional nature. It is easy to say what the church is not: it is not one corporate organization, elders do not work for a congregation, local churches are not units of an annual conference corporation, bishops are not chief executive officers, general agencies—especially the GCFA and GCOM—are not executive committees for the denomination as a whole. It is much harder to say what the church is.

The connection has grown from a chemistry of ecclesial traditions of order and the church's mission in changing social contexts.

It is a set of evolving practices far more than it is an entity capable of exact description and definition. There are any number of points, in fact, at which the UMC would be much better off if Disciplinary enthusiasts had resisted the impulse to write legislation. In many ways the connection cannot be legislated; it must be lived.

The UMC is an amalgam of ecclesial polities—Catholic, Anglican, Reformed, pietistic, and evangelical. Its unique connection brings together a mutual accountability that originated in small groups, with the fierce independence of preachers convicted by the power of the Holy Spirit with a word from the Lord. It combines both a democratic principle of conference and an organic principle of episcopacy. To advance its autonomy and participation it has ensured that crucial decisions are made not by executives but by conferences. To advance its continuity and organization for mission it has maintained an episcopacy.

In all legal issues, the UMC will be best served by both its clergy and laity being steeped in this basic, synthetic character of its polity. The more consistently and clearly church leaders can articulate and practice the United Methodist connection, the less civil courts and judges will undertake to define it for themselves.

CONCLUSION

Issues for the Future of United Methodist Polity

I write this book at a time when many voices are declaring that The United Methodist Church is in crisis. A whole vocabulary for addressing critical change has evolved—new paradigm, downsize, local, global, quality, vision, discernment, leadership, revitalization. Many clergy and lay leaders are calling for major restructuring of the denomination. Some argue that basic elements of the system of ministry and mission—including appointments and apportionments—must be fundamentally reformed.

Yet it is also true that the basic character of United Methodism as a unique synthesis of ecclesial political traditions persists in many forms. Conferences assemble, address a remarkable range of issues, and disperse to be in ministry. Bishops articulate new directions for the church, travel incessantly, preach and teach across the connection. United Methodist people are bound together in a network of friendship and collegiality that has amazing depth and resilience.

I have argued that viewing the contemporary church through the lens of crisis fails to recognize the gifts and strengths that church traditions bring to present needs. It is a disservice to faithful lay and clergy members constantly to declare or imply that their service is ineffective and the structures through which they work are inadequate. The United Methodist connection has always been a challenge to maintain. To meet and make decisions in conference requires deep commitment, energy and attention. To assign pastors where they are most needed and best able to serve is exceedingly complex. To worship and serve as a congregation means continually swimming against the tide of American privatism and consumerism. And no ecclesial role is more daunting than trying to be a bishop of integrity.

319

Enormous social changes have swept the U.S. and indeed all the nations in which United Methodism is active. But the followers of Wesleyan Methodism invented the connection precisely in order to spread the gospel in a world that was already changing rapidly when Wesley began his movement. In good United Methodist fashion, the way to work through these challenges is a blend of churchly tradition, evangelical experience, and lively pragmatism. The changing chemistry of this synthetic polity is recorded in a book, to be sure, but it is most basically a lived practice. It comprises the ways in which institutional traditions and habits persist as well as the avenues through which people seek change. It is in continual interaction with shifting social contexts, trends, and events. United Methodist polity requires its people above all to be practical theologians, enacting their theological affirmations in response to changing situations of the church's mission.

This book has named many issues that will challenge United Methodist polity now and in the years ahead, to which United Methodist people will need to bring all the resources of the connectional tradition. I would summarize them in five categories. First is a cluster of related questions about ordained ministry and itineracy. The growing number of clergy retirements accompanied by the rising costs of maintaining a full-time pastor will mean fewer ordained elders in full connection in the future. United Methodism needs to develop a system for meeting the pastoral needs of the many smaller local churches and circuits who can no longer expect to receive or support an elder under appointment. These churches are among the most loyal to United Methodist traditions, but there is danger of their feeling excluded or isolated from conferences dominated by larger churches and full-time clergy.

The itineracy itself needs continual study to find ways for it to place elders most appropriately. In particular, the church needs to address both the recruitment of new pastors and the high attrition rate among clergy. Many pastors remain in the itineracy for ten years or less; according to one study, a third of the clergy ordained elder in the decade between 1974 and 1983 left parish ministry within ten years, and half of those leaving either terminated or located. The growing disparity between salaries paid by smaller and larger churches may be one factor. Holding a covenant together among clergy some of whose income is four or five times that of others is going to be difficult. Another factor may be the inflexibility of the present clergy system, in which clergy are limited in effect to lifetime service in one conference "seniority system" with little opportunity to move throughout the connection.[1]

The itineracy system must continue to seek a balance between its guarantees of appointment under the elders' covenant and the needs and wishes of local churches. The guarantee under the bishop's exclusive power to appoint makes possible the placement of women as pastors and the appointment of clergy across racial lines to a much greater extent than in other denominations. On the other hand, the system forces the connection to develop a broad consensus, for example, about the ordination of self-avowed practicing homosexuals, since if gay and lesbian pastors were admitted to annual conferences they would enjoy the same guarantee of appointment.

Some congregations want a larger role in the selection of their pastors. While some seek to move toward a call system, most would settle for the possibility of proposing names of elders to be considered. Incorporating this desire in a just system of guaranteed appointment will be a huge challenge, and is part of the reason some people advocate removing the guarantee altogether.

Another ministry issue revolves around the diaconate. United Methodism got along for twenty years with a hybrid category to certify and legitimate the crucial roles of professional staff persons in churches. Diaconal ministry is now giving way to an order of deacons with clergy status. Yet a permanent diaconate of persons not under itinerant appointment by the bishop is a major innovation for United Methodist polity, and will require years of practice for the church to live into it.

A second issue is how to support mission both locally and globally. As clergy insurance and pension costs soar, annual conferences resist increases in budgets for conference and general agencies. For generations the UMC has supported a cadre of expert specialists in missions, education, social action, and other connectional concerns. But in some agencies half or more of these positions have been eliminated.

The challenge now is to reform and create structures through which the church can continue its evangelical witness in a world devastated by poverty, overpopulation, ecological disasters, and social injustice. United Methodist people respond in remarkable generosity to the needs of people in crisis. Programs for training, placing, and coordinating lay volunteers in mission are growing rapidly. United Methodist people are attracted to hands-on activities in which they can see practical results and meet new friends in the fellowship of Christian service.

At the same time, general agencies are one of the key strengths of the United Methodist connection. They provide support services in many areas of church administration and ministry. They enable the whole church to carry forward its calling to develop an educated, committed ministry and a dynamic mission. These basic functions of denominations must continue in some form in the future.

A third and closely related issue is the possibility of creating a structure for a global connection, less U.S.-centered, with all regions of the church participating on an equal (proportional) basis as peers. Both the Council of Bishops and the General Council on Ministries have been developing proposals for the General Conference to become a global body for the two purposes of constituting basic regional governing units and setting broad policy for the church as a whole. It would meet less often, and rotate among regions of the world. Regional conferences would have latitude for adopting forms and procedures useful in particular cultures—much as Central Conferences do now.

These plans must contend particularly with the economic disparity among world societies. United Methodism's fastest growth is in Africa and the Philippines, where the standard of living is vastly lower than in the U.S. American United Methodists would have to be committed to bearing much of the cost of global gatherings and administrative units.

A global church also opens the possibility of autonomous Methodist churches becoming partners with United Methodism in forming some new ecclesial body that carries on the Wesleyan Methodist tradition. The activities of the World Methodist Council and meetings of the World Methodist Conference every five years have brought these groups together for worship, study, and fellowship. A new church would call them into working together toward a common polity and mission as well.

At the same time a global Methodism is emerging, United Methodism is fully involved in a fourth issue for American churches. Mainstream Protestant denominations have been working for many years toward a new church, catholic, evangelical, and reformed, inclusive of many traditions arising from the Protestant Reformation and welcoming people of all ethnicities and backgrounds. The UMC is at the point of entering into covenant communion with other denominations committed to mutual recognition of membership, ordination, and sacraments, as well as a shared mission.

The Church of Christ Uniting (COCU), now Churches Uniting in Christ, will take years to emerge (conversations began nearly fifty years ago). Each tradition will have to discover how to bring its own ecclesial gifts and graces to the communion, while continuing to teach both its own distinctives and the values of a new covenant relationship with other churches. The drive toward organic union of church bodies so prevalent in the first half of the twentieth century has given way to a desire for polities that are more flexible, local, and practical. But what form that will take remains to be seen.

Finally, the church will face a perennial issue of how to define itself through its polity. In the American context, after all, the church is a voluntary association comprised of a variety of human beings as diverse as humanity itself. It depends on its people seeking and knowing God's call and guidance. It is governed by ecclesial discipline, not a rule of law. Whatever the *Discipline* may say, each local church and annual conference has its own ways of doing things, its local cultural traditions and expectations, its unique forms for expressing Christian faith.

In particular, in many areas of church life both clergy and laity actively resist demands that take away their sense of the church as fellowship or even extended family, or limit their local autonomy and initiative. While agencies and conferences may be anxious to get things in writing and add mandates to keep everyone on the same page, many United Methodists are going to continue singing their own tunes at their own pace.

The word "shall" appears over 2,000 times in the *Discipline*.[2] But all the imperatives in the world can neither create nor maintain a connection. That can only be built out of a shared sense of discipline and mission. The "shalls" are appropriate for people under common discipline. But their proliferation severely strains a consensus that grows far better from appeals to people's desire to work together than from rules and demands.

At the same time as some United Methodist people resist the "shalls" and want to cut material from the *Discipline,* there is an increasing need for more precise legal definitions and policies that govern church operations. Especially as United Methodists seek redress in civil courts instead of through church procedures, civil law will pressure the church to redefine ministry vocations as professional career employment, bishops as chief executive officers, and local churches as corporate employers. In fact, the church has been sloppy and inconsistent in many policy areas, especially in keeping accurate records and in handling lay employees. District and episcopal offices are not staffed or financed to maintain the kind of files and procedures one would expect in government or corporate business. Many clergy and lay leaders prefer to run the church from scrap paper stuffed in pockets and purses. Too many agreements and contracts have been informal and ill-considered.

If the church does not want the courts to define its polity, then some of these habits will have to change. Local churches and conferences will have to take much greater care in personnel and property matters. But this must be done, not so much to satisfy the civil courts, as to preserve the autonomy of the church. There may well be points at which the church must claim its freedom to define its polity in its own ecclesial language, in the traditions of discipline long held among Methodist people. In order to do so, the church must have its own house in order.

As United Methodism meets challenges and changes in these five areas, it must give far greater attention to its polity than it has in the past. The church has relied greatly on oral tradition to pass along its distinctive practices. But this has led to an unfortunate neglect of the ecclesial foundations and historical contexts from which United Methodist polity has grown. Few studies comparable to this one have been published in this century, and I consider this one only a beginning. Many areas of political practice need research and reflection, among them:

- the emerging place of the local church in connectionalism;

- the effects of women's leadership on practices of polity, as women have moved from roles exclusively in gender-specific organizations to offices of the whole church;

- the place of men in the church, the ways male assumptions have shaped polity and practice, and the shifts that occur as male roles change and women come into leadership;

- the role of the Judicial Council in shaping polity and influencing the church's direction;

- the impact of American "establishment" Methodism from 1880–1920 on contemporary polity and understandings of the connection;

- the differing political perspectives and practices of rural, urban, and suburban churches;

- comparison of the contemporary rhetoric of crisis and use of business management concepts with earlier periods, especially the 1890s;

- comparison of United Methodist polity with the polities of other denominational traditions, especially in the context of cultural trends and social change; and

- the global nature of the church as it has emerged not just in this generation, but over the last two hundred years.

The current flourishing of Wesley studies is encouraging to everyone who wants to see new generations of United Methodists immersed in the unique theology and spirituality of Methodist tradition. The church needs comparable studies now that capture the Methodist experience of being church and its distinctive ecclesiology.

Polity is a lived practice, worth little, as Wesley said, if it does not lead people to discover the unfathomable love and hope of life with Christ. Over the generations United Methodist people have discovered disciplines and avenues of education and mission that have brought countless people to that new life. The time has come to claim the gifts of this rich tradition, to learn these ways well, and to seek forms and practices for a vital church of the future.

Notes

Foreword

1. I first learned this image from the writings of Erik Routley on the significance of liturgy, and have found it profoundly true for the church's organizational life as well. See Routley, *Church Music and the Christian Faith* (Carol Stream, IL: Agape, 1978), 89.

Introduction

1. These denominations have in common their origins in or near the colonial period, when they drew their adherents mainly from English and Scotch-Irish (and some German) immigrants. They have exemplified the "White Anglo-Saxon Protestant" (WASP) social stratum that has had broad influence historically in shaping American culture. Clearly other denominations have moved into the "mainstream" of American society in the twentieth century, including Lutherans, Roman Catholics, and Baptists. Yet the five denominations named still have a social status and influence disproportionate to their numbers in the general population. For a full discussion see Wade Clark Roof and William McKinney, *American Mainline Religion: Its Changing Shape and Future* (New Brunswick: Rutgers University Press, 1987).

2. Recitation of decline and the dire consequences that may result has long been a popular rhetorical device in America. One form of this speech was known as the jeremiad, which would appeal to the audience's nostalgia for a golden age when the pure ideals of society or church were valiantly upheld by all; detail the failings of the current generation; and conclude with a Deuteronomic crisis: now is the time to choose life or death. I would argue that in recent times, however, this art form has followed the trajectory of its own narrative line. It has itself declined into tiresome repetition and self-fulfilling prophecy, serving only to persuade people that there is no hope.

3. See the statistical review section of the *General Minutes 2000* (Nashville: United Methodist Publishing House). See also the *Yearbook of American and Canadian Churches* (Nashville: Abingdon Press, 1990), 284-85, which last printed a fifty-year comparison table for all major denominations in 1990.

4. Milton J. Coalter, John M. Mulder, Louis B. Weeks, *The Re-Forming Tradition: Presbyterians and Mainstream Protestantism* (Louisville: Westminster/John Knox Press, 1992), 25.

5. Douglas W. Johnson and Alan K. Waltz, *Facts and Possibilities. An Agenda for The United Methodist Church* (Nashville: Abingdon Press, 1987), 31.

6. Richard B. Wilke, *And Are We Yet Alive?* (Nashville: Abingdon Press, 1986), 26.

7. Johnson and Waltz, *Facts and Possibilities*, 89-91. Estimates vary, however; *Churches and Church Membership 1990*, based on census data, estimates the United Methodist proportion of the total population at 4.5 percent (Table 1). Martin B. Bradley, et al., eds. (Atlanta: Glenmary Research Center, 1992), 3.

8. Dean M. Kelley, *Why Conservative Churches Are Growing* (New York: Harper and Row, 1972). Roger Finke and Rodney Stark make a similar argument in applying marketing theory to American religious history, in *The Churching of America 1776–1990; Winners and Losers in Our Religious Economy* (New Brunswick: Rutgers University Press, 1992).

9. Stanley Hauerwas and William H. Willimon, *Resident Aliens: A Provocative Christian Assessment of Culture and Ministry for People Who Know That Something Is Wrong* (Nashville: Abingdon Press, 1989), 12.

10. *Churches and Church Membership 1990*, ix.

11. "United Methodist Church Membership over 1000, Attendance over 500" (Office of Research, National Program Division, General Board of Global Ministries, UMC, 1993).

12. For a recent study of changes in associational life in America, see Robert D. Putnam, *Bowling Alone: The Collapse and Revival of American Community* (New York: Simon and Schuster, 2000).

13. For in-depth, balanced studies of current generations, see Wade Clark Roof, *A Generation of Seekers* (San Francisco: Harper and Row, 1993); Dean R. Hoge, Benton Johnson, Donald A. Luidens, *Vanishing Boundaries: The Religion of Mainline Protestant Baby Boomers* (Louisville: Westminster/John Knox Press, 1994); and Douglas A. Walrath, *Frameworks: Patterns of Living and Believing Today* (New York: Pilgrim Press, 1987).

14. Roof and McKinney, *American Mainline Religion*, 158-62.

15. Robert Wuthnow, *The Struggle for America's Soul: Evangelicals, Liberals, and Secularism* (Grand Rapids: Wm. B. Eerdmans, 1989), 183.

16. David Roozen and Carl Dudley, "A Premature Obituary," *Christian Century* 110:26 (Sept. 22-29, 1993), 889-90. This issue is entirely devoted to articles on contemporary denominationalism.

17. Summarized in a news item, "Measuring Mainline Vital Signs," *Christian Century* 111:37 (December 21-28, 1994), 1214.

18. *Background Data for Mission* (Research Office, National Program Division, General Board of Global Ministries, UMC, March 1993).

19. Council of Bishops of The United Methodist Church, *Vital Congregations—Faithful Disciples: Vision for the Church*, Foundation Document, Thomas E. Frank, principal writer and consultant (Nashville: Graded Press, 1990), 9-11.

20. *Vital Congregations—Faithful Disciples*, 21.

21. *Vital Congregations—Faithful Disciples*, 76-78.

22. Quoted in Thomas E. Frank, "Ecclesial Vision and the Realities of Congregational Life," *Quarterly Review* 12:1 (Spring 1992), 8.

23. *A Form of Discipline, for the Ministers, Preachers, and Members of the Methodist Episcopal Church in America* (New York: W. Ross, 1787).

24. 1 Corinthians 13:1.

25. General Council on Ministries, "Summary Report of Annual Conference Vision and Structure Statements," Thomas E. Frank and Beth Givens, consultants (Dayton, 1994).

26. United Methodism has a particular way of understanding congregations as "local churches," local mission outposts of a national and international connection. United Methodist polity is quite unlike forms of congregationalism—each congregation constituted on its own and deciding the degree of its cooperation with others. Thus the church's task will be to discover new ways for the mission orientation of United Methodist polity to empower congregations for ministry— both as local churches and as a connection. See chapter 3 on "The Constitution of United Methodism" and chapter 6 on "The Local Church."

27. *Vital Congregations—Faithful Disciples*, 84.

1. Polity as Ecclesial Practice and Practical Discipline

1. From a June 25, 1746, letter to "John Smith," Wesley, *Works*, 12:80-81. The letter is also quoted and discussed in Gerald F. Moede, "Bishops in the Methodist Tradition: Historical Perspectives," in Jack M. Tuell and Roger W. Fjeld, *Episcopacy: Lutheran-United Methodist Dialogue II* (Minneapolis: Augsburg, 1991), 52; and in Henry D. Rack, *Reasonable Enthusiast: John Wesley and the Rise of Methodism* (Nashville: Abingdon Press, 1989, 1992), 294.

2. Aristotle, *The Politics*, trans. by Carnes Lord (Chicago: University of Chicago Press, 1984), Book 1:2 (35-38), and 4:8, 9 (129-32).

3. See Acts 2:44-47, Galatians 3:28. For origins of the Christian use of *ekklesia*, especially in contrast to the emerging Jewish use of *synagogein* in the intertestamental period, see Wayne A. Meeks, *The First Urban Christians: The Social World of the Apostle Paul* (New Haven: Yale University Press, 1983), 80, 108; Fenton John Hort, *The Christian Ecclesia* (London: Macmillan and Co., Ltd., 1914), 4-7, 13-14; and Peter C. Hodgson, *Revisioning the Church: Ecclesial Freedom in the New Paradigm* (Philadelphia: Fortress Press, 1988), 24-28.

4. Recent ecumenical statements of ecclesiology building on classical consensus include the *Baptism, Eucharist, and Ministry* document of the World Council of Churches, Faith and Order Paper No. 111 (Geneva: World Council of Churches, 1982), and *The COCU Consensus: In Quest of a Church of Christ Uniting*, Gerald F. Moede, ed. (Princeton: Consultation on Church Union, 1985).

5. Leonardo Boff, *Ecclesiogenesis: The Base Communities Reinvent the Church*, trans. Robert R. Barr (Maryknoll, N.Y.: Orbis Books, 1986).

6. For a similar definition that I have found very helpful, see James W. Fowler, "Practical Theology and the Shaping of Christian Lives," in Don S. Browning, ed., *Practical Theology* (San Francisco: Harper and Row, 1983), 148-66. Contemporary voices in ecclesiology include Letty M. Russell, *Church in the Round* (Louisville: Westminster/John Knox, 1994); Jürgen Moltmann, *The Church in the Power of the Spirit: A Contribution to Messianic Ecclesiology* (London: SCM Press, 1977); Hodgson, *Revisioning*.

7. See the parable of the unfaithful servant in Matthew 24:45-51.

8. Ephesians 4:4, 12-16.

9. *Oxford English Dictionary.* "Discipline" is a multifaceted word. In academia, it refers to a field or method of study, usually comprised of a distinct body of texts and approaches, through which the scholar practices investigations of knowledge. To learn a discipline in the academic sense is to master the method and the primary questions in the literature.

"Discipline" in another sense refers to punishment or censure for transgressions of the rules. In ecclesiastical history, the "discipline" was an actual tool of punishment, "a whip used to inflict chastisement on the body as a means of mortification." *New Catholic Encyclopedia* 4:895.

10. Wesley, *Works,* 8:275. The Minutes soon became a standard for examining and admitting new preachers; see Richard P. Heitzenrater, *Wesley and the People Called Methodist* (Nashville: Abingdon Press, 1995), 174-75.

11. For evidence of this connection, especially through the practices of John Wesley's mother Susanna, see Russell E. Richey, *The Methodist Conference in America: A History* (Nashville: Kingswood Books, 1996), 16.

12. Wesley, *Works,* 8:278.

13. Wesley, "Thoughts Upon Methodism" in *Works,* 13:258.

14. Early changes in American Disciplinary materials are described in Frank Baker, "The Doctrines in the *Discipline*" in Frank Baker, *From Wesley to Asbury: Studies in Early American Methodism* (Durham, NC: Duke University Press, 1976), 162-82.

15. *Oxford English Dictionary.*

16. See discussion in Rack, *Reasonable Enthusiast,* 237ff.; and Heitzenrater, *Wesley,* 138-39.

17. Henry H. Knight III, *The Presence of God in the Christian Life: John Wesley and the Means of Grace* (Metuchen, NJ: Scarecrow Press, 1992), 12-13, 192.

18. David Lowes Watson, "Aldersgate Street and the General Rules: The Form and the Power of Methodist Discipleship" in Randy L. Maddox, ed., *Aldersgate Reconsidered* (Nashville: Kingswood Books, 1990), 36-37.

19. David Lowes Watson, *The Early Methodist Class Meeting: Its Origin and Significance* (Nashville: Discipleship Resources, 1985), 87.

20. For a thorough discussion of the means of grace and the practices of Christian life in Wesleyan Methodism, see Randy L. Maddox, *Responsible Grace: John Wesley's Practical Theology* (Nashville: Kingswood Books, 1994), 192-229. Quotation from the Introduction, 19.

21. 1 John 4:19.

22. Wesley, *Works,* 8:301.

23. Wesley, *Works,* 8:322. See Knight's helpful discussion in *Presence,* 5 and passim.

24. Wesley, *Works,* 8:315-16.

25. Wesley, *Works,* 8:273.

26. Wesley, *Works,* 8:322.

27. Rack, *Reasonable Enthusiast,* 241.

28. Rack, *Reasonable Enthusiast,* 249.

29. For a survey of the resources Wesley provided for spiritual guidance and formation of Methodist people, see Steven Harper, "John Wesley: Spiritual Guide," *Wesleyan Theological Journal* 20:2 (Fall 1985), 91-96.

30. The term may also have referred to a theological method associated with Arminianism, another name to which Wesley was amenable. See Richard P. Heitzenrater, "What's in a Name? The Meaning of 'Methodist'" in *Mirror and Memory: Reflections on Early Methodism* (Nashville: Kingswood Books, 1989), 13-32. On the gradual narrowing of the term to apply only to Wesley's connexion, see Heitzenrater, *Wesley,* 181, 215-16.

31. Rack, *Reasonable Enthusiast,* 237.

32. Heitzenrater, *Wesley,* 319.

33. See W. Stephen Gunter, *The Limits of "Love Divine": John Wesley's Response to Antinomianism and Enthusiasm* (Nashville: Kingswood Books, 1989).

34. Wesley, *Works,* 8:314, 316.

35. Rack, *Reasonable Enthusiast,* 248.

36. Wesley, *Works,* 8:299.

37. See data in Watson, *Class Meeting,* 131.

38. John J. Tigert, *A Constitutional History of American Episcopal Methodism,* 6th edition, revised and enlarged (Nashville: Publishing House of the M. E. Church, South, 1916), 58-59.

39. See Randy L. Maddox, "Social Grace: The Eclipse of the Church as a Means of Grace in American Methodism," in *Methodism in Its Cultural Milieu,* Proceedings of the Centenary Conference of the Wesley Historical Society (Oxford: Applied Theology Press, 1994), 131-60; and Richey, *The Methodist Conference,* 134.

40. Frank Baker, "American Methodism: Beginnings and Ends," in *From Wesley to Asbury,* 183-205.

41. Rack, *Reasonable Enthusiast,* 202ff. describes Wesley's controversy with the Moravians over "stillness."

42. Rack, *Reasonable Enthusiast,* 307-08, 420-22.

43. Heitzenrater, *Wesley,* 19-25.

44. See Richard P. Heitzenrater, "The Church of England and the Religious Societies," in *Mirror and Memory,* 35-45; and Rack, *Reasonable Enthusiast,* 14.

45. Rack, *Reasonable Enthusiast,* 525.

46. For a comprehensive study of Wesley's relationship with Anglicanism, see Frank Baker, *John Wesley and the Church of England* (Nashville: Abingdon Press, 1970).

47. On this point in relation to episcopacy, see for example James K. Mathews, *Set Apart to Serve: The Meaning and Role of Episcopacy in the Wesleyan Tradition* (Nashville: Abingdon Press, 1985), 39.

48. Wesley, *Works,* 5:492-504.

49. Rack, *Reasonable Enthusiast,* 208-11; Heitzenrater, *Wesley,* 192.

50. Wesley, *Works,* 13:251-52.

51. However, Coke continued to have episcopal ambitions in the Church of England. See Rack, *Reasonable Enthusiast,* 516-17.

52. William A. Williams, *The Garden of American Methodism: The Delmarva Peninsula, 1769–1820* (Wilmington: Scholarly Resources, 1984), 90; quoted in Russell E. Richey, *Early American Methodism* (Bloomington: Indiana University Press, 1991), 56, 64. See also Nathan Hatch's claim that Methodist lay preaching broke down "the wall between gentleman and commoner" by making the priesthood less of a profession for the sons of gentility; Nathan O. Hatch, *The Democratization of American Christianity* (New Haven: Yale University Press, 1989), 85.

53. Albert C. Outler, ed., *John Wesley* (New York: Oxford University Press, 1964), 9-10. For a thorough discussion of John Wesley and ancient Christianity see Ted A. Campbell, *John Wesley and Christian Antiquity: Religious Vision and Cultural Change* (Nashville: Kingswood Books, 1991). Campbell writes, "[In some cases] Wesley's use of Christian antiquity can be demonstrated to have intentionally called upon ancient Christian customs and beliefs as patterns which Wesley wanted to see reinstated by the Methodists" (107). These included love feasts and weekly fasts.

54. Hatch, *Democratization*, 87-89.

55. For more discussion of Wesley and scripture, see Maddox, *Responsible Grace*, 36ff.

56. Wesley, *Works*, 7:238; Rack, *Reasonable Enthusiast*, 514, 524.

57. Gerald F. Moede, *The Office of Bishop in Methodism: Its History and Development* (Zurich: Publishing House of the Methodist Church, 1964), 38-39. See also Campbell, *Christian Antiquity*, 90-93.

58. Rack, *Reasonable Enthusiast*, 513, 519.

59. Rack, *Reasonable Enthusiast*, 208-09.

60. Patricia V. Bonomi and Peter R. Eisenstadt, "Church Adherence in the Eighteenth Century British American Colonies," *William and Mary Quarterly* 39 (April 1982), 245-86.

61. Donald E. Byrne, Jr., *No Foot of Land. Folklore of American Methodist Itinerants*, ATLA Monograph Series, No. 6 (Metuchen, NJ: Scarecrow Press, 1975), 240-41.

62. Hatch, *Democratization*, 55.

63. Rack, *Reasonable Enthusiast*, 497.

64. Moede, *Office of Bishop*, 42.

65. Rack, *Reasonable Enthusiast*, 499-500. Wesley also explored what he thought to be a distinction in the ancient church, between "the 'extraordinary' ministry of those who preached and propagated the faith [and] the 'ordinary' ministry of those who maintained the church's order and doctrine, and who administered the sacraments"—corresponding to a distinction between apostles and pastors. Campbell, *Christian Antiquity*, 89-90.

66. Rack, *Reasonable Enthusiast*, 298, 507.

67. A well-known use of this phrase is a chapter heading in Frederick A. Norwood, *The Story of American Methodism* (Nashville: Abingdon Press, 1974), 94.

68. Hatch, *Democratization*, 49-56.

69. Methodism was not alone in this trend, and unquestionably was influenced by other Protestant groups. Note this generalization, for example: "In recent

times the tendency among Churches using the English tongue is to forgo as far as possible the right of discipline, preferring to trust almost wholly to the effect of the public exposition of the truth from the pulpit and to the conscience of the church member." David S. Schaff, "Discipline (Christian)" *Encyclopedia of Religion and Ethics* (New York: Charles Scribner's Sons, 1908), 4:715-20.

70. Randy Maddox has outlined the transformation of Methodist discipline from mutual accountability to individual privacy, and from a focus on love of God and neighbor to a preoccupation with moral rectitude and duty, in "Social Grace," esp. 139-45. The journey of Methodism's social stance from countering the culture of gentility to a privatized, domesticated religion is explored in A. Gregory Schneider, *The Way of the Cross Leads Home: The Domestication of American Methodism* (Bloomington: Indiana University Press, 1993).

71. Rack, *Reasonable Enthusiast*, 408.

72. Outler, *John Wesley*, 27, 119.

73. Theodore H. Runyon named Wesley's central concern "orthopathy"— right experience or the right heart—as a third way beyond either orthodoxy (right belief), or orthopraxis (right practice). See "The Importance of Experience for Faith" in Maddox, *Aldersgate Reconsidered*, 93-107, and "A New Look at 'Experience'," *Drew Gateway* 57:3 (1988), 44-55. Gregory S. Clapper coined the term "orthokardia" in an effort to capture the same concern, in *John Wesley on Religious Affections: His Views on Experience and Emotion and Their Role in the Christian Life and Theology* (Metuchen, NJ: Scarecrow Press, 1989), 156-59. See also Randy L. Maddox, "John Wesley—Practical Theologian?" *Wesleyan Theological Journal* 23 (Spring/Fall 1988), 122-47; and Knight, *Presence*, 12.

74. Rack, *Reasonable Enthusiast*, 237.

75. Stanley Ayling, *John Wesley* (Cleveland: William Collins Publishers, 1979), 288.

76. For a summary of American Methodist attributes that were the source of its characteristic appeal, see Frank Baker, "American Methodism: Beginnings and Ends."

77. "In 1776 the Methodists were a tiny religious society with only 65 churches scattered throughout the colonies. Seven decades later they towered over the nation. In 1850 there were 13,302 Methodist congregations, enrolling more than 2.6 million members—the largest single denomination, accounting for more than a third of all American church members [34.2 percent]." Finke and Stark, *Churching*, 56. The scale of U.S. society in 1850 must also be kept in perspective; the total population was about 23 million (with an obvious undercounting of the African slave population), and the sweeping immigrations of southern and eastern European, Asian, Hispanic, and other peoples had not yet begun. United States Census Office, *7th Census, 1850*.

78. General Council on Ministries, The United Methodist Church, "Results of the Survey of Annual Conference Members, May-June 1994," Thomas E. Frank, Scott Thumma, and Karen DeNicola, consultants (December 1994), 6.

79. Quoted by Roy H. Short, *Chosen to Be Consecrated: The Bishops of The Methodist Church, 1784–1968* (Lake Junaluska: Commission on Archives and History, 1976), 75.

80. On practices of theology and the role of teaching in the church, see L. Gregory Jones, "Toward a Recovery of Theological Discourse in United Methodism," *Quarterly Review* 9:2 (Summer 1989), 16-34. On the American neglect of Wesley's practical theological method and the possibility of its recovery, see Randy L. Maddox, "An Untapped Inheritance: American Methodism and Wesley's Practical Theology," paper for the Duke Divinity School research project on "United Methodism and American Culture."

81. Richey, *Early American Methodism*, 95, 112 n. 31.

2. Denomination and Polity in America

1. Nathan O. Hatch, "The Puzzle of American Methodism," *Church History* 63:2 (June 1994), 187.

2. Ernst Troeltsch, *The Social Teachings of the Christian Churches*, 2 vols., trans. Olive Wyon (London: George Allen and Unwin, Ltd., 1931), 1:331ff., 2:691ff., 2:993ff.

3. Finke and Stark, *Churching*; the authors try to establish their case for the strength and growing "market share" of denominations that hold sectarian views, in the Southern Baptist tradition, 187-98, and the decline of the mainstream, 249-55.

4. Alexis de Tocqueville, *Democracy in America*, 2 vols. (New York: Alfred A. Knopf, 1945, 1966; originally published 1835 and 1840), 1:303-05.

5. Craig Dykstra and James Hudnut-Beumler, "The National Organizational Structures of Protestant Denominations: An Invitation to a Conversation," in Milton J. Coalter et al., eds., *The Organizational Revolution: Presbyterians and American Denominationalism* (Louisville: Westminster/John Knox Press, 1992), 311-12.

6. Russell E. Richey, "Denominations and Denominationalism: An American Morphology," in Robert Bruce Mullin and Russell E. Richey, eds., *Reimagining Denominationalism: Interpretive Essays* (New York: Oxford University Press, 1994), 80-82.

7. Conrad Wright, "The Growth of Denominational Bureaucracies: A Neglected Aspect of American Church History," *Harvard Theological Review* 77:2 (1984), 183-85.

8. Richey, "Denominations," 82-84.

9. Dykstra and Hudnut-Beumler, "National," 317. On Methodism see William McGuire King, "Denominational Modernization and Religious Identity: The Case of the Methodist Episcopal Church," in Russell E. Richey, Kenneth E. Rowe, and Jean Miller Schmidt, eds., *Perspectives on American Methodism: Interpretive Essays* (Nashville: Kingswood Books, 1993), 343-55.

10. Dykstra and Hudnut-Beumler, "National," 318-28.

11. Richey, "Denominations," 89.

12. As Wright ("Growth," 188) put it, "Our present denominational organizations are an amalgam of two quite different sorts of structure [discipline and mission or benevolence]; and it raises the question of whether the two are really compatible." Robert Bellah has referred to the church as "virtually the only effectively functioning institution in our civil society." Address on "Changing Themes

in Society: Implications for Human Services," Lutheran Social Services, San Francisco, April 28, 1995.

13. R. Stephen Warner, "The Place of the Congregation in the Contemporary American Religious Configuration" in James P. Wind and James W. Lewis, eds., *American Congregations*, 2 vols. (Chicago: University of Chicago Press, 1994), 2:54-99.

14. William H. Swatos, Jr., "Beyond Denominationalism? Community and Culture in American Religion," *Journal for the Scientific Study of Religion* 20 (1981), 223. See also C. C. Goen, "Ecclesiocracy Without Ecclesiology: Denominational Life in America," *Religion in Life* 48:1 (Spring 1979), 17-31.

15. William R. Hutchison, "Protestantism as Establishment," in William R. Hutchinson, ed., *Between the Times: The Travail of the Protestant Establishment in America 1900–1960* (Cambridge: Cambridge University Press, 1989), 3-18.

16. Warren J. Hartman, "The EUBs Had Reservations Then and Now," *Circuit Rider*, 16:10 (Dec. 1992–Jan. 1993), 4-6.

17. Bellah and his colleagues argue that "a real community" continually retells its "constitutive narrative," and is thus a "community of memory." Robert N. Bellah, Richard Madsen, William M. Sullivan, Ann Swidler, and Steven M. Tipton, *Habits of the Heart: Individualism and Commitment in American Life* (New York: Harper and Row, 1985), 153.

18. For studies of organizational culture generally, see Peter J. Frost et al., *Organizational Culture* (Beverly Hills: Sage Publications, 1985); Joanne Martin, *Cultures in Organizations: Three Perspectives* (New York: Oxford University Press, 1992); Edgar H. Schein, *Organizational Culture and Leadership* (San Francisco: Jossey-Bass Publishers, 1985, 1992). Studies of organizational culture in religious organizations include James F. Hopewell, *Congregation: Stories and Structures*, ed. by Barbara Wheeler (Philadelphia: Fortress Press, 1987); Thomas Edward Frank, *The Soul of the Congregation: An Invitation to Congregational Reflection* (Nashville: Abingdon Press, 2000); and Melvin D. Williams, *Community in a Black Pentecostal Church: An Anthropological Study* (Waveland Press, 1984).

19. Of course, the name of the UMC now combines an appeal to its historic methods with a political term, "united," which refers both to a theological claim of unity in one Body of Christ and to the union of MC and EUBC polities; see p. 117.

20. For the history of United Methodism's cross and flame logo, developed as a unifying symbol of the new united church in 1968, see Edwin H. Maynard, "The Cross and Flame: A Personal Memoir," *Methodist History* 34:4 (July 1996) 203-13.

21. David Morgan, *Icons of American Protestantism: The Art of Werner Sallman, 1892–1968* (New Haven: Yale University Press, 1996); or see Morgan, "Sallman's Head of Christ: The History of an Image," *Christian Century* 109:28 (October 7, 1992), 868-70.

22. Charles Edgar Welch founded the Welch Grape Juice Company in 1869, ran for governor of New York on the Prohibition Party ticket in 1916 and was a regular delegate to the MEC General Conference from 1908 to 1924. *Who Was Who in America*, Volume 1, 1897–1942 (Chicago: A. N. Marquis Company, 1942), 1318.

23. See Gwen Kennedy Neville, "Places and Occasions in the Transmission of Denominational Culture: The Case of 'Southern Presbyterians'," in Jackson Carroll and Wade Clark Roof, eds., *Beyond Establishment: Protestant Identity in a Post-Protestant Age* (Louisville: Westminster/John Knox Press, 1993), 142-56.

24. Robert L. Wilson and William H. Willimon, *The Seven Churches of Methodism* (Durham, NC: The J. M. Ormond Center, Duke Divinity School, 1985). Wilson and Willimon identified seven regional cultures of United Methodism: Yankee, Industrial Northeastern, South, Midwest, Southwest, Frontier, and Western. As they noted, "Regional differences are rarely discussed openly because the church's leaders want to maintain unity" (2).

25. George Cheney, *Rhetoric in an Organizational Society: Managing Multiple Identities* (Columbia, SC: University of South Carolina Press, 1991), 23.

26. Cheney, *Rhetoric*, 16-17. See also Swatos, "Beyond Denominationalism?"

27. Richey, *Early American Methodism*, chap. 6.

28. General Council on Ministries, "Summary Report of Annual Conference Vision and Structure Statements," 8.

29. Robert Wuthnow, *The Restructuring of American Religion: Society and Faith Since World War II* (Princeton: Princeton University Press, 1988), 9-10.

30. Cheney, *Rhetoric*, 14.

31. *1999 Annual Report*, General Board of Pension and Health Benefits, Evanston, Illinois.

32. *Background Data for Mission* (Sept.-Oct. 1993).

33. *General Minutes 2000*.

34. *Newscope* 23:1 (January 6, 1995).

35. See the special issue on "Patterns of Financial Contributions to Churches," Dean R. Hoge, ed., *Review of Religious Research* 36:2 (December 1994), as well as Dean R. Hoge, Charles Zech, Patrick McNamara, Michael J. Donahue, *Money Matters: Personal Giving in American Churches* (Louisville: Westminster/John Knox Press, 1996).

36. See for example David G. Downey, *Militant Methodism: The Story of the First National Convention of Methodist Men* (Cincinnati: Methodist Book Concern, 1913), in which speakers such as S. Earl Taylor pleaded for support of missionary enterprises.

37. Roof and McKinney, *American Mainline Religion*, 107-26.

38. Roof and McKinney, *American Mainline Religion*, 162-77.

39. William B. McClain, *Black People in the Methodist Church: Whither Thou Goest?* (Cambridge, MA: Schenkman Publishing Company, 1984); Grant S. Shockley, ed., *Heritage and Hope: The African American Presence in United Methodism* (Nashville: Abingdon Press, 1991); James S. Thomas, *Methodism's Racial Dilemma: The Story of the Central Jurisdiction* (Nashville: Abingdon Press, 1992).

40. Peter J. Paris, *The Social Teaching of the Black Churches* (Philadelphia: Fortress Press, 1985), 10 and passim; see also Donald G. Mathews, "Evangelical America—The Methodist Ideology," in Richey et al., *Perspectives on American Methodism*, 28.

41. These figures are based on the *General Minutes 2000* and on the summary table in *Background Data for Mission* 5:3 (March 1993). Statistics vary widely,

however; Roof and McKinney estimate 435,000 black UM members in 1974 (*American Mainline Religion*, 142); *Newscope* (I am not sure of the date) printed a figure of 242,000. The UMC has not been consistent in collecting data and some annual conferences fail to turn in statistics of ethnicity.

42. Thomas, *Methodism's Racial Dilemma*, 43.

43. Lawrence N. Jones, "Timeless Priorities in Changing Contexts: African Americans and Denominationalism," in Carroll and Roof, *Beyond Establishment*, 229, 242.

44. H. Richard Niebuhr, *The Social Sources of Denominationalism* (Hamden, CT: Shoe String Press, 1954; originally published by Henry Holt and Co., 1929), 6, 25.

45. Contra Niebuhr's judgment, Andrew Greeley argued that the ethnicity represented in denominationalism is a source of strength for ethnic groups; see Russell E. Richey, *Denominationalism* (Nashville: Abingdon Press, 1977), 249-50, and (in the same volume), Martin E. Marty, "Ethnicity: The Skeleton of Religion in America," 251-72.

46. Frank, "Ecclesial Vision;" see also Hopewell, *Congregation*, 11.

47. Jean Miller Schmidt, "Denominational History When Gender Is the Focus: Women in American Methodism," in Mullin and Richey, *Reimagining Denominationalism*, 214.

48. The United Brethren Church approved women's ordination in 1889, and the Evangelical United Brethren later accepted it, but very few women were ever ordained. J. Bruce Behney and Paul H. Eller, *The History of the Evangelical United Brethren Church*, ed. by Kenneth W. Krueger (Nashville: Abingdon Press, 1979), 160, 360-61. For a startling contrast in gender language, compare the *Disciplines* of 1968 and 1972.

49. Schmidt, "Women in American Methodism," 213-14.

50. Schmidt, "Women in American Methodism," 215.

51. For a parallel account see Joan C. LaFollette, "Money and Power: Presbyterian Women's Organizations in the Twentieth Century," in Coalter, ed., *Organizational Revolution*, 199-232.

52. Statistics from the UMC Division of Ordained Ministry.

53. For perspectives on how contemporary women are finding their place in varied forms of church, see Rebecca Chopp, *Saving Work: Feminist Practice and Theological Education* (Louisville: Westminster/John Knox Press, 1995); and Miriam Therese Winter, Adair Lummis, Allison Stokes, *Defecting in Place: Women Claiming Responsibility for Their Own Spiritual Lives* (New York: Crossroad, 1994).

54. Dale E. Soden, "Men and Mission: The Shifting Fortunes of Presbyterian Men's Organizations in the Twentieth Century," in Coalter, ed., *Organizational Revolution*, 233-53.

55. General Conference authorized a study Commission on the Status and Role of Women in 1968, funded its work to begin in 1970, continued it as a study commission in 1972 and made it a standing commission in 1976.

56. As Craig Dykstra and others have argued, in the contemporary American culture of technology, productivity and consumption, practices are too readily understood as individual deeds or as organizational functions that

accomplish some goal or produce a tangible object. But to reduce the practices of the church to mere utility is to miss the depth and richness of Christian ways of being. Congregations do not worship in order to make people feel better about themselves. A local church does not open a soup kitchen in order to solve society's hunger problem. These practices of the church—the practice of praise, or the practice of service—have their own intrinsic values as they express a whole outlook and way of life.

Nor are practices simply contemporaneous actions. They are acts with a history in many times and places. They are the outgrowth of a continuous but ever-changing community of believers whose ways have accrued over time. They fit together in patterns unique to the community that sustains them. They constitute shared, communal life; in a real sense, communities *are* their practices. See Craig Dykstra, "Reconceiving Practice," in Barbara G. Wheeler and Edward Farley, eds., *Shifting Boundaries: Contextual Approaches to the Structure of Theological Education* (Louisville: Westminster/John Knox Press, 1991), 47 and passim.

57. I am indebted for the categories of this discussion to Coalter, *Re-Forming*, 281-85.

58. Tigert, *Constitutional History*; Nolan B. Harmon, *The Organization of The Methodist Church*, 2nd revised edition (Nashville: The Methodist Publishing House, 1948, 1962); Jack M. Tuell, *The Organization of The United Methodist Church*, rev. 1997 edition (Nashville: Abingdon Press, 1997); Robert L. Wilson and Steve Harper, *Faith and Form: A Uniting of Theology and Polity in the United Methodist Tradition* (Grand Rapids: Francis Asbury Press, 1988).

59. *The Presbyterian Presence* series addressed the lack of organizational studies of the church with *The Organizational Revolution*.

60. Mathews, *Set Apart to Serve*, 185, n. 3.

61. Roy H. Short, *United Methodism in Theory and Practice* (Nashville: Abingdon Press, 1974), 23.

62. *Doctrines and Discipline of The Methodist Church 1939* (New York: Methodist Publishing House, 1939), 1-2.

63. Robert Emory, *History of The Discipline of The Methodist Episcopal Church* (New York: Lane and Sandford, 1844), 3-4.

64. The 1888 MEC Commission on the Constitution, charged with regularizing the paragraphs to be considered constitutional, was even given the wrong paragraph numbers for their study and had to recheck them through the journals of the General Conference (General Conference *Journal* 1896, MEC, 337).

65. The *Discipline* included a glossary of terms from 1948 (MC) to 1980 (UMC), except the year of union in 1968. The glossary was prefaced,

> This glossary, like the index, is not part of the law of the Church but rather a guide to that law. (1980 *Discipline*, p. 633)

Yet fears of civil court interpretations of glossary terms, especially construing the UMC as a corporation, caused the glossary's removal. For definitions now, see Alan K. Waltz, *A Dictionary for United Methodists* (Nashville: Abingdon Press, 1991).

The *Discipline* still includes an Index, which inevitably defines entities by listing their component and related parts. This is very helpful to the reader, but care must be taken to avoid misuse of the Index in civil court proceedings.

3. The Constitution of United Methodism

1. *The United Methodist Book of Worship* (Nashville: The United Methodist Publishing House, 1992), 106, 92, 95.

2. General Conference 2000 adopted several constitutional amendments to the Preamble that, following adoption by the aggregate members of annual conferences, removed some of the language about the union quoted here. But the sense of The United Methodist Church as self-constituted remains in any case.

A striking contrast on this point can be found in comparing the United Methodist Constitution with one of the major documents of the Second Vatican Council, the Dogmatic Constitution on the Church *(Lumen Gentium)*, promulgated by Pope Paul VI in 1964. Here the word "constitution" means a papal statement on a question of fundamental importance to the faith. It clearly does not mean a document that brings something into being. For Vatican II, the church was the given reality in continuity with the apostles and "the teaching of previous councils," a holy mystery, the one Church of Christ, a sign of "the unity of the whole human race." *The Sixteen Documents of Vatican II* (Boston: Daughters of St. Paul, n.d.), 109.

3. General Conference *Journal*, MEC, 1896, 338. The MECS was content with its historic understanding that the Restrictive Rules, including a rule on representation in General Conference, comprised the church's constitution (though it was not so titled). The EUBC had a considerably longer Disciplinary section titled "constitutional law," including the basic units and powers of all conferences, local churches, and forms of ministry.

4. Paul Washburn, *An Unfinished Church: A Brief History of the Union of the Evangelical United Brethren Church and The Methodist Church* (Nashville: Abingdon Press, 1984), 74-5.

5. Tigert, *Constitutional History*, 15.

6. Tigert, *Constitutional History*, 323-24, 403.

7. General Conference 2000 decided to weigh church membership more heavily in the proportion of delegates from each annual conference to the General Conference, resulting in a shift of delegate numbers from northern and western conferences to southern conferences (¶502.3).

8. Herbert E. Stutts and J. Hamby Barton, "History of the Episcopacy," in *The Study of the General Superintendency of the Methodist Church: A Report to the General Conference of 1964.* The Co-ordinating Council of the Methodist Church, January 1964, 38; Tigert, *Constitutional History*, 323-24.

9. Stutts and Barton, "History of the Episcopacy," 46, 84; Mathews, *Set Apart to Serve*, 209-11.

10. Moede, *Office of Bishop*, 184; Mathews, *Set Apart to Serve*, 210.

11. John M. Moore, *The Long Road to Methodist Union* (New York: Abingdon-Cokesbury Press, 1943), 192-93.

12. Already in 1958 James H. Straughn was complaining that the Northeast in particular was not taking the jurisdiction seriously as a programmatic unit; see his *Inside Methodist Union* (Nashville: The Methodist Publishing House, 1958), 141.

13. See chapter 2, n. 39.

14. Harry Wescott Worley, *The Central Conference of the Methodist Episcopal Church: A Study in Ecclesiastical Adaptation, or a Contribution of the Mission Field to the Development of Church Organization* (Foochow, China: The Christian Herald Mission Press, 1940), 119-20.

15. John L. Nuelsen, *Die Ordination in Methodismus* (1935), quoted in Moede, "Bishops in the Methodist Tradition," 59.

16. Mathews, *Set Apart to Serve*, 47.

17. Jack M. Tuell, "The United Methodist Bishop and *The Book of Discipline*," in Tuell and Fjeld, *Episcopacy*, 76.

18. James M. Buckley, *Constitutional and Parliamentary History of the Methodist Episcopal Church* (New York: Methodist Book Concern, 1912), 187-88.

19. Thomas B. Neely noted this long ago in *The Evolution of Episcopacy and Organic Methodism* (New York: Phillips and Hunt, 1888), 439.

20. Moede, "Bishops in the Methodist Tradition," 59. The EUB tradition was even clearer on this issue, with bishops serving only one four-year term at a time and no laying on of hands indicating ordination or consecration.

21. Mathews, *Set Apart to Serve*, 264.

22. Murray H. Leiffer, "The Episcopacy in the Present Day," in *Study of the General Superintendency 1964*, 169.

23. As Neely put it, "[The Methodist Episcopal Church has] not a government *by* bishops, but a government *with* bishops." *Evolution*, 442.

24. William F. Warren, *Constitutional Law Questions Now Pending in the Methodist Episcopal Church, with a suggestion on the future of the episcopacy. Containing also the new constitution, to be acted on by the General Conference of 1896, and a paper on the man and woman question* (Cincinnati: Cranston and Curts, 1894), 23.

25. Straughn, *Inside Methodist Union*, 161.

26. Tigert, *Constitutional History*, 403.

27. Behney and Eller, *History*, 383.

28. I am grateful to William J. Everett for his thoughts about the relationship of annual conferences, political conventions, and forms of republican governance.

29. Buckley, *Constitutional and Parliamentary History*, 387.

30. Short, *United Methodism in Theory and Practice*, 12.

31. EUBC *Discipline* 1967, ¶¶34-35.

32. Prior to merger, the EUB term for the governing body of a congregation was "Local Conference"—even more explicitly indicating oversight of all the spiritual and temporal interests of the local church on behalf of the connection. EUBC *Discipline* 1967, ¶52ff.

33. Predecessor bodies did incorporate as a general church; the EUBC, for example, had a general church Board of Trustees to serve as a corporation to "receive and administer new trusts and funds" as well as property of all kinds. The UMC has no such corporation or executive unit for the general church or denomination as a whole (EUBC *Discipline* 1967, ¶1950ff.).

34. For further discussion of major sources of constitutional order in United Methodism, see William J. Everett and Thomas E. Frank, "Constitutional Order in United Methodism and American Culture," in Russell Richey, et al., ed., *Connectionalism: Ecclesiology, Mission, and Identity* (Nashville: Abingdon Press, 1997).

4. History, Theology, and the *Discipline*

1. The first *Discipline* of the EUBC (1947), offered another appeal to providence:

> In the eighteenth century it pleased the Lord our God to awaken persons in different parts of the world who should raise up the Christian religion from its fallen state and preach the gospel of Christ crucified in its purity. (3-4)

From 1830 to 1939 Methodist Protestants, of course, used their historical statement for a narrative explanation of their opposition to episcopacy and desire for lay representation.

2. Russell E. Richey, "History in the Discipline," in Thomas A. Langford, ed., *Doctrine and Theology in The United Methodist Church* (Nashville: Kingswood Books, 1991), 193-94.

3. Albert Outler, for years one of the leading interpreters of United Methodist tradition and theology, exemplified United Methodist attitudes in his General Conference presentation of the new 1972 statement of "Our Theological Task."

> Christian truth, if it ever could be fully stated in propositional form, would then be the creed to end all creeds, the doctrine to end all doctrinal formulations and only have to be repeated thereafter till people understood it properly . . . our emerging historical consciousness . . . has altered this static view of dogma beyond all recognition and control.

"Introduction to the Report of the 1968–72 Theological Study Commission," in Langford, *Doctrine and Theology*, 23.

4. Pragmatism as a constructive philosophy of social vision has thrived throughout American history, in the work of C. S. Peirce, William James, and John Dewey, and more recently among feminist and liberationist theologians such as Rebecca Chopp and Cornel West. This continuing interest makes an intriguing dialogue with United Methodist theological traditions in their common focus on practices of social justice. See Rebecca Chopp, *The Power to Speak: Feminism, Language, God* (New York: Crossroad, 1989), esp. 30-39; and Cornel West, *The American Evasion of Philosophy: A Genealogy of Pragmatism* (Madison: University of Wisconsin Press, 1989). See also Randy Maddox, "Untapped Inheritance."

5. Rack, *Reasonable Enthusiast*, 509-10.

6. Behney and Eller, *History*, 358.

7. Richard P. Heitzenrater, "In Search of Continuity and Consensus: The Road to the 1988 Doctrinal Statement," in Langford, *Doctrine and Theology,* 103.

8. Richey, "History in the Discipline," 200.

9. For this debate, see Richard P. Heitzenrater, "At Full Liberty: Doctrinal Standards in Early American Methodism," and Thomas C. Oden, "What Are 'Established Standards of Doctrine'? A Response to Richard Heitzenrater," in Langford, *Doctrine and Theology,* 109-42. Oden has published a book-length version of his views entitled *Doctrinal Standards in the Wesleyan Tradition* (Grand Rapids: Francis Asbury Press, 1988). See also Thomas W. Ogletree, "In Quest of a Common Faith: The Theological Task of United Methodists," in Langford, *Doctrine and Theology,* 168-75, esp. 174. Richey criticized the Disciplinary inclusion of a particular scholarly viewpoint (even though he agreed with it) to interpret such a critical issue, in "History in the Discipline," 201.

10. Ogletree, "Quest," 174.

11. Heitzenrater, "In Search of Continuity," 101.

12. "Our Theological Task" is written in first person plural as a statement of United Methodist people. It also consistently capitalizes Church, whether in reference to United Methodism or to the Church catholic (e.g., compare the second paragraph on p. 75 with the fifth paragraph on p. 83). This gives the statement an inherent ambiguity—to whom is it addressed and for whom does it purport to speak? all Christians, or United Methodist Christians? Does the statement hope through its ambiguous language to point toward United Methodism's role in an emerging ecumenical consensus in theology?

13. Ted A. Campbell, "The 'Wesleyan Quadrilateral': The Story of a Modern Methodist Myth," in Langford, *Doctrine and Theology,* 154-61 (Smith quoted on 158). In the same book, see also Geoffrey Wainwright, "From Pluralism Towards Catholicity? The United Methodist Church After the General Conference of 1988," 223-31; and Langford, "The United Methodist Quadrilateral: A Theological Task," 232-44.

14. Bishop Nolan B. Harmon's *Understanding The United Methodist Church* (Nashville: Abingdon Press, 1955, 1977) is striking in this regard. Over half the book is devoted to expounding the Articles of Religion and the General Rules (along with Wesleyan teachings). Clearly Bishop Harmon thought of these as the twin pillars of United Methodism, the documents that gave the church its distinctive witness and purpose. Their relationship was simple: "Doctrine has to do with what one believes, discipline with what one does" (75). These must be consistent with each other.

While acknowledging that "Methodists have never been too doctrinally serious," Bishop Harmon quoted the MC bishops' address to the 1952 General Conference:

Our theology has never been a closely organized doctrinal system. We have never insisted on uniformity of thought or statement . . . [But] there are great Christian doctrines which we most surely hold and firmly believe. (24-5)

342

Is Bishop Harmon's approach an anachronism? One wonders how many laypersons and pastors in United Methodism would be prepared to teach a class about the church on the basis of explaining the Articles and Rules.

15. Richey points this out for "Our Doctrinal Heritage" particularly, calling it "a strategy of primitivism" or "reform through recovery"; "History in the Discipline," 200-201.

16. Tuell, *Organization,* 41-42. The heading on *Discipline* p. 69 is editorial, referring to the source of this particular edition of the General Rules in the MC *Discipline.*

17. Maddox, "Social Grace," 147-49. As Maddox points out, Wesley's oftenquoted appeal for "social" holiness represented not so much an effort to address social issues per se, but a conviction that holiness can only be sustained in community with other persons. In Wesleyan theology the Christian practices of social action are a response to grace, not a blueprint for broad social reform. On this point, see Theodore R. Weber, "Breaking the Power of Cancelled Sin: Possibilities and Limits in Wesleyan Social Theology," *Quarterly Review* 11:1 (Spring 1991), 4-21.

Steven M. Tipton (as primary researcher) explores the contemporary relationship of United Methodist and American public life in chapter 6 on "The Public Church," in Robert N. Bellah, Richard Madsen, William M. Sullivan, Ann Swidler, and Steven M. Tipton, *The Good Society* (New York: Alfred A. Knopf, 1991), 179-219.

18. Thomas A. Langford, "Conciliar Theology: A Report," in Langford, *Doctrine and Theology,* 181.

19. Quoted in Albert C. Outler, "The Wesleyan Quadrilateral—in John Wesley," in Langford, *Doctrine and Theology,* 76.

20. See the arguments over property deeds in Heitzenrater, "At Full Liberty," 113-14, and Oden, "Response," 130-31.

21. Albert C. Outler, "Do Methodists Have a Doctrine of the Church?" in Dow Kirkpatrick, ed., *The Doctrine of the Church* [papers of the 1962 Oxford Institute of Methodist Theological Studies] (New York: Abingdon Press, 1964), 26-7.

22. Outler, "Doctrine of the Church," 24-5.

23. For further discussion of United Methodism's "ecclesial location" and contribution to ecumenical dialogue, see Geoffrey Wainwright, *The Ecumenical Moment: Crisis and Opportunity for the Church* (Grand Rapids: Wm. B. Eerdmans, 1983), chapter 11, and *Methodists in Dialog* (Nashville: Kingswood Books, 1995); and John Deschner, "United Methodism's Basic Ecumenical Policy," in Richey et al., *Perspectives on American Methodism,* 448-59.

5. The Ministry of All Christians

1. *Lumen Gentium,* ¶¶9-17.

2. *Lumen Gentium,*¶33. The scriptural quotation is Ephesians 4:7.

3. *Lumen Gentium,* ¶10.

4. *Lumen Gentium,* ¶¶18, 31.

5. *BEM,* ¶¶1, 3, 5.

6. *BEM,* Ministry section, ¶6.

7. *BEM,* Ministry section, ¶13.

8. *The COCU Consensus,*¶¶21, 24, 18.

9. The Mission Statement in the 1992 *Discipline* was itself condensed from a much fuller document written by a General Conference study commission on mission and adopted in 1988.

10. *The COCU Consensus,* 45-6.

11. *BEM,* 21.

12. ¶139 was added in the wake of the Pacific Homes case of the 1970s, in which an appellate court did indeed hold the entire UMC liable in a lawsuit over an agency owned by one annual conference. The court argued that the UMC was a single corporate hierarchy with the Council of Bishops as its executive authority. See chapters 3, 12, and 13 for further discussion of the corporate nature of the UMC.

6. The Local Church in United Methodism

1. Quoted and discussed in Richey, *The Methodist Conference,* 166-68.

2. R. Sheldon Duecker addressed some of the points of stress and change in the relationship of local church and connection in *Tensions in the Connection: Issues Facing United Methodism* [Into Our Third Century Series, Alan K. Waltz, ed.] (Nashville: Abingdon Press, 1983).

3. Note Professor Leiffer's name as consultant on the copyright page; his role was confirmed for me in a conversation with Alan K. Waltz.

4. Richey, *The Methodist Conference,* 165.

5. 1963 EUBC *Discipline,* ¶52.

6. *Vital Congregations—Faithful Disciples,* 10, 64. The bishops' document on *Vital Congregations—Faithful Disciples* was not a statement of polity. Theologically its use of "congregation" was intended as a translation of the New Testament *ekklesia*— an attempt to capture the sense of church coming into being as Christians gather for worship and service. The bishops' choice of the term congregation, of course, both reflected and reinforced its increasing use in United Methodist rhetoric.

7. Membership vows are normally taken in public, but exceptions may be made (¶223).

8. This wording expresses a systems model of church that has been advocated throughout the 1980s and 1990s by the General Board of Discipleship and its general secretary, Ezra Earl Jones. The *Discipline* charges GBOD with helping local churches become "communities of growing Christians" (¶1101.2).

7. Called and Set Apart: Ordered Ministry in United Methodism

1. 1787 *Discipline,* Section II.

2. Wesley's letter to America, 1784, in Wesley, *Works,* 13:251-52.

3. "Early American Methodists were consistent with Wesley in their judgment that preaching was not related to ordination. . . . Methodist ordination was not, however, the 'absolute ordination' of Catholicism in that it was tied to the traveling ministry." Dennis M. Campbell, *The Yoke of Obedience: The Meaning of Ordination in Methodism* (Nashville: Abingdon Press, 1988), 74.

4. Norwood, *Story of American Methodism,* 136.

5. Gerald O. McCulloh, "The Theology and Practices of Methodism, 1876–1919," in *The History of American Methodism,* 3 vols., Emory Stevens Bucke, ed. (New York: Abingdon Press, 1964), 2:659.

6. For more discussion, see Campbell, *Yoke of Obedience*, 86-89.

7. Behney and Eller, *History*, 257.

8. Statistical reports obtained from the Division of Diaconal Ministry, General Board of Higher Education and Ministry, Nashville.

9. For thorough discussion of the new diaconate, see Margaret Ann Crain and Jack Seymour, *A Deacon's Heart: The Ministry of the Deacon in The United Methodist Church* (Nashville: Abingdon Press, 2000) and Ben L. Hartley and Paul E. Van Buren, *The Deacon: Ministry Through Words of Faith and Acts of Love* (Nashville: General Board of Higher Education and Ministry, 1999).

10. Norwood, *Story of American Methodism*, 133.

11. Johnson and Waltz, *Facts and Possibilities*, 38.

12. Campbell, *Yoke of Obedience*, 78-9.

13. Norwood, *Story of American Methodism*, 137. Asbury and Coke are quoted here as well.

14. "A Charge to Keep I Have" (1762) is one of many Charles Wesley hymns that express and reinforce the dynamics of the Methodist preaching movement.

15. "Worn-out preachers" was standard terminology in early America, referring to those who either located or retired from itinerant ministry.

16. From the Large Minutes, Wesley, *Works*, 8:324-25. The 1996 *Discipline* substitutes the word "service" for "preaching"—a historical travesty (¶305).

17. From the Large Minutes, Wesley, *Works*, 8:310.

18. Peter Cartwright, *Autobiography*, with introduction by Charles L. Wallis (New York: Abingdon Press, 1956), 64; quoted in Gerald O. McCulloh, *Ministerial Education in the American Methodist Movement* (Nashville: United Methodist Board of Higher Education and Ministry, Division of Ordained Ministry, 1980).

19. From the Large Minutes, Wesley, *Works*, 8:315.

20. *Christian Advocate and Journal* (July 18, 1834), 186.

21. Short, *Chosen to Be Consecrated*, 80.

22. Nolan B. Harmon, "Structural and Administrative Changes," in Bucke, *History*, 3:9-10.

23. Donald H. Treese, "Reaffirming the Covenant in Itineracy," in Donald E. Messer, ed., *Send Me? The Itineracy in Crisis* (Nashville: Abingdon Press, 1991), 79. See also John E. Harnish, *The Orders of Ministry in The United Methodist Church* (Nashville: Abingdon Press, 2000).

24. Lyle E. Schaller, "Who Is the Client? The Clergy or the Congregation?" in Messer, *Send Me?*, 87-99.

25. William H. Willimon and Robert L. Wilson, *Rekindling the Flame: Strategies for a Vital United Methodism* (Nashville: Abingdon Press, 1987), 109.

26. The 1984 General Conference debate on the "self-avowed practicing homosexual" phrase is instructive; see 1984 *Journal of the General Conference*, 337ff., esp. 344.

8. Superintendency in United Methodism

1. J. Robert Nelson, "Methodism and the Papacy" in *A Pope for All Christians?* ed. Peter J. McCord (New York: Paulist Press, 1976), 156; quoted in Moede, "Bishops," 62. Moede suggests that later changes to the *Discipline* have

corrected this somewhat. But I would argue, not much. United Methodist episcopacy relies heavily on oral tradition and inherited practice.

2. An intriguing ecclesiological question is whether a bishop can refuse to ordain a candidate whom the conference has elected. The episcopal address of 1844 argued not, since a bishop only affirms what the elders have voted to do. But presumably the bishop could speak out at the point in the liturgy when objections to an ordination are called for. The question arose recently in the case of an annual conference electing to membership a "self-avowed practicing homosexual" whose ordination appeared to conflict with ¶304.3. For older history of ordination, see Harmon, *Organization*, 87.

3. Discussion of the term "general superintendency" may be found in Leiffer, "Episcopacy," 148.

4. Mathews, *Set Apart to Serve*, 223.

5. Mathews, *Set Apart to Serve*, 206-07.

6. Short, *Chosen to Be Consecrated*, 28.

7. Roy H. Short, *History of the Council of Bishops of The United Methodist Church, 1939–1979* (Nashville: Abingdon Press, 1980), 195-96.

8. Mathews, *Set Apart*, 209-10.

9. See chapter 13 for more on complaints and charges.

10. Gerald F. Moede, "Episcopacy as Point of Unity" in Tuell and Fjeld, *Episcopacy*, 117.

11. In fact, the general conference of 1787 made clear that Thomas Coke was general superintendent with Asbury only when Coke was in the U.S., that is, traveling the American connection. Tigert, *Constitutional History*, 233.

12. Harmon, *Organization*, 88.

13. Short, *Chosen to Be Consecrated*, 50-51.

14. A letter from Quayle quoted in an article by J. Ralph Magee (elected bishop himself in 1932), "Area Episcopal Supervision: Has It Succeeded?" *Zion's Herald* (January 21, 1920), quoted in Nolan B. Harmon, "Structural and Administrative Changes," in Bucke, *History*, 3:33-34.

15. Stutts and Barton, "History of the Episcopacy," 100.

16. See *Journal of the 1952 General Conference of The Methodist Church*, 179.

17. Further discussion of these issues may be found in Harmon, *Organization*, 44-67; and Tigert, *Constitutional History*, 335. See also James E. Kirby, *The Episcopacy in American Methodism* (Nashville: Kingswood Books, 2000).

18. *Leadership and Servanthood: Episcopacy and Superintendency in The United Methodist Church*. Report, Recommendations, and Proposed Legislation of the 1972–1976 Quadrennial Commission for the Study of the Offices of Bishop and District Superintendent, The United Methodist Church, January 1976, 41-42. See also Leiffer, "Episcopacy," 148; and Jack M. Tuell, "The United Methodist Bishop and *The Book of Discipline*," in Tuell and Fjeld, *Episcopacy*, 74-76.

19. The Western Jurisdiction has twice elected someone from another jurisdiction: Gerald H. Kennedy from Nebraska in 1948 and Leontine T. Kelly from Virginia in 1984.

20. Stutts and Barton, "History of the Episcopacy," 95; Short, *Chosen to Be Consecrated*, 17-18.

21. Joshua Soule refused election in 1820 because he thought the General Conference had violated the Third Restrictive Rule by changing "the plan of our itinerant general superintendency." He was elected again in 1824. Franklin Parker refused election in the MECS in 1930.

22. Short, *Chosen to Be Consecrated,* 37, 96. Ann Eliza Scarritt was the daughter of Dr. Nathan Scarritt of Kansas City, a prominent Methodist preacher and businessman after whom Scarritt College was named. William McKinley was a Methodist layman from Ohio.

23. See Judicial Council Decision No. 745.

24. Tigert, *Constitutional History,* 393, 399.

25. Stutts and Barton, "History of the Episcopacy," 57, 65, 74, 77, 84. Even in its 1912 action the MEC asked only that bishops preside at least three of the four years of a quadrennium in a particular annual conference. Mathews, *Set Apart to Serve,* 215. See also Harmon, *Organization,* 63-65.

26. *Journal* of the Uniting Conference, 1939.

27. Short, *Chosen to Be Consecrated,* 38.

28. See Judicial Council Decision No. 735.

29. Over forty years ago Nolan B. Harmon edited a volume of essays on the district superintendency titled *The District Superintendent: His Office and Work in The Methodist Church* (Nashville: The Methodist Publishing House, 1954). Murray H. Leiffer conducted two studies of district superintendency. The first was titled *The Role of the District Superintendent in The Methodist Church* (Evanston: Bureau of Social and Religious Research, Garrett Theological Seminary, 1960). Ten years later the second was published as *The District Superintendency in The United Methodist Church* (Evanston: Bureau of Social and Religious Research, Garrett Theological Seminary, 1971). Like other Leiffer studies, these were based on surveys and interviews, and a second volume of the 1970 interviews was published under the title *What District Superintendents Say—About Their Office and The Issues Confronting Them* (Evanston: Bureau of Social and Religious Research, Garrett Theological Seminary, 1972). While extremely helpful in portraying the opinions and practices of district superintendents, these studies not only are somewhat dated, but in any case did not explore the ecclesiological grounding of the office.

I have also benefited from an unpublished paper by my colleague and former district superintendent J. C. Montgomery, Jr., "Reflections on the Role and Functions of the District Superintendency."

30. Richey, *The Methodist Conference,* 165; Behney and Eller, *History,* 353.

31. This concept was added as a result of the superintendency study report to the 1976 General Conference; see n. 18 above.

32. Annual Conference Survey 1994, General Council on Ministries.

9. General, Jurisdictional, and Central Conferences and the General Agencies

1. For General Conference history see Tigert, *Constitutional History;* Buckley, *Constitutional and Parliamentary History;* Thomas B. Neely, *A History of the Origin and Development of the Governing Conference in Methodism, and especially of the General Conference of the Methodist Episcopal Church,* 7th edition (Cincinnati: Jennings and Graham, 1892). See also chapter 3 above.

2. James M. Buckley told of a delegate who lectured on capital punishment for an hour and a half at one General Conference before the conference had a chance to adopt its rules; *Constitutional and Parliamentary History*, 367.

3. "Survey of Delgates to the 1992 General Conference of The United Methodist Church," Office of Research, General Council on Ministries (Dayton: January 1992), 1, 7.

4. Bishop Short lamented the passing of the bishops' hymn in his *History of the Council of Bishops,* 108. Bishops and spouses sang in 1996, however.

5. Johnson and Waltz, *Facts and Possibilities*, 116.

6. This is the argument of King, "Denominational Modernization."

7. This story is told fully by one of the opponents of women's participation, James M. Buckley, in *Constitutional and Parliamentary History,* 305-19. For the story of women's representation in the church see Rosemary Skinner Keller, "Creating a Sphere for Women: The Methodist Episcopal Church, 1869–1906," in Richey et al., *Perspectives on American Methodism,* 332-342, and Jean Miller Schmidt, "Women in American Methodism."

8. Behney and Eller, *History*, 231, 285. For a full account of the history of lay representation in The Methodist Church and its predecessor bodies, see Harmon, *Organization,* 116-123.

9. Report of the GCSRW to the 1992 General Conference, *DCA*, 783.

10. *Newscope* 20:1 (January 3, 1996); Robert Lear, "Choosing Delegates," *Interpreter* 39:3 (April 1995), 17; Bob Lear, "General Conference Points to the Future," *Interpreter* 37:5 (July-August 1992), 5.

11. *DCA* for the 2000 General Conference.

12. For a typical complaint of this type, see Duecker, *Tensions in the Connection,* 66-69.

13. See page ii of the *Discipline* for this rule and the names of committee members.

14. *The Book of Resolutions of The United Methodist Church, 2000* (Nashville: The United Methodist Publishing House, 2000), 5. All resolutions expire after eight years (¶510.2.a).

15. For accounts of the history and purpose of the ethnic caucuses, see Grant S. Shockley, ed., *Heritage and Hope; Justo L. Gonzáles, ed., Each in Our Own Tongue: A History of Hispanic United Methodism* (Nashville: Abingdon Press, 1991); Homer Noley, *First White Frost: Native Americans and United Methodism* (Nashville: Abingdon Press, 1991); and Artemio R. Guillermo, ed., *Churches Aflame: Asian Americans and United Methodism* (Nashville: Abingdon Press, 1991).

16. Annual Conference Survey 1994, General Council on Ministries.

17. *Good News* 28:5 (March/April 1995), 4.

18. *United Methodist Reporter* 139:9 (July 24, 1992), 3.

19. Bishop Hazen Werner was the last U.S. bishop to serve an episcopal assignment outside the U.S., in Hong Kong and Taiwan from 1964–68. See Mathews, *Set Apart to Serve*, 209-11.

20. While general agencies are amenable to General Conference, they are not corporate "agencies" of the General Conference as "principal," in legal parlance. The language of ¶701.1—referring to "master-servant" and "principal-agent,"

both relationships with legal precedent—is intended to clarify this relationship in such a way that general agencies will be amenable to General Conference but General Conference as an entity will not be liable for general agency actions. General Conference, as stated above, is not incorporated and has no continuing existence.

21. The General Commission on Status and Role of Women at first did not adopt this tradition, as an effort to break the hold of male leaders at a time when all bishops were men. The GCSRW president for 1992–96, though, was a female bishop.

22. *Journal of the General Conference, 1972,* 2:1942-43.

23. This concern is spelled out in Leiffer, "Episcopacy," 46, 112-13, 120-21, 125, 128.

10. Annual Conference

1. Richey, *The Methodist Conference,* 21-26.

2. John Wesley used his brother Charles's hymn, "And Are We Yet Alive" (1749), for opening Methodist conferences and societies, and it is widely sung as annual conferences gather today. Russell Richey notes the revival of this "conference hymn" in connection with Methodism's American centennial, in " 'And Are We Yet Alive': A Study in Conference Self-Preoccupation," *Methodist History* 33:4 (July 1995), 249-61.

3. The General Council on Ministries 1994 survey of annual conference members indicated that many respondents would like to see more time and attention given to worship, study, and fellowship at annual conference sessions.

4. Harmon, *Organization,* 135-36.

5. See chapter 3 above on the constitutional place of the annual conference.

6. See for example Willimon and Wilson, *Rekindling the Flame,* 70-79.

7. A constitutional amendment to allow lay members of the BOM to vote on conference relations was approved by the 1996 General Conference and subsequent annual conferences (¶31).

11. Church Property

1. The PCUSA did permit congregations to opt out of the union of northern and southern Presbyterian branches in 1983 under certain conditions. The Methodists and EUBs were much more protective of their trust clause, and only a few EUB congregations in the Pacific Northwest and Canada withheld their participation in the 1968 union.

2. For a clear and thorough discussion of church property, see Tuell, *Organization,* 144-52. See also the *Legal Manual* published each quadrennium by the General Council on Finance and Administration (Evanston, IL).

3. Rack, *Reasonable Enthusiast,* 246, 498. Model Deed quoted in Buckley, *Constitutional and Parliamentary History,* 164.

4. Quoted in Buckley, *Constitutional and Parliamentary History,* 83.

5. 1798 *Discipline,* 173.

6. Thomas C. Oden explores the history of deeds of settlement and what standards of doctrine were expected to be propagated from Methodist pulpits; see *Doctrinal Standards*, 43-48.

7. See General Conference resolutions on "Investment Ethics," 427-31; and "Economic Justice," 403-11, in *Book of Resolutions 1992*.

8. The contemporary manifesto for this concern is Robert K. Greenleaf, *Servant Leadership: A Journey into the Nature of Legitimate Power and Greatness* (New York: Paulist Press, 1977). See also such publications as *Trusteeship*, a magazine for trustees of colleges and universities, and *In Trust*, a similar publication for theological schools.

9. See tables in *2000 General Minutes*.

10. GCFA *Legal Manual 1997–2000*.

11. See General Conference resolutions on "Annual Accessibility Audit," 157; "The Church and Persons with Mental, Physical, and/or Psychological Disabilities," 304; "Communications Access for Persons Who Have Hearing and Sight Impairments," 256; and "Compliance with the Americans with Disabilities Act for Employers," 158; all in the *Book of Resolutions 2000*.

12. The bishops advocated a stewardship in keeping with the General Rules, in *Vital Congregations—Faithful Disciples*, 127-30. See also Theodore W. Jennings, Jr., *Good News to the Poor; John Wesley's Evangelical Economics* (Nashville: Abingdon Press, 1990), and M. Douglas Meeks, ed., *The Portion of the Poor: Good News to the Poor in the Wesleyan Tradition* [papers of the 1992 Oxford Institute of Methodist Theological Studies] (Nashville: Kingswood Books, 1994).

12. Judicial Administration

1. For a fuller account of the history of judicial administration in Methodist bodies, see Harmon, *Organization*, 189-213.

2. Judicial Council protocols and procedures are available in the GCFA *Legal Manual* and are published in the bound volumes of Judicial Council decisions.

3. This material is based on interviews with three persons familiar with legal issues facing the church: Stephanie Anna Hixon, one of the two general secretaries of GCSRW; Craig R. Hoskins, former general counsel for GCFA and attorney specializing in church law; and Mary Logan, general counsel for GCFA.

4. The *Discipline* requires that all general secretaries as well as associate or assistant general secretaries be United Methodist, but specifies no ecclesial personnel rights and protections even for a United Methodist layperson serving in such a capacity. Clergy in such positions would have at least the regular clergy appointment system and complaint procedure on which to rely.

5. Judicial Council Decision No. 698. Some have argued that the Council improperly ruled that earlier provisions were "unconstitutional," since the UMC constitution guarantees a right to trial, that is, a right to a church trial, and the fair process provision of ¶2701 refers to fairness within that church trial context. The church's trial procedures may appropriately be quite different from those of a civil court.

6. I am grateful to William J. Everett for details and interpretation of the Pacific Homes case. See our joint article, "Constitutional Order in United Methodism and American Culture."

7. For many years the UMC and predecessor bodies referred only to pastoral "support," not to salaries. That is, pastors in the traveling connection received support for their work, and local churches were making a contribution to that support on behalf of the whole connection. For income tax purposes, clergy drawing on this theoretical pool of "support" were arguably "self-employed." Now that pastors understand themselves to be receiving "salaries" from local churches, with even insurance and pensions often direct-billed to the local church, it is harder to argue for "self-employment." The 1994 Weber v. Commissioner of Internal Revenue decision removed clergy salaries from the self-employment category for income tax purposes (though not Social Security payments). But the secular courts did not specify who the employer is—annual conference or local church.

Conclusion: Issues for the Future of United Methodist Polity

1. On clergy attrition, see Rolf Memming, "United Methodist Ordained Ministry in Transition (Trends in Ordination and Careers)" in William B. Lawrence, Dennis M. Campbell, Russell E. Richey, eds., *The People(s) Called Methodist: Forms and Reforms of Their Life* (Nashville: Abingdon Press, 1998), 129-48.

2. DeLane Wright, a former student in my polity class and now a pastor in Iowa, sent me a paragraph he wanted to propose for the *Discipline:*

It shall be, as it should be, that from this day, the word *shall* should be and the word *should* shall be defined wherever either word shall be used in the *Discipline,* or should be, shall it be determined that *should* shall be added or that *shall* should be added to any sentence wherever it should be suggested.

It goes on to tie the tangles ever tighter—not unlike the *Discipline* itself at points.

Index